101 DAMNATIONS

Also by Ned Boulting

How I Won the Yellow Jumper
How Cav Won the Green Jersey
On the Road Bike

NED BOULTING

101
DAMNATIONS

DISPATCHES FROM THE 101ST TOUR DE FRANCE

YELLOW JERSEY PRESS
LONDON

Published by Yellow Jersey Press 2014

2 4 6 8 10 9 7 5 3 1

First published in Great Britain in 2014 by
Yellow Jersey Press
20 Vauxhall Bridge Road,
London SW1V 2SA

www.vintage-books.co.uk

A Penguin Random House Company

Penguin
Random House
UK

global.penguinrandomhouse.com

A CIP catalogue record for this book
is available from the British Library

ISBN 9780224099936

Penguin Random House supports the Forest Stewardship Council®
(FSC®), the leading international forest-certification organisation.
Our books carrying the FSC® label are printed on FSC®-certified paper.
FSC® is the only forest-certification scheme supported by the
leading environmental organisations, including Greenpeace.
Our paper procurement policy can be found at:
www.randomhouse.co.uk/environment

Printed and bound by CPI Group (UK) Ltd, Croydon, CR0 4YY

To George. For his casual return.

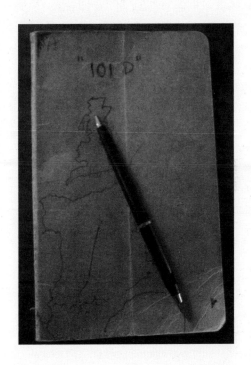

CONTENTS

Part 4

Epilogue

PARIS

'That is to say, I loved it.'

Something remarkable played out day after day, throughout July, before my eyes. But at the moment when Vincenzo Nibali clutched his cap and the Italian anthem bounced playfully off the darkening Parisian sky, I could not quite grasp the significance of what it was that I was witnessing. Perhaps there was none.

Later that evening, in the company of my colleagues, we made for a restaurant and tore into steak and chips. Absolved for the first time in almost a month of the need to be fit and proper broadcasters, we could now lift off the yoke of our accreditation and slip the knots that had tied us to the Tour de France.

Perhaps I'd best explain. For the last twelve summers my job has been to talk to the riders both before and after they have ridden their bicycles. These questions, and their corresponding answers, are then broadcast on television, either live, or more likely in the nightly highlights show on ITV4. Most days I go to the start of the race and then drive like a maniac to get to the finish in time to see who wins, and then talk to the winner. Repeat and fade.

Every day, our small team operates from a big white truck that parks up among a huge number of other trucks at the finish line of the race, ready to receive, analyse and re-broadcast the day's events. French television provides us with a live feed of the race footage itself, so all we do is add on all the other bits: the chats, the features, the interviews.

Now the Tour was done and it was time to eat, our conversation turned to anything other than the bike race. Our crew was almost all there, sawing away at faux filet and gulping down Brouilly, save one or two. Gary Imlach had justifiably retired early to his hotel after anchoring a forty-fourth consecutive broadcast. Phil Liggett and Paul Sherwen, who commentate on the action as it unfolds from a booth on the finishing line, were also absent. They had disappeared off into the Paris night, each in his own separate direction, perhaps clutching better invitations than the one we could offer.

But Chris Boardman, our expert analyst, and Matt Rendell, the cycling writer who contributes in dozens of different ways, were both tucking in, deeply involved, in Chris's case at least, with a mojito, which he was sipping as if it were keeping him alive. Around us sat the ten critically important people who make sure that the show gets on the air looking and sounding right. Chatting away at the far end were Liam MacLeod and Jim Sefton, the cameraman and soundman respectively, with whom I travel round France: my surrogate July family.

So there we were, scattered around the restaurant, perching on too many chairs around tables that were too small, and generally cluttering the place up. It was an inoffensively average bistro, furnished in red, and located just round the corner from the Place de la Concorde. It was the kind of establishment that would have expected to have closed at around ten o'clock on a regular Sunday night, were it not for the cursed, noisome annual presence of the Tour de France and its army of hangers-on. The laughter and the wine flowed easily.

It was late already when our party broke table and left. We had outstayed our welcome, and the young, immaculately coiffed waiter, who had at first been so solicitous to our needs, had run out of patience with our tiresome demands for beer and food and wine to be brought to the table in seemingly endless measures. The orders had kept him in constant motion, until suddenly he'd had enough and a bill appeared at our table with all the finality of a bailiff's notice. He hovered over us with his credit card machine. It was time to move on.

So we drifted up the street, a dozen of us, refugees from the race. One of our party had identified a bar, which, rumour had it, might still be open and happy to serve us. This seemed unlikely, but such was the momentum of the evening, no one had any better suggestions, except to gather around the minibar in one of our hilariously small hotel rooms and share a tube of Pringles and a can of gin-and-tonic. So now, too catatonic to take the initiative, most of us were strung out along the pavement's length, happy to follow the leader, walking slowly past shuttered antique shops, art galleries, and the lit windows of fashion houses. There was a male mannequin in a skirt and shawl, pointing heavenward. This was another bit of France, I was forced to concede, which knew nothing of cycling, and cared still less.

I dropped to the back of our line, and there I found Matt Rendell, walking alone.

'Hello, Matt.'

'Aaah. Bloody hell.' This was Matt's usual greeting.

In 2003, on the eve of my first Tour de France, on a similarly sultry night near Les Invalides, this was the man who had taken me to one side and sat me down in a terrible cafe. Here, over a pale and flaccid pepperoni pizza, he proceeded to tell me in most earnest tones that everything I was about to witness would leave me overwhelmed, breathless, confused and dazzled. But with luck, too, it might also leave me with a lifetime's infatuation. I recall how I had toyed with my meal, fiddled with the stem of my wine glass, and not really listened to him, wishing all the while that I could have been anywhere else. I remember how an ink-black Paris sky was brewing up a violent storm above us as we ate. The thunder had broken sometime during the night, and by morning, on the glistening wet pavements, I had found myself for the first time in my life face to face with the Tour de France.

Now, eleven years, and twelve Tours later, I paced in step with my friend and asked him a simple question.

'Did you enjoy it?'

'What?'

'The Tour.'

'No, course not.'

I looked at him, knowing what was coming. He glanced at me, resettling his glasses on his nose in that familiar way of his that normally signals the fact that he is coming, imminently, to the point.

'That is to say, I loved it.' And then, in summary, he concluded, 'Both of those things.'

I clapped him on the shoulders, and grinned, understanding perfectly. We walked on a few more paces, ambling now. Matt must have guessed my mood, and been alert to the almost imperceptible slackening of the pace. It was too late for me now to follow the rest of them to another bar, I was too tired. So, as the rest of them forged ahead, he presented me with an exit strategy.

'Here,' he said suddenly. 'If you go up there, and then take the second left, you get to the hotel.' He pointed up a side street. We were near to the Madeleine, close to the Hotel Alison, where we always stayed when the race came to Paris. I understood what he meant.

Wordlessly, I shook his hand, and smiled at him, then I did as he said, leaving him to catch up with the others. I turned right and then took the second left, and, as the streets grew quieter, my own question came back to me.

It had been a race that had conspired, over three grossly distended weeks, to produce a series of shocks and horrors, thrills and grave disappointments. From Yorkshire's glorious self-fulfilling prophecy, with its huge, welcoming embrace, to the desolation of the cobbles of Flanders, the sweep of the race had been immense. Naturally, there had been the usual smattering of farce, too. But some images that sprang to mind were not so funny. They involved riders in pain, clutching at legs, chins, elbows and wrists. They were pictures of rain, and mud. It is, after all, a hell of a long way from Leeds to Paris.

Had I enjoyed the Tour? Of course, not.

Had I loved the Tour? Yes. Both of those things

Before I knew it, all I could hear were my own footsteps, and Paris, closing softly in on midnight.

PART 1

GARITY

'Percy Shaw, the inventor of cats' eyes? From Halifax?'

About a week before the Tour de France began, I was retweeted by Arthur Scargill.

That sentence looks every bit as unusual written down as I thought it might. It's not something I was ever expecting to happen.

Out of a casual spirit of celebration, I had penned something bland and optimistic about the Grand Départ in Yorskhire, and posted it on what broadcasters tend to refer to as a 'social network', when what they really mean is Twitter. I forget what my inoffensive tweet was now, but it must have read something along the lines of 'Looking forward to the start of the #TdF in Yorkshire.'

I did not imagine, for a second, that the former leader of the National Union of Mineworkers would read my tweet and deem it worthy of wider agitprop distribution. But before I knew it, Scargill, the scourge of the Thatcher Revolution, the coal-faced crusader of the Left, had picked up on it, shared it with his followers and added something along the lines of 'So proud of God's Own County #YellowJersey.'

Two things amazed me about this. No, three things, actually.

The first was that Scargill was still alive. I don't intend this to be unkind, but I had assumed, given that he had been publicly invisible for the best part of thirty years, that he might no longer walk among us. To the best of my knowledge, he'd not yet appeared on *Celebrity Big Brother* dressed as a cat. Indeed the last I had seen of him, he'd been wearing a donkey jacket and shouting through a megaphone as a row of police horses bared their Conservative teeth at him. And that was several decades ago. I lose count.

The second was that Arthur Scargill liked cycling. The miners' leader with the bushy comb-over had never seemed to me to be the cycling type. Not that I'd ever wondered if he was, if truth be told. But, now that I was confronted with the reality, I found it hard to imagine him as a coffee-sipping, Bianchi-loving Continental aficionado of all things vélo.

But there it was, his affection for the Tour de France was on Twitter, and therefore verifiable fact.

And the third was that Arthur Scargill followed me on Twitter. This one was perhaps more weird than the other two put together, like discovering Neil Kinnock hiding in your airing cupboard.

Evidently this was going to be a summer that challenged preconceptions.

'We'd made a film to show them about Yorkshire,' Gary Verity recalls with a grimace. 'And the bloody DVD player wouldn't work.'

In 2010 the chief executive of Welcome to Yorkshire travelled to the French capital in the hope of buying, or at least renting, the Tour de France. But things didn't quite go according to plan. In a meeting room in Paris, faced with a panel of hard-nosed, inexpressive French cycling administrators, he found himself in a position of some discomfort.

The Frenchmen waited in awkward silence while another DVD machine was brought to the room. That one wouldn't work either.

'Well, don't worry about that,' said Philippe Sudres, one of the Tour's most venerable directors. 'Just tell us about it anyway,' he intoned, probably in the French equivalent of a John Le Mesurier voice.

Improvising wildly, now that he no longer had his info-mercial to fall back on, the Yorkshireman started to reel off great names of his county's estimable past in a last-ditch effort to sell the land of his birth to these Parisian sophisticates.

He subconsciously edited out Geoffrey Boycott, on the fair assumption that the men at the helm of the Tour de France would not necessarily be up to speed with the more nuanced aspects of 1970s' test cricket. But, he hoped, the prestigious Yorkshire icons left on the list would carry enough cultural heft to bowl over the men he was trying to woo.

'Yorkshire puddings, Yorkshire bitter, Bettys' Fat Rascal?'

This was his opening salvo, accompanied by a winning smile. There was no response, save for the raising of a few Gallic eyebrows.

'Treacle tart? Yorkshire Tea?'

'David Hockney? Barbara Hepworth? Henry Moore? The Brontës?'

There was an exchange of glances between Christian Prudhomme, the director of the Tour and his two lieutenants Cyrille Tricart and Sudres. Then Tricart, an archetypal, poker-faced, bespectacled bureaucrat, answered, 'We don't know about the Brontës.'

Undeterred, but by now beading a little at the brow, Verity ploughed on.

'J. B. Priestley? Joseph Priestley, who discovered oxygen?

'No.'

'Percy Shaw, the inventor of cats' eyes? From Halifax?'

'No.'

'Harry Brearley, the inventor of stainless steel?'

It was desperate stuff. Verity drew breath. He had just made a startling realisation, which looked likely to sink his bid at the first attempt.

'They'd literally never heard of Yorkshire.'

*

The Yorkshire Miracle (let's just call it that straight from the off, and leave ourselves no further space for hyperbole) had been a few years in the making. And it was, as is now well documented, almost entirely the brainchild of Gary Verity, who, for some reason I often, and embarrassingly, call 'Garity', even to his face. The fusion of his two names is too difficult to avoid.

When the day of the race finally dawned, Verity, the man who dreamt the whole thing up in the first place, was in his element. He strode from person to person, stage to stage, launch to launch and lunch to lunch as if his knighthood depended on it. He was a considerable presence, exuding marketing, breathing branding and sweating Yorkshire from every pore of his body. From the tip of his crocodile skin shoes to the glint of his bicycle-themed cufflinks, Gary Verity is all about the show. In fact he's quite a bulldozer of charm. He is a tall man, with a cheeky, willing smile and luxuriantly floppy hair, occasionally parted down the middle and relaxed, at other times wonderfully quiffed. But his great gift, and by extension one of Yorkshire's greatest gifts, is his prodigious ability to talk. He starts quietly but quickly picks up both volume and pace, until the words slide forth, avalanche-like, fluid and unstoppable. His happy countenance, ubiquitous blue blazer, sporting an enamel 'Y' on the lapel, and banana-yellow slacks became a potent symbol of the opening weekend of this year's race.

Right up until midnight the evening before the 2014 Tour de France, every weather forecast you'd care to look at predicted heavy rain for Stage 1. And in the end, unfathomably, the sun shone brilliantly.

God's Own County, they call it. And maybe they're right. God was responsible, ultimately, only with a bit of facilitating from Garity, perhaps working on a sub-contract.

*

Verity made his name and his numerous quids in various different guises, riding the New Labour good years of boom and more boom before the bust, as something of a 'career chief executive'. He went 'troubleshooting' in Hong Kong with Royal Insurance. He returned home to the Bradford and Bingley, where he took control of their ailing property division, converting a £1m monthly loss-maker into a £1m monthly profit machine. A couple of other jobs later, doing wondrously fiscal things at places like Prontaprint, he pitched up in the chief executive's role on the Yorkshire Tourist Board.

At the time, he would have us believe, it was a fairly unambitious institution, boasting, 'tea shops around village greens'; the kind of place you might drift around wondering if your aunt would like a tea towel for Christmas, and appeasing your children by giving them fifty pence to spend on a leather tassled bookmark.

Part of his thinking in dropping out of the world of commerce involved the wish, indeed the need, to spend as much time as he could with his wife Helen, who had been diagnosed with terminal cancer, and to be there for his baby daughter Lilly. It goes without saying that this long period of Helen's illness changed everything for all of them.

'I became a bit more reflective, and I started thinking and wondering what I could do for Yorkshire that would be a game changer. I wanted to leave a legacy for Helen. I know I'm not discovering cures for the world's diseases, and I know I'm not feeding half the world's poor or anything, but . . .'

Helen died just before Christmas in 2009.

One morning, Gary nicked himself shaving when he hit upon the big idea. 'Why not the Tour de France? It was almost too obvious. It was such an obvious fit!'

Somehow, he got hold of an email address for Jean-Etienne Amaury, whose family still owns the Amaury Sports

Organisation (ASO), which in turn owns the Tour de France.

Amaury is, as near as spit, a royal, and looks like it, too. In fact, he is only ever glimpsed stepping either into or out of helicopters, or with heads of state on carpets leading up to banquet halls. This was, therefore, something of a long shot.

Dear Monsieur Amaury,

Gary typed impatiently. The cursor on the screen winked excitedly back at him, waiting for its next instruction.

I'd like to do the Grand D . . .

At this point, there would, I am sure, have been a brief hiatus while he figured out how to write an *e* with an acute accent on the keyboard.

. . . Départ in Yorkshire at your earliest convenience. Please let me know your thoughts.

There really wasn't much more to say at this point. So he just signed off.

Astonishingly, he received a reply a few days later.

We'd like to discuss your idea. Please come to Paris and we will buy you lunch.

That brief email exchange set into motion an extraordinary chain of events. There were further visits to Paris, negotiations, setbacks. At their next meeting it became very clear that some seriously big hitters were also queuing up for a piece of the action. ASO were in receipt of bids from Barcelona, Florence, Utrecht and Vienna. And there was interest too from Edinburgh, as well as a list as long as your arm of French towns. And yet, somewhere, somehow, within the innermost workings of the highly secretive heart of ASO, the Gary Verity sales pitch was beginning to take seed.

He stuck to his task. The breakthrough came when someone at ASO realised that the Yorkshire terrier was from Yorkshire.

Now the French for this kind of dog is the borrowed English word, *le Yorkshire*. This was an unexpected and critically important revelation for the French, as well as for Verity's team. Having drawn a blank with the Brontë sisters and umpire Dickie Bird, they suddenly had found a winning association in these unremarkable small dogs, the kind that are popular with wealthy Parisian women of a certain age, and whose urine is to be found in vast quantities at the base of the horse chestnut trees on the Champs-Élysées. The sort of women who own this sort of dog are the sort of women who are married to the sort of men who work at a high level for ASO. This dog-related synergy was good news for Yorkshire.

One after another the pieces of the jigsaw fell into place. Barcelona withdrew, citing the complete collapse of Spain's economy as an excuse, and Christian Prudhomme, the race director, in the company of five-time Tour winner Bernard Hinault, was invited to a lavish helicopter tour of Yorkshire.

The sun shone, the place sparkled, and it was a triumph. In fact, it was corporate showing-off on a grand scale, and it worked. Prudhomme and Verity got on famously; it was the start of a genuine friendship.

'For whatever reason, I got the DNA of it,' recalls Verity. 'From that very first meeting, which is why I came back to Yorkshire and said, "We're going to get this." I genuinely did. I genuinely understand what the essence of the Tour is. And once you understand that you can see how it's survived a hundred and eleven years, and all these crises.

'There is an unwritten set of values about the Tour that have meant its survival through all the trials and tribulations. It is largely free, it is open to all, it is hugely physically challenging. It's like a huge adventure, a thousand times bigger than that. It's that. Multiplied up. If you're French, of course it's the link between urban and rural France. It returns back to the centre.

'Christian has said to me on numerous occasions, "You understood what the Tour was, from the first moment we met."'

Some time later, the deal was done, and in 2012 they announced that it had come to pass. Florence, Edinburgh, Utrecht, Barcelona and the rest of them would have to wait.

All that remained was to throw a big party. Yorkshire did that bit too, staging a lavish affair to which I, along with hundreds of others, was invited.

The announcement of the Grand Départ in Yorkshire, fully a year and a half before the event itself, coincided with Lance Armstrong's appearance on Oprah Winfrey. It is hard to say which was more dramatic, or received more column inches.

Normally such things are not set to music. A more standard affair, whether the host is Liège or Brest, Utrecht or Strasbourg, would be to invite a smattering of local and cycling press to an arid press conference in a Novotel, where after a PowerPoint and a Danish pastry, they'd be sent on their way with a free Biro, a hat and an artisan sack of lavender. That's about all that's required really, all that the owners of the Tour, the imperious ASO, expect when they point their finger of fortune in your direction. Besides, Christian Prudhomme would normally have one eye on his Festina timepiece, to ensure that he didn't miss the last TGV home to Paris. The bartering for the right to host the Grand Départ is usually the domain of the unitary authority, the council worthies and the local dignitaries, of spreadsheets and feasibility studies, market research and infrastructure contracts. Vast, gleaming, bronze organ pipes do not normally have a role to play.

Unless you are Garity.

At the climax to Yorkshire's celebratory dinner, a huge curtain parted in the main atrium of Leeds City Hall to reveal the biggest organ pipes I have ever seen, in full cry and encircled by an orchestra and a vertiginously terraced choir all bellowing at the tops of their voices.

I sat back on my gold-sprayed wedding-reception style chair, and let drop the folded cardboard name card that I had been fiddling with throughout dinner.

The choir belted out a string of inspirational anthems to the accompaniment of timpani crashing, harp-plucking, baroque bombast. I looked around the room, aware that a Pavlovian grin had broken out across my face, and remarked that pretty much everyone in the vast dining room was undergoing the same reaction to this musical onslaught of the senses. We had been wined, yes, and dined, but this was something else: now we were being forcibly serenaded by a couple of hundred impressively exuberant Yorkshiremen and -women. As they cranked up 'What Have You Done Today to Make You Feel Proud', I finally took notice of what it was that this misfit, unlikely-sounding Yorkshire Grand Départ was all about.

Suddenly I got it. It was the expression not so much of the proud will of a venerable county (however much it can lay claim to being the home of British Cycling heroics), as the sheer charismatic chutzpah of this man in charge. Somewhere, behind the scenes, Gary Verity was probably peeking out from behind black drapes to see if he could gauge the mood in the room by studying the faces of his illustrious guests as they turned and listened to his after-dinner entertainment. If he had harboured any lingering doubts at this point he would have known that the project was going to succeed whatever hurdles were still to be overcome. He and his million-man choir had simply blown everyone away.

Eighteen months later, hundreds of drivers, from Spain, Sweden, Russia and Portugal pointed their vehicles in the rough direction of Yorkshire, and, for the first time in their lives, typed 'Leeds' into their sat-navs.

DÉPART

'No one has understood what will happen out there today.
They will turn up in their millions. It will be an
amazing thing.'

It was a disorientating experience to see all the Tour de France paraphernalia spread out on a piece of waste ground in Leeds city centre. The Tour had erected its sprawling tented village, which constituted its mobile headquarters, about half a mile from the railway station. This swiftly assembled, and then even more swiftly dismantled, village was known (rather inappropriately) as the Permanence.

So strong were my annual associations with this Tour de France environment that the whole display played havoc with my sense of geography, tricking me repeatedly into thinking that I was abroad. The signage was in French, most of the languages being spoken were not English, and even the rays of sunshine that beat down on the makeshift courtyards between marquees felt unusually strong for Yorkshire.

It was curiously unsettling, and not altogether mediated by the presence of a truly terrible burger van knocking out gristly sausages in stale baguettes to a bewildered clientele, more used to being served foie gras and gazpacho. I queued up behind a German, who asked for a 'beef pattie'. The man looked at him as if he were simple. 'We can do you a burger, pal.'

But even that strong hint that all was not quite as exotic as it might seem did not convince me that this event was actually, really, genuinely happening in Yorkshire.

It was to this central point, in the days preceding the race, that the entirety of the Tour's international entourage would be drawn. Everyone involved with the race had, at some point, to gravitate there to gather information, register radio signals and collect the all-important stickers for their cars, without which it would be impossible to navigate the route, as well as press flesh and shake hands with colleagues new and old.

Even the riders made it down to the Permanence. Team by team, and over two solid days, their buses would pull up, and deliver thin men in liveried tracksuits, wearily trudging into the press conference room to deal with a firing squad of unanswerable banalities.

'Arnaud, what are your ambitions for the Tour de France?'

'I hope to ride well, and maybe, if I am fortunate, get a stage win.'

'Frank, do you think you can get a top-ten position, or maybe higher?'

'I don't know. We will have to see. The Tour is long, and we haven't started yet.'

On the morning of the race, as I waited for our first live broadcast from the start line in Leeds, I was ambushed by a silver-haired, deeply tanned man with bright, manic eyes, outstanding teeth and immensely natty attire. He lunged towards me.

'Ha! You don't recognise me!' he trilled. Then he turned to the similarly finely turned-out lady to his right. 'I said he wouldn't recognise me.'

'Of course I do.' I didn't. That is to say I almost did, and figured that if I bluffed for just a few more seconds, his name might emerge, winking like a safety beacon through the fog of general disorientation. Silver hair, British, Tour de France, obviously met him before, has a wife—

'Barry Hoban! Good morning, sir!' It came to me in the nick of time.

The West Yorkshire-born cyclist, accompanied by his wife Helen, was a guest of honour at the Tour. In 1967, the day after the death of Tom Simpson, Barry Hoban had been accorded the honour of an uncontested stage win by the peloton in recognition of Britain's loss. After that he went on to win many more races, including seven more Tour stages, a national record that stood until 2009 when it was overhauled by Mark Cavendish.

We stood there, fighting the loudspeakers that emitted a constant ear-splitting drone. I placed my hand across his shoulder and angled my head towards him so that I might make myself better heard, and at the same time, listen to what he had to say. He was talking about Cavendish. Hoban was certain that it would not be the Manxman's day, and predicted instead a stage win for Peter Sagan.

He sighed, and looked back at me with real regret. 'Just wish I was bloody forty years younger.' He would have backed himself over Yorkshire's testing, windy roads that he knew so well from long and lonely training rides. Hoban was never short of self-belief when he rode, and none of that had diminished in his seventies.

But one thing he told me stuck in my memory. He was quite specific about it, quite adamant. 'No one has understood what will happen out there today. They will turn up in their millions. It will be an amazing thing.'

He knew better than anyone the scale of the event we were all about to witness.

And all the way down the course, his prophecy was holding true. In Leeds city centre, all morning, as the drizzle gave way to bright sunshine, the railway station released wave after wave of spectators, trudging in packs up the hill towards the start, where they took their place alongside the tens of thousands of others who had already beaten them to it. There they stood, for hour after hour, immobile for the crush, unable and unwilling to relinquish their position by the roadside for fear that they would lose their spot altogether. And when the pavements were full, they climbed lampposts, or jumped up on railings, reaching balconies, any vantage point. It really was an astonishing sight.

What we did not know at the time, and what only later became apparent when the helicopters became airborne and pointed their cameras down at the race, was that the same thing was happening across the entire 190 kilometres of the race route, even the unlovely parts. Along the bleaker reaches of suburban Leeds, on ring roads and dual carriageways that bisected industrial estates, they had arrived in scarcely credible numbers. Stretches of road whose equivalent in France on a regular Tour stage might be populated by one man and his Yorkshire terrier, were flanked ten deep with people straining to glimpse the Tour de France pass by. Some time later, as we drove out of town, our route passed over a flyover above the race route, where they stood in just such overwhelming numbers, patiently awaiting the arrival of the riders. That was the moment at which I understood the magnitude of the event. But all this would only come fully to light as the race got underway, and would prove Barry Hoban quite correct in his patriotic assertion that it would be 'an amazing thing'.

In the meantime, at the start line, the countdown to the race was gathering serious momentum. We were now minutes from the 11 a.m. roll out. Rider after rider, muscles twitching, and nerves fluttering, pushed their way through the hordes to mount the steps and sign on. Each one was cheered as if he were personally delivering a message from the Queen that we could all have next year off and she was going to pay for it.

Whether it was Markel Irizar or Martin Elmiger, Julien Simon or Michał Gołaś, they all got the same fevered reaction from the gathered masses, penned in by barricades under the watching Victorian splendour of City Hall.

'And now, ladies and gentlemen, please welcome on stage the former national junior time-trial champion of Italy, and fourth-placed rider in last year's inaugural London–Surrey classic, Cannondale's Fabioooo Sabatiiiniiii!'

A crescendo of applause, whistles and clapping. It is probable that Fabio Sabatini may go through the rest of his life without once hearing his name received with such rapture again. I hope for him that this is not the case, but it is a possibility.

I stood, with Jim and Liam, as we waited to go live on ITV. We were right on the start line, one foot either side of it, straddling anticipation and fulfilment. Christian Prudhomme, the tall, loping figure clad in standard-issue blue shirt and chinos, the uniform of the organisation of the Tour de France, came striding towards us along the start straight where, very soon, the riders would begin to gather. The crowd at the side of the road spotted him, and, perhaps because most of them had been there for five hours and had seen very little except for the cursed publicity caravan, they went wild, even at one point chanting his name in a football-terrace style.

'Only one Christian Prudhomme . . . walking in a Prud-homme wonderland.'

This, I am prepared confidently to announce, is the first time that a Yorkshire crowd has sung out loud the name of a French sports administrator.

He looked stunned by such a euphoric reception, a little caught out by it. But he still had sufficient wits about him to avoid stepping in something just past the start line, which looked suspiciously like a dog turd.

*

And then they were off. It didn't take long before the oldest man in the peloton attacked. Jens Voigt, riding his valedictory lap of France (and Yorkshire) had put his nose in the wind and was 'off on one'.

Originally away in a break of three riders, alongside Nicolas Edet and Benoît Jarrier, he attacked the pair of them, and ended up riding most of the day alone to crest the summit of the côtes of Cray, Buttertubs and Grinton Moor on his own, a dot of Trek Factory black, bobbing and weaving through a sea of spectators, thirty, fifty, a hundred deep in places.

After taking the third ascent unopposed he could relax a notch, his unlikely goal of a polka-dot jersey at the end of the day was complete. He pushed on until he could push no longer, and was then unceremoniously swamped by the lead-out trains. But his last Tour de France was already a triumph.

Out on the road, Yorkshire had become one giant village fete, with 'chuck the welly' competitions, beer tents, cake stalls and bit of a bike race thrown in for good measure.

After leaving Leeds, we embarked on an improbable race of our own: to get to a tiny little spot on the map called West Tanfield. It was to here, we understood, that the royal party of the two princes and Kate would be helicoptered from Harewood House.

I had been detailed with filming them arriving at West Tanfield and, ridiculously, trying to 'grab a word'. I suspected that you don't get to just 'grab a word' with the Windsors. They probably keep you waiting for hours, and then they talk to you only if they see fit, and only if the request has first passed through layers of ever more obscure authority, until the arrangement has been rubber-stamped by those in whose power it is to withhold or dispense soundbites from hereditary aristocrats and their spouses about sporting events.

Anyway, even if I wasn't exactly in a mood to fly the meta-phorical bunting for our future king and his soldiering brother, then West Tanfield obviously was up for it, and who was I to spoil the party?

Besides, the village had a menacing resident who was perfectly capable of doing 'spoiling the party' all on his own. An encounter with him reminded me, not for the last time, that although I was driving a French-registered, fully accredited Renault Espace, I was decidedly not in France. It was true that the bike race passing through was indeed the Tour de France, but it was also evident that not everyone shared the love and reverence for its noisy passage as they do in its mother country. There were one or two hearts and minds that had yet to be won over, and one of them lived on the main road into West Tanfield.

We drove into the outskirts of the village in a tearing hurry, scouring the blue summery skies above us for signs of royalty and rotor blades. Pulling up on a grass verge, we jumped out of the car and started to assemble our kit.

'You can't park here.'

A bloke, stripped to the waist, with a can of Stella in his hand, and a fag loosely hanging from his lip, had appeared from the house directly next to us. He had one of those concreted driveways in which Britain specialises that boast an unusual number of vehicles, all in different states of decay.

'Why?' We were already on the Tour, and had hair-trigger belligerence as a default setting when confronted with anything as irritating as a request to move the car.

'Cos I said so,' he replied, straightforwardly. 'Get it moved.'

'Do you own this piece of land?' I offered, getting quickly into fairly complex legal territory, which, without the help of Her Majesty's Land Registry, might be difficult to resolve. Especially with Stella Man, whose house was surrounded by oily engines.

'I do, as it happens. And I don't want your car on it.'

'Right!' I said, as if I had won the argument. But instead of resting my case, I jumped back in the car, and did exactly what he said, moving it to the other side of the road.

'God save the Queen!' I yelled back at him, irrelevantly.

Then I legged it after Liam and Jim. I had no idea what I meant by 'God save the Queen', but, in the absence of anything like threatening talk in my verbal armoury, it was the best I could come up with under pressure. He turned and walked away. Anyway, I had left the encounter with a clean conscience and an unpunched face. Just.

I filmed my piece to camera, in which I rambled on about festival atmospheres and expectations being exceeded. Devoid of any soundbites from the very important helicopter passengers, this bit of sycophantic padding was all we managed to get out of our visit to West Tanfield (the 'grab a word' policy had pulled up breathtakingly short). I hoped that I had not sounded too much like Nicholas Witchell (not that I've anything against Mr Witchell, who I'm sure is very nice. It's just that, you know . . .), and then we jumped back into the Espace, and drove off, without making further eye contact with Stella Man.

And so the race closed in on Harrogate. After Jens Voigt was caught not much happened for a while on the road, and so the director reverted to the helicopter shots, whose camera operator was instructed to go off in search of colourful images. At one point he cut to a shot of deflated hot air balloons, lying like giant colourful condoms side by side in a field. As the race rattled past them, they each fired up their burners into the air, saluting the passage of the Tour. More than one rider turned to look, as they streamed past the field. They would have felt the heat blasts from the flames on their faces.

Things were getting closer. At the finish line in Harrogate we all now squinted at the giant screen, watching the sprinters' teams get organised. All the years of anticipation. All the months and weeks and column inches. All the crowd. All for this.

Somewhere in the stand, the town's most famous resident for the day, Mark Cavendish's mother Adele, was trying to contain her nerves, while Peta, his wife, could hardy bring herself to watch.

Those who had been close to Cavendish knew that something was going to happen. In hindsight, I suspect they all knew that this would not work out. He had been almost impossible to be around for weeks, if not months, leading up to this race. The size of the occasion, the lure of the opportunity and the cost of failure were never far from the brittle surface of his equanimity. It is rare that sprinters get the chance to wear, albeit briefly, the yellow leader's jersey. It remains the only leader's jersey Cavendish is missing from his Grand Tour collection. In 2013 he had been presented with a chance, but had crashed close to the finish. And now this year he had one more, possibly final, opportunity, in Great Britain, and in the town in which his mother lived. The British public expected him to deliver. The pressure must have been immense. In short, in the words of one of his closest associates, he'd been a 'right fucking nightmare'.

But what would be his undoing? The climb? The sprint? The aura of invincibility around his formidable German rival Marcel Kittel?

From where we all stood, or sat, up on top of that hill, with the grassy park overrun by the Tour's absurdly swollen caravanserai to one side, and the beery hordes of British cycling fans to the other, amid the genteel architecture of Harrogate's most sought-after addresses, we did not see it coming. Cavendish hit the pedals in fury, just one rider among many either already on the brink of maximum effort or just about to discover what it is like to have no more to give, and then give more.

No one predicted the fall. No one ever sees them coming, that's the point of them.

When it happens, it happens in an instant.

The row of riders, head on, shimmers towards the line, hunched low against their frames in effort. In the heart of all that forward intent, that fluid motion, a bike arrows into the tarmac, bringing with it another. The back wheels suddenly rear up above the line of riders' helmets, describe violent circles in the turbulent air directly over the race. And then, following on, the riders themselves, toss up and then drop hard into the middle of the damage. The perfect surface of the race shatters into jagged edges.

A bruised race. And a raging heart.

PETA

'Time stops. You think, just get up. Just get up.
Please, just get up.'

'An almighty crash.'

Even if we didn't see it coming, that's not to say that anyone was entirely surprised. In fact, when the dust settled (there was no dust, just noise), there was no great shock left in us.

'Cavendish is down.' Yes, he was. And Marcel Kittel powered beyond his prone and tangled figure to repeat the salt in the wound act of 2013, by taking that rarest of prizes, the sprinter's yellow jersey for the second year in a row.

We saw David Cameron clutch his face in photogenic horror, annexing for himself the right to be forever remembered as the first prime minister ever to be caught in a state of disappointment at a bike race of international importance. But what we didn't see, as the director chose to linger on politicians, was the discreet disappearance from the stand of the rider's wife.

Peta Cavendish went down the steps at the back of the grandstand and walked away from the scene with her head lowered. She had been here before.

'When I think of Mark, I think of this massive smile. The whole of his face is a big smile. He loses all of his eyes, and you just see these big eyelashes.' This is what Peta Cavendish sat down to tell me, before the race, before Harrogate, before the fall, when all things still seemed possible on this most auspicious Tour.

'That's what I think of Mark.'

I've seen this winner's smile, too. I've sat frighteningly close to it in fact, close enough for me to feel the radiated heat coming off his frame as his engine starts to cool down and click in front of me. Twenty-five times on the Tour de France, watching his face do just that. When he is caught up in the delight and success, his toothy grin is profoundly infectious. So it's true, what she says. I can second that. And I'm not even married to him.

When Peta talks about the Cav she met, she sometimes looks genuinely cross, especially when she recounts his foibles, his off-handedness with people. But she does so with that kind of indulgent exasperation that you get with people when they only half mean it. What amuses me most when she recalls her first encounters with Cavendish is her own brazen lack of knowledge. Neither of them had the faintest idea who the other one was. The Internet searches in their separate hotel rooms later that night must have been rather a shock to both parties.

'When he said to me, "I'm a cyclist," I thought, That's weird. Why would you tell me what your hobby is? I knew the Tour de France existed, but I couldn't have told you if it was every year, and I'd never watched it in my entire life. I thought that if you were a cyclist on the Tour de France, you'd probably still have to have a real job as well.'

This admission is remarkable for two reasons. Firstly, that Mark Cavendish, who is spectacularly dismissive of people who don't 'get' cycling, didn't walk away from her there and then. Although, this speaks volumes for the former Page Three girl Peta Todd's charms, which are many and considerable, and only a portion of which are superficially apparent to anyone searching on the Internet.

But it is also a remarkable admission for another reason. This meeting took place some four years ago. Those understandable levels of honest ignorance about the Tour among the British public were quite ordinary back then, quite commonplace.

In the winter of 2010, Mark Cavendish was a niche name like any number of others. He had all the public profile of a winter Olympian or a county cricketer. And yet, barely a year later, he was the World Champion, the Green Jersey and BBC's Sports Personality of the Year. And a year after that, Wiggins won the Tour, the Olympics, SPOTY (Wimbledon, a General Election, the Lottery, and *The X Factor*) all in one year. And then the secret was well and truly out. It really had been that sudden.

This had all happened in the time it took for Cavendish to meet Peta, for them to move to Essex and start a family. Not that everything which surrounded their smooth progression into married life was as unruffled and serene as that makes it sound.

For her part, Peta spent hours in front of the TV and with her nose in books trying to understand this all-consuming sport in which she was now partly implicated. She read up on its history. She quickly discovered, for example, who Eddy Merckx was. This was useful, because a few weeks later they were both entertained for dinner. By Eddy Merckx.

Her application and willingness to learn paid off. She started to pick the abstruse locks of a sport that yielded up its secrets unwillingly. Yet there were familiar obstacles to overcome, as anyone who has recently discovered the sport will testify. She remembers her bafflement, which found expression in repeated conversations like this, which her new partner tried patiently to answer:

'Why've they let that lot get away?'

'It's the breakaway.'

'Well, why did they let them break away?'

'Because it's the breakaway.'

'Well, why don't they catch them?'

'They will.'

'When?'

'Right at the end.'

'So why did they bother getting into a breakaway.'

'Because . . .'

'Because what?'

'Because it's a bike race.'

Anyone who has had to learn the sport from scratch can identify with that kind of question being met with that kind of answer.

All the time, as she was struggling with the convoluted grammar of cycling, she was also trying to understand this growling, charming little millionaire who had swept her off her feet. He was not long out of the clutches of a former Miss Italy, and before her there'd been the end of a long-term relationship with his childhood sweetheart.

'He had personal problems. The split from Melissa was really hard for him. There was a lot of stuff going on,' she recalls. 'It's no secret. I've said it to his face. When I met Mark, I googled him. I thought, if I hadn't met you, I'd think you were an arrogant little prick.'

He was still at HTC at the time, cocooned in that famously effective sprint train that ran riot through France every July. But, despite all the success on the bike, Peta felt that there was no one really looking out for his best interests. Instead, she felt, too many people in his entourage were taking advantage of his 'bad boy' image and turning it to suit their own purposes.

'Whether he was throwing something onto the ground and screaming and shouting, or whether he was standing on the top of the podium crying his eyes out, it made the press. Mark kicking off, or having a fight, or calling someone this, that and the other . . . it made the press. No one cared whether he was a nice person. He had people around him who thought of him as a commodity.'

She has a point, although it sits a little uneasily with the launch, just before last year's Tour de France, of Cavendish's own line of clothing (Cvndsh), using the catchy slogan 'Fst as Fck'. That went fairly far down the road of turning his bad-boy image into a commodity. Nevertheless the 'angsty teenager' of 2010, when the couple first met, has given way, ever so gradually, to a more moderated version of the man. Most of the time, that is.

Here's a recent and puzzling example from my working life on the 2013 Tour de France. It was the day of the team time trial in Nice. Omega Pharma–Quick Step went off early, and, powered by the fuel-injected turns of speed from Cavendish (he is a brilliant teammate for this discipline), set the fastest time by a decent margin.

He rode over the finish line, and came to rest in the run-out zone. I walked joylessly over to where Cavendish stood, astride his bike, towelling himself down and necking a Coke. We went through the usual routine, making him aware that I was there, but naturally allowing him time to recover. In his own time, then.

When I judged that the moment had come, I stepped in, 'Great ride, Mark. How well was the plan executed out there today?' I planted the microphone towards him. And as I did this, a couple of newspaper journalists did the same, but there really weren't more than about four of us.

And then? Nothing. He just looked dead ahead. I held the microphone out for what felt like a ridiculous length of time because, frankly, it was a ridiculous length of time; long enough at least for me instinctively to scroll back through our encounters over the previous days, hunting for a clue. What had I said, or done, which might possibly have upset him? What was there in my question that might have deserved his scorn? I couldn't imagine. So I continued to hold my grin in place and my microphone arm extended, until . . .

. . . he just rode off. I still wonder what that was all about, and have come up with no plausible explanation. The following morning, he was happy to talk, when I ambushed him at the hotel.

Peta has since dropped me a useful piece of advice, which I shall use in the future. 'Before it actually happens, I can see it coming. When he's really stressed, or he's tense or he's annoyed, his jaw muscles flicker badly.

'They really go. They're really prominent, over-developed because of how he clenches his jaw on the bike. And when he's trying to bite his tongue and he's getting really annoyed I can see them going. Sometimes, someone will be asking him a question and I think, I wish I could just pick that person up and move them because they don't even know what's about to happen. And I do.

'It's very hard, because he's only ever going to be interviewed at two points: he's won and everything's fantastic and the boys all did a fantastic job and they rode out of their skins and blah, blah, blah. Or something went wrong and he didn't win and someone's about to ask him how it feels. If I'd just spent five hours in the saddle and I'm hurting and I'm tired and I'm hot and I'm nowhere near home and I'm going to stay in a shit hotel sharing a room with another bloke who's going to snore all the way through the night and I've not done my job and I'm not happy, and then two seconds afterwards, when my emotions are high and my adrenalin is high, someone asks me how I feel . . . I'd probably want to say, "How the fuck do you think I feel? I feel like shit. How do you feel?"

'There's no middle ground. He's either really happy or really upset. Very few people know Mark's personality because you've got these two extremes and there's so much in between that you don't see.'

This polarity reaches its annual zenith at one particular point in the calendar: during the Tour de France. It is a race, according to Peta, that Cavendish 'holds up on a pedestal, in an ivory castle, with unicorns surrounding it'.

During the Tour there is an unbridgeable distance between him and his family. When Peta is back at home in Essex, and can only talk to him on the phone, she has to deal with certain signature problems, not least his accent. He 'kind of mumbles', with the result that she often doesn't understand him, but, rather than constantly asking him to repeat himself, she tries to guess what he might have said. Generally this doesn't work. In fact, if she slips up, he's on to her in a flash: 'Why haven't you been fucking listening to what I'm saying?'

'I get it in the neck all the time. I rang him the other day. He answered the phone, and I said, "All right, boy?" And he said, "I'm fucking trying to get dressed." So don't answer the phone! And then he rang me back, and said, "You all right, girl?" And then he said, "I've got to go. I'll ring you back."'

'Sometimes it drives me mad. Because even if I've got the hump with him, which happens, if he's at a race, especially a big race, I'll have to just suck it up. My feelings become less and less important. I won't say anything, because I can be distracting. I know he's got to focus. But there've been occasions when sometimes that isn't realistic, and I have to say, "Well actually you're a fucking idiot."

'There have been so many occasions when I have turned up to races and been furious with him, not really wanting to speak to him. But I'm "doing my bit", and then I've had to stand and do interviews outside the bus all about how proud of him I am and it's all so lovely . . . And I'd love to say, "Actually, I tell you what, he's a selfish bastard." But I can't. I just have to stand and smile and be there and let him kiss the baby.'

There is, and by now you may have picked up on it, a risk that all this weight of evidence as well as the robust language in which it is couched, might lead you to conclude that life in the Cavendish household is tempestuous at best and down-right dysfunctional at worst, the kind of the real-life soap that Channel 5 might decide to make their flagship Saturday night post-pub viewing. But this is far from being the case. Probably.

There is, however, considerable understanding for what it is that her husband does. Peta understands his job in great detail, every last pedal turn and nuance, in fact. Despite her bluster, those hackles that rise to match his, she does get it. Peta's unaffected passion for the sport bubbles over whenever she talks about its nobility and its aura. Hers was a headfirst induction into the intricately balanced ecosystem of the pro-fessional peloton. The first time she watched her new boyfriend racing, she had to fire up the computer and log on to a semi-legal webstream in the middle of the night, just in time to catch Mark Cavendish on his back on the hot tarmac, his head lolling from side to side as he writhed in pain.

'There was blood. His helmet was cracked. And I thought, 'Oh my God. This is dreadful.'

When he did eventually sit up, his helmet comically pushed to the back of his head, he looked around as if he had not the faintest idea what his name was or how he'd come to be sitting in the middle of an Australian highway with a helicopter thrashing its blades overhead. On the other side of the world, in the middle of a darkened house, Peta Todd was abruptly brought face to face with the tenuous, broken clasp with which bike riders embrace their best friend and worst enemy: danger.

'I didn't know if that was normal. Is that what happens? I didn't know if I could really do this. If you do this every time you race, that's not for me. I can't do it.'

I once saw an interview, filmed in 1968, with the wife of André Darrigade, the French sprinter whose record of twenty-two Tour stage wins Cavendish overhauled in 2012. She is sitting alongside him a year or so after his retirement, reflecting on their new life running a newsagent in Biarritz. She is asked whether she had married a champion.

'No. I married a man. There's been a lot of joy, but a lot of pain, too. A lot of worrying. I was always very nervous, quite a pessimist. I was always afraid that something would happen to him. I was always afraid that he would fall, that above everything else. In the last year, I could think of nothing else. I was enormously concerned. I wanted him to stop.'

This unspoken fear, and the unforgiving consequences of every moment where luck deserts you, are never far from the surface. Peta Cavendish has grown to understand, if not necessarily accept this. 'As a sprinter, especially, you are in those dicey situations all the time. He purposefully involves himself every day in the most heated, the most volatile point of the whole bike race.'

She recalls one night after a race, looking after baby Delilah on her own in a hotel room directly above her husband's (he sleeps separately from them during a race, in order not to be disturbed), listening to him screaming in agony. One floor below, Mark Cavendish was having grains of tarmac picked out of red raw wounds from another crash, on another day, in another race. This is their everyday.

'If they crash, to everyone else watching, it might seem like it takes seconds, that they get up straight away. To me if feels like they're on the floor for an eternity before they stand up. Time stops. You think, just get up. Just get up. Please, just get up.'

When Wouter Weylandt died due to a crash at the 2012 Giro d'Italia, Peta Cavendish was badly affected by the experience. 'I just sat there, and felt so guilty. My first reaction had been, I am so pleased that that's not Mark. I was just consumed with this sense of guilt. There was someone else, the same as me, watching, and realising that it was actually their partner. And I felt dreadful. All the riders were so shaken by it. They all questioned whether it was really worth it. It's a bike race.'

And again, in 2013, that question reared its head in very different circumstances. It happened the day after Cavendish had been involved in a crash, which had brought down Argos Shimano's Tom Veelers. Some, many even, laid the blame for this racing incident squarely at Mark Cavendish's feet. It goes without saying that the view was very different from within the Cavendish entourage. But the rights and wrongs of Tom Veelers' painful encounter with the seafront in Saint-Malo are only of secondary relevance here.

What mattered more, and what shocked Cavendish to his bones, was what happened the following day, when he was pushing on along the time-trial course, quite alone, and flanked by boisterous cycling fans.

Suddenly he spotted someone lurching forward from the crowd and flinging a liquid at him. It was urine. The accompanying abuse left him in no doubt that this was someone who'd made his mind up about Mark Cavendish.

'Pissgate.' That's how Peta recalls it, and tries to smile it off, but can't really.

It stunned him. For this to happen on the Tour de France, a race that had borne him aloft on an enduring high ever since his maiden win in 2008, was unthinkable. For once, it left him speechless. In public he said nothing, leaving his *directeur sportif* Patrick Lefevere to invent the funniest cycling spoonerism I have ever heard, when he described his rider's assailants as 'goolihans.'

Only to his wife did Cavendish articulate the real depth of his humiliation.

'That was the most upsetting day. He was looking forward to the time trial. I was out, I wasn't watching. He rang me afterwards and I said, "How did it go, boy?" "It was fucking terrible." He sounded like he was crying. "I feel sick, I feel sick."

'He was heartbroken. The respect he had always felt for the Tour in particular, and he'd been treated with the ultimate disrespect. He'd been treated like an animal.

'We all tried to suggest to him that he should have his say, and address it, telling him that he was the victim. But he didn't want to say anything about it. He was so embarrassed. He was mortified.

'It was a really hard, horrible Tour. I was just hoping that Mark didn't log on to read what was being written about him. It was dreadful. I felt helpless. He just shut everyone out and walled up. He didn't talk about it.

'Some of the stuff that was written on Twitter to me after that Tom Veelers crash was absolutely disgusting. Horrendous. "I hope Delilah never sees Mark again. I hope he ends up in hospital."'

It was difficult to say, that Saturday afternoon in Harrogate, what might remain of the 2014 Tour de France for Cavendish. But it didn't look at all good as he lay grimacing, slumped against the sloped angle of the Vittel crash barriers.

I ran to the finishing line to see him crossing on his bike, minutes after the rest of the race, the expression on his face as torn as his clothing, his right arm cradled uselessly.

I knew exactly what I had to do next. As soon as I was done interviewing Marcel Kittel, in all his deserved and generous delight, I gathered up Liam and Jim and we set off in pursuit of the injured rider. One man at the wheel, another programming the sat-nav, and me on the phone. At first we believed he'd been taken to Leeds General Infirmary. Then we were suddenly pulling a three-point turn on a hill as we re-programmed our destination for a clinic in Harrogate. And finally I got a call from someone on his team, telling me that he had been taken back to their hotel. A quarter of an hour later, I was there too.

The first person I bumped into was Dave Brailsford, walking through the lobby of the hotel (where Team Sky were also resident). He'd just seen Cavendish coming back from hospital. 'It's not a collarbone. He's dislocated his shoulder. Mark doesn't break bones.'

'Thanks, Dave.' I made to go. 'Hey, how about Froomey?' Amidst all the confusion and chaos around Cavendish, Chris Froome had sprinted to an unlikely sounding fifth place. So there was nothing wrong with his form.

'Doing what he's paid to do, at long last.' A wink, a chuckle, and with that, the knight of the realm hopped cheerily on his bike and went off up the road for a ride.

Then Peta Cavendish appeared, walking slowly towards the hotel with her daughter on one arm, and her son trailing limply behind.

'What's for dinner?' he asked, repeatedly, in that particular way that kids do when they really, really want to know what's for dinner.

They'd made their own way straight from the hospital. 'It's not great, for him, Ned. He's torn a ligament. Between you and me, I don't think he'll start tomorrow. But you know what he's like . . .' And with that she slouched off in the direction of the one hotel room you would have not wanted to be within a hundred miles of.

And there we left Mark Cavendish, down and out, and not so much at a crossroads in his career as standing in the middle of a roundabout he couldn't get off, while traffic roared all around him.

MILLAR

'I'm not designed for this. My legs can't do this.'

David Millar was not there to ride his bike, which made a change.

Instead of hurting himself for three weeks in the name of sport, and to his immense chagrin (he would like me using that word, I suspect) he had been deselected by his team at the last minute. This was a considerable blow to a rider not necessarily known for his stoicism and graceful acceptance of setbacks.

He had invested much in this race, not least emotionally. It would have been a thirteenth and final Tour. His farewell season had been constructed around his participation in an event that had given him everything, and to which he had returned over and over again throughout his turbulent, terrible, tremendous career.

A film crew had been following him for months, making a movie with the aspirational title *The David Millar Project*. Their focus, inevitably, would be the Tour de France, which would form the narrative meat of the film. And his shoe sponsor had created especially for him a series of bespoke cycling shoes inspired by every race he entered that year. The series bore the understated name 'An Eloquence of Motion', which, if we are honest with ourselves, is not only extremely 'David Millar', but is also probably the best name ever given to a range of shoes since 'Clarks Commandos'.

But tragically, we will now never know what symphony of textures and colours they had composed to cushion the feet of David Millar during the month of July, because he wasn't on the race.

I spoke to him by phone an hour or so after he'd stolen a march on his team's PR operation by self-announcing his non-selection and making plain his extreme dissatisfaction.

'I'm so sorry to hear your news, David.'

'F***,' he began, and 'f***' was roughly how he continued.

Ten minutes later, he was still talking, and I was still listening. But, being a sneaky media type, I had an ulterior motive for the phone call. I wanted to get him to join us, at least for the three stages in the UK, as part of the ITV presentation team. I had long felt that he'd be an interesting, articulate addition to our line-up, and had made the unconscious assumption that one day this would come to pass. What I hadn't anticipated was quite how precipitously it might happen.

'So, have you got any idea what your movements are right now?' It was the Monday before the race was due to start, and he would have had to change his itinerary overnight.

'No idea.'

'Well—' I was about to make him a suggestion, before I was interrupted.

'I'll come and work with you lot, if you'll have me.'

'You took the words out of my mouth.'

'Well, let's do it.'

And so the deal was done. But it wasn't until I arrived at the finish line of Stage 1 in Harrogate that our paths finally crossed. Here, stowed away in the fenced-off enclave of the technical area, and far away from the colossal crowds that had gathered along the high street, I found him tucking into a plate of salmon and noodles provided by our ever-astonishing Tour de France caterers Philippe and Odette. He was washing it all down with a plastic cup of wine, which struck me as an entirely reasonable, if unconventional, approach to live broadcasting. But it was very David Millar.

We sat down to talk, and after a while we were joined at the lunch table by Vin Denson, a former teammate of both Barry Hoban and Tom Simpson. He had brought along two jerseys which he unpacked from a Morrisons shopping bag and laid out on the table in front of us. The first was Vin's own British National Road Race champion's jersey, a beautiful heavy garment that still boasted oil stains on the front, and flapjack stains at the rear where he had stowed his snacks during whichever race he had last entered in the red, white and blue bands. And the other jersey was yellow. It was, it transpired, the genuine article: a Tour de France *maillot jaune*, but not just any one. That very jersey which now lay on the trestle table in front of us was Tom Simpson's first ever, and therefore Great Britain's first. It was won on Stage 12 of the 1962 Tour, and worn on the road the next day. Vin had come into its possession after Simpson's death.

I gazed at it. I am not someone who usually finds life in inanimate objects. But here was an artefact in vivid context, the bright yellow of its cloth reflected up at our three-way gaze like a buttercup under our chins, lighting the scene with strange intensity. Vin had ridden the ill-fated 1967 Tour in the Great Britain team alongside Simpson, and said later, 'Although I knew I was a grown man, I remember being almost hysterical in tears. I felt as if something inside me died when Tom died.'

The meaning of this lunchtime encounter was not lost on David Millar. He wore the yellow jersey in the 2000 Tour, and he, like Simpson, abused his body and his sport, chasing more success. If he was the lucky one, then he understood very well his good fortune. I recalled Millar's last stage win on the Tour, in 2012, when, minutes after outsprinting Jean-Christophe Péraud (for whom the 2014 Tour held much in

store) to take the win, he shouted across to me, 'Ned! Is it true that today's the anniversary of Simpson's death?'

Yes it was, I told him, exactly forty-five years.

Now, two years after that, he held up Tom Simpson's yellow jersey and shook Vin Denson firmly by the hand. Perhaps, in all this, there was also, for Millar, the strong sense that his race was done, and that his story, his endeavours, like those of Simpson and Hoban and Denson, had already passed into history. If it meant all that to me, I can only guess at what it might have meant to Millar.

So much changes, so quickly in this sport, as in others. But at its heart, there is a common ground that defies the shifts of the generations. Otherwise Denson and Millar would not have recognised each other as riders, as Tour riders.

*

That night, as Cavendish lay uncomfortably in a hotel, imagining the prospect of the race continuing without him, my guts fired a warning salvo.

I had been ill only once before on the Tour, in 2003, when a foolishly pre-emptory impulse to immerse myself in the culture of the event had prompted me to eat a plate of snails. A few hours later they returned, at speed, to the open air, faster than snails are supposed to travel. It had been days before I felt right again.

This time it started with a headache, then a sweat, and then became a strapping, constant pain across the midriff, just south of my ribcage. I lay in bed, closed my eyes and tried to remember what life had been like before my innards had decided to take up Pilates. I couldn't, and so instead I gave up and fell asleep.

Dawn broke over York. To my astonishment, I had survived. But I woke with my head pounding, and, bearing in mind that we had just completed day one of a twenty-three day journey (rest days are a misnomer), I was filled with an unshakeable gloom. I wanted only to get going, and get it done.

Before leaving the others the previous night, I had casually suggested that we should set off the following day at 'a loose 8.30'. The addition of the word 'loose' was designed to soften the blow of what I really meant, which was 8.30. It was a mistake to use that word, as I soon found out.

I was on the pavement, ready to leave at about 8.25, on the off-chance that the rest of the team felt the same urge to jump the gun. It turns out they didn't. At 8.45 I rang Liam, and at 8.46, when I had left a voicemail message, I rang Jim. There was no answer. At 8.59, I rang David Millar, who picked up.

'Hello?'

'David. It's Ned.'

'Aah. Good morning.'

'Yup.' How did I broach this? Which words should I use to suggest that I was quietly going mad at having been stood up and waiting on the pavement for half an hour? I have often witnessed the difficulty recently retired sportsmen and -women have at adapting to the strangely sapping rigours of working for television, with its endless hours of standing by and checking to see if everything works. Quite understandably, they tend to assume that you just swan up five minutes before the programme goes on air, do your bit, and then leave. So it comes as quite a shock when someone has to tell them they need to be on site two hours before they are needed, and will only be free to travel on when all the work is done. Often, after one chastening foray into the media, they are never seen again. So how to tell David Millar to please get a move on?

'Um. Where are you?' I glanced at my watch, which had just ticked over past 9 a.m.

'Just . . .' he paused as I heard the angle of his mouth expand to accommodate the razor blade, '. . . shaving. Won't be long.' I almost thought he might add, 'dear boy' in a Frank Muir sort of a voice, but luckily he refrained.

In a split second, I calculated forwards from there. Shaving, showering, packing, breakfast, loading the car . . . another half an hour? My headache throbbed. This was going to be a long Tour.

It wasn't quite that long a wait, but when at last we were all together and on the road, the definition of 8.30 had been stretched to breaking point. Liam picked up on my huff.

'Well, you did say, "loose".'

'I . . .' didn't know what to say. So I kept my mouth shut, as did we all. No one spoke really until Millar's BlackBerry suddenly buzzed with an incoming message.

'Cav's out.' I glanced over at where he sat. 'Just texted me. He's going to be at the start line. But then he's going to bail.'

At last we pulled up at York Racecourse, and went off in search of the injured, abandoned sprinter.

It is extraordinary how quickly silt settles on the fault lines and sudden tears in the bedrock of the Tour. What had seemed unimaginable twenty-four hours earlier – a race without the presence of the one-man headline generator Mark Cavendish – was already part of the bald fact, history and continuing narrative of this edition.

Besides, Stage 2's jagged profile on the approach to Sheffield was attention-grabbing enough, and brought into play a whole raft of riders who might win neither flat stages nor mountain stages but who fancied their chances on this silly, fascinating, horrible but beautifully designed parcours, with its back-loaded proliferation of short, sharp climbs.

One by one, as David Millar and I presented live from York, the fancied riders shuffled past us, and on to the start line for the roll-out. One of them had been brought down the previous day by Mark Cavendish. Simon Gerrans, the perennially smiling, perennially pugnacious Australian all-rounder, stopped to tell us that he was OK after the fall the day before, and that Cavendish had called him to apologise. Then there was most people's favourite for the stage Peter Sagan, and there were riders like Michael Albasini, or Jan Bakelants, Thomas Voeckler, or even Alejandro Valverde. It was one of those days that fell fabulously between a number of competing stools (hard to picture, that metaphor, I know).

It could be a sprint, but probably not. It could mean a breakaway gets up the road with a dangerous lead. It might end with a showdown of the big general classification favour-ites. It might be a damp squib. In fact, the more you discussed it, and the more riders thought about it as they pushed their bikes towards the start, the more you were able to make a case for almost anyone winning the stage, and with it the second yellow jersey of the Tour. Except, possibly, Andy Schleck. Or Fränk.

So, David Millar and I stood side by side, talking occasionally to the camera, occasionally to riders and occasionally to each other, with a packed grandstand behind us. The crowd's frighteningly high levels of enthusiasm showed no signs of abating in the glaring absence of either of the pin-ups of the British Cycling scene, Bradley Wiggins and Mark Cavendish. In fact, I suspect that there were many more people gathered there to watch the start of a bicycle race than the racecourse usually gets on race day.

Millar at least looked the part, in this setting. He had decided, presumably while he was luxuriantly shaving himself in the mirror that morning, and probably humming some of Schubert's lesser-known lieder, that today would be the day that he would broadcast to millions of viewers at home wearing a trilby. And trilbies were very 'horse'.

Now, it must be said, there are few precedents for headgear of any description in the sports broadcasting world. In fact, now that I try to think of them, all I can come up with is John McCririck and his profoundly affected deerstalker. The beard, of course, has had the occasional outing (Jimmy Hill), and the moustache has regularly been aired (one need only think of Des Lynam), but by and large sportscasting (to give the profession the kind of disdainful name it probably merits) is the land of the sports casual shirt and the short back and sides. And woe betide you if you stray, as Jake Humphrey never does, out of these narrow confines.

So trilbies are indeed a rarity. And, in and of themselves, there is nothing wrong with them. Indeed, I seem to recall a winter in my early twenties during which I chose to sport the peaked cap of a Hanseatic merchant sailor, until I thought better of it, presumably after catching an accidental glimpse of myself in the reflection of a shop window. But Millar's rather fine chestnut-coloured felt trilby had the unforeseen consequence of making him look even more vast than he in fact was.

David Millar stands at something over six foot two inches. I am something approaching five foot ten. Add to that four-inch differential the extra two inches that Millar's chapeau lent him, and he appeared giant, alongside my laughable stature. In cutlery terms (why not?), he was a fork next to my teaspoon. Add to the basic mathematics of his *hauteur* (again, I use a French term, as this is David Millar we are talking about) his absurd skinniness, then the overall effect was of a man on a badly adjusted television set. To understand what I mean, try watching a widescreen film scrunched into an old 4:3 TV. Everyone looks like David Millar, as if they'd been turned on one side and left between the pages of a heavy stack of books like a pressed flower.

You get my point. He was tall.

After York, we stopped en route to take in the splendour of Jenkin Road.

This was the steep climb just a few kilometres from the finish line in Sheffield, which ran through the heart of a 1940s housing estate. Famously, at one point, a few hundred metres from the 'summit', the gradient is so unkind, that the pavement (or 'sidewalk', as I mysteriously, and somewhat humiliatingly found myself saying on air that evening) has been fitted with a handrail, so that you can pull yourself up it, Sir Edmund Hillary-style, without the sherpas.

We parked the Espace and walked up the hill; Liam and Jim striding ahead carrying all the equipment, me and Millar lagging behind, until even I got bored of keeping his relaxed pace, and dropped him.

'I'm not designed for this. My legs can't do this.' I heard him complain as I continued up the climb. At one point I looked back to take in his languid form zig-zagging up the hill to lessen the gradient. He stopped briefly, took off his trilby, wiped the sweat from his brow, and then continued his ascent.

Lining the road was an array of houses, some of which had touchingly embraced the occasion, some of which still weren't sure how to react, and others that had double-locked the front doors, drawn their curtains and turned their backs on the whole bloody inconvenience. But mostly the residents of Jenkin Road, an unpretentious community of Sheffield people, had decided to get behind the race. Tables had been dragged out onto the pavement, kids flitted around with chalk and balloons, bunting was going up from lamppost to lamppost, and a few of the houses had even been decorated with a rash of bright red circular stickers, as if they had succumbed to German measles late in life. Homemade banners welcomed the race in dozens of different ways.

At the top of the road, when the almost-retired-yet-still-technically-elite athlete finally made it, we recorded a quick chat about what impact the severity of the climb, so close to the end of the stage, might have on the race. As we did our bit, a steady stream of riders made it up the hill to warm applause from the waiting crowd.

Then we headed downhill again, pausing briefly at Newman's Convenience & Off-Licence, so that the quadruple Tour de France stage winner could surprise the shopkeeper by heading for the fridge, and plonking a four pack of Stella Artois down on the counter. He was, after all, on his holidays. Sort of.

After the elegant spa-town delight of Harrogate, which had closed down entirely for the day to embrace the Tour, Sheffield was sending out more mixed messages about how it wanted to display its wares. It had cleared a space for us, right enough. But it wasn't exactly centre stage. Rather than looping through the middle of town, we parked up instead next to the monolithic facade of Sheffield Forgemasters steelworks and the less monolithic but significantly more modern exterior of the Motorpoint Arena, handily placed also for Toys R Us and Nando's. Now, I have nothing against working cities, and God knows the Tour de France takes us through some pretty utilitarian settings, but I was surprised that this was Sheffield's image of choice for their most important shop window in a generation.

Was this an oversight, a lack of consideration? Or was it perhaps quite deliberate? And if that were the case, then I admire their stance. Who needs 'pretty' when you've got steel! Let Harrogate and York do 'pretty'. We know who we are.

The gallic sous-chef Romain, who slaves away in the mobile kitchen every day preparing the most fantastic regionally based cuisine for the TV production crew, has a rare talent for words, even in his second language. As soon as we got to the finish line, we sat down for a coffee at his canteen, and took in the architectural scene that surrounded us.

'Thank you for taking us to Sheffield.' He gestured expansively with a wooden stirring spoon, as drops of stock flew off it in the direction of the steelworks. 'It makes me wonder why we even bother with France.'

We sat down with David Millar, an hour or so before the scheduled finish, as the riders were just starting to do battle with the three-mile ascent of Holme Moss and the multitudinous crowd that had turned it into a flattened-out version of Alpe d'Huez for the day, and we spoke at length about his career. Unable to find a quiet spot suitable for the intimate, reflective nature of the interview, we ended up sitting on a couple of upturned flight cases, just round the access ramp at the back of the Motorpoint Arena. It was the humblest of settings in which to ask Millar to reflect on the closing of a most troubled and rewarding chapter of his life.

But we spoke for an hour, more or less. He trawled patiently and thoughtfully through the early years, his descent into the bespoke hell of his own creation when he was caught red-handed with the paraphernalia of a doper, and his painful adaptation to life after the punishment. But when it came to describing the redemptive power of his last ever stage win, on the 2012 Tour de France, his throat caught. He recalled lying down on the tarmac, immediately after winning the sprint, and blocking out the mayhem around him, just focusing on the sky above him, and trying to frame the moment for ever in the simplest terms, catching the fly in amber.

He broke off, and looked down, suddenly finding himself sobbing, at the realisation that he would never race the Tour again. Now, there are good locations in which to find yourself confronted with a sudden sense of your own mortality, and

of the fleeting essence at the heart of your existence, and there is the access road at the back end of the Motorpoint Arena in Sheffield.

We cut the camera, and waited for him to recover his composure.

Selfishly, I, too, was struck by a sudden onrush of change. Here, after all, was the rider whose ill-fated Prologue ride in 2003 had kick-started my own bumpy career in the sport (and, quite incidentally, provided me with the title for a book). That Tour had ended with a stage win in the final time trial in the pouring rain. He'd finished so early, and had to wait for so long before Lance Armstrong, in the yellow jersey, came over the line seven seconds slower than him, that he'd already changed out of his cycling shorts, and was on to his fourth beer of the afternoon. That's why, he told me, on all the photos of the podium, when he reaches his arms into the air, you can see his boxer shorts.

Everything he had done since, from his disgrace to his rehabilitation, had formed the backbone of my understanding of the race. He had always been generous with his time. I had spoken to him over and over. He had never ducked a request, never refused to answer a question. I thought he'd be on the race for ever.

And yet here he was, perched uncomfortably on a flight case opposite me, drawing deep breaths and fiddling with the band of the felt trilby he clutched between his hands. The hat suddenly looked flippant. It was, most unequivocally, over.

When we were done we walked slowly, and wordlessly, back to the TV compound. I wanted to say something to him, but I couldn't articulate the thought. It was something that pointed towards how changed it all seemed, how suddenly. There was no Wiggins on the race, no Cavendish any longer. No Millar. One or other of them had been involved in every Tour I'd covered. I suppose I just wanted to tell him I'd miss his story.

Once inside the perimeter fence of the compound, he turned right, and went to use the toilet. I hung back and waited for him to return, thinking that I would tell him these things to his face when he came back. But after a minute, I felt the moment had passed.

The next day, he left us, and went off to train for the Commonwealth Games. And today, right now, in fact, as I sit here typing, he is out on the track dressed in the blue of the country of his parents' birth. He may believe he is still looking for a suitable way to sign off. But he did that already. And there's no need.

On Jenkin Road, Vincenzo Nibali attacked. The Sicilian rode away from all the others, from Contador and Froome, from Peter Sagan and all the opportunists, who thought they might have a chance. They were mistaken. It was the first glimpse of a pure, brilliant talent that would light up, and to some degree, define the character of the 2014 Tour.

When I spoke to Nibali later about the climb of Jenkin Hill, he mistook Froome for Wiggins, and then quickly corrected himself with a shy giggle when he realised his error. I spoke to him in English, shamed by my lack of Italian, and he answered in Italian. Often, over the coming weeks, I would only get the gist of what he was saying, and await a translation later. But the Wiggins/Froome confusion was as clear to understand as it was funny to hear. What did he care, though? He sat there answering questions in the sunshine. And in yellow.

We climbed back in the car and headed south to Cambridge. Somewhere near Peterborough, though, the sun peeped out again, and a rainbow raced briefly alongside our southbound trajectory. The race was fast gathering its rhythm.

At first, the eye tries to absorb all the detail through the passing of each stage. But after a few days, it wearies of the task, and takes a different approach, allowing a whirr of colour to flit unfocused through its field of vision, save for the picking out of a vibrant detail, every now and again.

TO DOVER

'Not one. He's never once thrown
his arms in the air on a bike.'

The following morning, a policeman stood guard outside our
bed and breakfast in Cambridge. It was a city I knew well.
The road on which we stayed the night before had been so
close to the race start that it was closed to traffic when we
woke up.

As we loaded the car, just down from where the bobby
stood sentinel, a trio of French gendarmes rode past on blue
motorbikes, the headlights unnecessarily on, their blue lights
superfluously flashing, and their knee-length biker boots
unfairly gleaming in the morning sunlight.

'Be honest,' I said to the Cambridge copper as he watched
them pass by. 'Would you, if you could, swap their uniform
for yours?'

He stood there stiffly in his heavy-looking black jacket and
completely ridiculous hat, which only Taiwanese tourists and
Spanish exchange students think is worthy of photographing.
The bobby's hat is a symbol of Britain and, according to esti-
mates, is therefore worth £12 billion to the economy, putting
it on a par with Wallace and Gromit. And Prince Andrew.

He looked at me. Then he looked up at his hat, without
taking it off, by tilting his head back slightly and rolling his
eyes skywards. Then he looked back at me.

'Err. Yeah.'

He turned away, as if the conversation had never happened.

*

Later on that morning, I spotted Jens Voigt trying on a policeman's hat, and almost doubling over with the mirth of it all, which completed the policeman's unarticulated thoughts.

Further down the road, at the start village, one of his colleagues from a different police force was buzzing, but for reasons which in no way related to his hat. Neither was it as a result of the third coffee of the morning, which PC Dave Solomon had snaffled as he stood there in his biking leathers. Rather, it was from anticipation of the day that lay ahead of him.

Already he had spent two days ploughing a furrow through the densely packed crowds of the Yorkshire hills, now he would lead the race on to the Mall, outside Buckingham Palace.

To be selected as lead motorbike in the convoy was a high honour. There had been some scepticism among the grizzled and fiercely protective gendarmerie as to whether or not this jumped-up Brit on his faintly underpowered bike and absurdly safety conscious hi-viz garb would be up to the job. Why, they probably complained, he doesn't even wear reflective aviator shades! But, acknowledging the sovereignty of the nation's roads, they had reluctantly been forced to agree that the British stages of the Tour de France should probably be policed by the British.

And so, on the magnificently named climbs of Midhopestones, Blubberhouses and Oughtibridge, it would be Dave Solomon's duty to part the crowds in the road with the nose of his motorbike, so that the Tour de France might pass through. This he had to do without inconveniencing the riders, nor allowing them a free ride, and preferably without killing, or even maiming, any of the spectators.

PC Solomon was just one of countless others who, already for the third time on the Tour, were going about their minutely specific task, preparing for the day's rigours. As we swung around the corner next to Christ's Pieces (this is the name of a park, not a holy relic) on our way to the start line, we came across the publicity caravan, parked up outside the row of houses where I used to live, as a student, back in the late seventeenth century.

I pulled up short, and brought the car to a stop, thrown completely off-balance by the unreal sight of a row of giant mobile Fruit Shoot drinks cartons, revving up their sound systems directly outside the front door to the student house where I used to live.

It was the very door I had pushed open wearily every evening over two decades previously, as I'd thought about how little revision I'd done, once again, for my modern languages finals. But here it was, almost entirely eclipsed by an absurdly overblown plastic blueberry which played music. I was stunned at the sight.

What had happened to my life? How had it come to pass that the oversized, lurid marketing float of an international sugary drink conglomeration now bore more comforting familiarity, more relevance, meant more to me, than did my academic home for those formative years in the late eighties/ early nineties?

When did Haribo replace Victor Hugo in my life? What had become of me?

Looking more closely at the unchanged wooden front door with its scuffed footboard, I realised I would no longer know how to address the ghost of my previous life. What could I possibly have to say to him? And what would he have made of the middle-aged cycling reporter in the Renault Espace gawping at the noisy fruit-liveried vehicle outside his door? Where would those two find their common ground?

I suppose if we hang around long enough, in the end it happens to us all, in differing ways. We grow up. And now, sitting in the car and staring at the rough, glossy front-door interface of a distant Tour-free past and an abrasively noisy present, I wondered about the future waiting just around the corner.

What did this new edition of the race mean? A partly unfamiliar array of names and faces to assimilate? So many of the old guard, those riders who had formed the backbone of the peloton as I had come to know it, were no longer riding, or were destined to fall away. It surely constituted another step away from what I had grown up with.

Put another way, I feared that the best of the years may well have been and gone, which is the inexorable fate of those who realise, with sudden shock, just how much time has marched on.

How else to explain my recent and unstoppable bout of weepiness, when listening to a poem by Pam Ayres?

I had been driving down a motorway, listening to Radio 2 (again, a portent of ageing) when she was introduced. Instinctively, I reached for the dial. Anything but Ayres, I thought. But then I heard the opening words of her exceptional poem about taking her children to university and returning home to a quiet house, changed for ever. I continued to listen, until I was, unmanfully (and dangerously, since I was in the fast lane of the M1), in floods of tears. This was neither normal, nor intended, nor dignified. But it happened, and there was no obvious excuse for it, beyond a recognition of the steady sweep of the minute hand, and the hour hand, across the face of the clock.

And now, it was time to get a grip. The Tour de France is not my teenage child. I have not just dropped it off at a hall of residence. I have stopped making sense.

Stage 3 came and went. There were the customary thick crowds all the way along, and in clumps through the Essex villages, even though this was a working Monday. But it was on the way into the East End of London that I really noticed the difference. Seven years previously, when the race had rolled out along the Woolwich Road, past the end of my street, there had barely been a soul out to watch it. Except of course my poor family, who had been dragooned into dutifully spectating.

Now, as we pulled off the North Circular Road somewhere near West Ham, and tried with only partial and fractious success to navigate a smart-arse short cut onto the race route, I noticed a significant difference. The folk of Tower Hamlets and Newham had got deckchairs out, filled the Thermos, packed the sandwiches and bagged a spot on the barriers. They weren't just there in pockets, they lined every stretch of the route, and by the time we got closer to Tower Bridge, along the Highway, they were already three deep on either side.

This was the scene which greeted the two breakaway riders of the day, Bretagne-Séché Environnement's Jean-Marc Bideau, who you are allowed never to have heard of, and Jan Bárta, the chunky Czech rider from NetApp Endura, which was the only team, rather humblingly, who hadn't turned up with a full-size bus, but lived instead in something which would probably be dubbed a 'Hoppa' if it were put into the service in, say, Maidenhead. I liked both those teams instinctively, the more so because a good few of NetApp Endura's riders had cut their racing teeth in British criterium races. Aussie Zak Dempster, a tall, gaunt, charming man, was taking just such a massive step up in his racing. Every so often over the coming weeks, I'd bump into him at the start, and watch his fatigue and growing sense of euphoria race each other neck and neck all the way to Paris. Good on them.

Bárta eventually dropped Bideau, who just couldn't hold his wheel, and was swept up by the inevitable bunch sprint that was starting to brew up menacingly at the pointy end of the peloton. But when I spoke to Bárta later it was evident, even for a rider of his calibre and class, that hurtling headlong into a capital city, with massive crowds roaring you along, was not something he expected to experience every day.

Marcel Kittel won again, with a bit more effort this time, but still comfortably. I watched him loping around good-naturedly behind the podium, nattering to the blissed-out Gary Verity, who was looking increasingly like a knight-of-the-realm-elect (despite, or even because of, his banana-yellow slacks), swapping a word with a sour-faced and mildly confused-looking José Mourinho, who seemingly only had a vague idea what he thought he was doing there, and then he was bounding up the steps to throw his arms aloft for the second time in just three days.

Kittel wore success well. A year ago he'd still been a wide-eyed debutant, now he was racking up the wins with all the alacrity of a young Mark Cavendish, and growing into his status as the 'patron' of the sprint. He came over to talk, with a broad, easy grin and an outstretched hand in greeting. And perfect hair. There was much to admire about Marcel Kittel.

And then the Tour was gone. David Millar also took his leave. We left him in London.

All around us, the trappings of the race were being dismantled as we went about our business on the Mall, putting together the various bits of script, voiceover and links which constituted the highlights show. To our left and right, the barriers were being removed.

A sizeable crowd hung around to watch us nipping in and out of our truck. Every time Chris Boardman poked his head out of the door, there were a few stray shouts of 'Chris!' It was a good hour and a half after the stage finish that we were finally done, and left the truck to make for our cars, parked up on Horse Guards Parade. By this time, the 'sizeable crowd'

had dwindled to a concentrated residue of the very bored and the very obsessive.

One man stopped me, as I sloped off, and good-naturedly demanded that I tell him which years I had ridden the Tour de France. When I pointed out that I wasn't Chris Boardman, he seemed undeterred. 'Yes, I know that, Ned. But which team did you ride for?'

Another man was furious. He had been trying, unsuccessfully, to blag a water bottle (or *bidon*) from one of the teams. 'Bloody Cannondale said they'd get me one. I waited for hours, and they didn't give me one. I wanted to get one for my daughter. It's bloody out of order, that's what it is.'

And, just when I thought I could make a bid for freedom and a release from conversations that made no sense, and to which I had no idea how to contribute, a hand was thrust out in front of me, and a beery face loomed at me, supported by a spindly neck and wiry frame.

'I've done fifteen marathons.' He stared intently at me, scrutinising me for my reaction.

'Right.' I smiled politely. 'Well done.' And I made to go, letting drop his hand in as tactful a way as I could. But he stopped me again.

'They all finished here, on the Mall.' It seemed he was going to continue. 'My personal best was here. I did three hours twenty-seven.'

'That's very fast.'

'Yes. It is. But do you know how I did it?'

'No.' I looked up the length of the avenue, hung on either side with its vast Union Jacks, at the receding shapes of Liam and Jim. 'How did you do it?'

'I was drunk.' Then he staggered off.

Over the rise of Abbott's Cliff, before the road dropped down into Dover, there was a thick summer mist. It was a soft, mild evening. Suddenly the vista of the Channel opened up before us, studded with a dozen white ferries ploughing back and forth. We pointed the nose of the car towards the docks, whose lights were now brightening as dusk fell.

The riders had all long since reached France, and already lay on the massage tables or beds in cheap hotels, having the heavy rigours of British roads squeezed out of their muscles. The rest of the Tour waited wearily on the dockside, as departure times slipped and the ships slowly filled up with the distended underbelly of the race. It was midnight by the time our ferry slipped its berth and grunted out into the water.

On board the *Pride of Kent*, I ate fish and chips with Team Sky's coach Rod Ellingworth. He opted for beans, and I had mushy peas. He's not often wrong about things, Rod, but he was hopelessly off target with that choice, just as he was when he contended, pointing a fork at me and chewing on

his battered cod, that Andy Schleck had never won a professional bike race, unless you counted the 2010 Tour which
was handed to him after Contador's suspension.

'Not one?' I so wanted to believe, but I was sceptical.

'Not one. He's never once thrown his arms in the air on a
bike.'

We googled it, just before the 3G signal loosened its grip,
and cast us into the Internet-free wilderness of the high seas.
Sadly, Rod's fact was torpedoed by the 2009 Liège–Bastogne–
Liège, which Schleck won. That aside, though . . .

Perhaps that's why I only paid scant attention to him when
he told me that he thought Thibaut Pinot might one day win
the Tour de France. Although, as the Tour progressed, I was
often to have reason to remember his prophecy, uttered with
great prescience, as he popped chips into his mouth.

Then, after taking my leave and wishing him a happy Tour,
I found a corner of the bar that didn't smell of lager and,
curling up against the wipe-clean plastic seating, fell sound
asleep, my stomach humming an unfathomably profound duet
with the ship's colossal, throaty engines.

PART 2

LILLE

'Kind of straight, straight, straight, then wuuuhhhhrrrr, then a bit of that, then wuuuhhrrr, and then whoosh.'

The next days simply dissolved. The passage of time started to warp, as it always does after three stages of every Tour I have covered. Timelines begin to accrue the mass of motorway asphalt, start villages find themselves grafted onto finish lines and the whole procession becomes confused, until it requires a three-second pause before you can answer the simple question, 'Where were we yesterday?' Even thinking about yesterday involves a brick-by-brick re-assembly of the consciousness, obliterated by the quotidian, same-thing-different-place paradox of life on the Tour.

But the first Continental stages of the race also started to dissolve in a more literal way: in water. It started to rain with such resolute intent, and from such gunmetal grey skies, that we feared the sun had detached itself and was pushing out into the galaxy towards a less gloomy solar system to illuminate. Good old Flanders.

We had shuddered into Europe, driving flat out from Calais along a stretch of terrifyingly unpredictable dual carriageway, arriving into Lille at a far from reasonable 3 a.m., where we had to unload all our gear at a city centre Ibis. After unpacking everything, I was forced to drive off again to park the car in a multi-storey car park so confusing that our designated level, reserved for Ibis hotel guests, was called Level 4½. It could only be accessed by means of a steep helter-skelter arrangement precisely the width of a Renault Espace without a centimetre to spare. It was harrowing, and when my head finally hit the pillow, with my innards still writhing, I fell instantly asleep.

Lille, in the early morning, was beautiful though. This was despite the constant, at times almost imperceptible, drizzle. Although I must have been there many times before, and certainly I had passed repeatedly through the international railway station, I don't think I'd ever seen the old town before. I am very fond of that kind of melancholic mercantile Northern European architecture, which talks of civic pride more than ecclesiastical excess.

We stopped in the main square to film a nostalgic look back at the 1994 Prologue in Lille: Chris Boardman's first Tour win.

'You'll have to tell me what I remember.' Chris doesn't do recollection.

'Why?'

'Because I can't remember anything I'm supposed to remember.'

In fact, and to his surprise, the Prologue course itself was still quite sharp in his memory. He had no idea which part of Lille it was in, but that scarcely mattered. The course was, in his words, 'L-shaped with a bit of a nipple.' He rode it, he told me, 'kind of straight, straight, straight, then wuuuhhhhrrrr, then a bit of that, then wuuuhhrrr, and then whoosh'. That final 'whoosh' had been enough to earn him the yellow jersey of the Tour de France. It had been, and still is, the fastest Prologue ever ridden on the Tour.

At the 2014 finish line, which had been rather banally plonked down next to Lille's hyper-modern football ground, the race had a hung-over feel. A lethargy seemed to spread like a contagion throughout the compound. Even the Tour de France itself, with its unwelcome return to early-season rain-capes and long leggings and spray on the camera lenses had a dutiful rather than exuberant look to it.

BUNCH: Shall we let a breakaway up the road?

REST OF BUNCH: Oh go on then.

BUNCH: Voeckler?

VOECKLER: Yup.

BUNCH: Maté?

VOECKLER: Seriously? Maté?

MATÉ: Please . . .

REST OF BUNCH: You two, off you go.

BREAKAWAY: See you later. Can you catch us at about 154 kilometres, please?

BUNCH: Whatever.

That kind of a day. There was some live entertainment, of sorts, on the finish line. A travelling brass and woodwind band had been freighted over from Opende in the Netherlands, called something like Bicycle Spectacular Crescendo.

Wearing Napoleonic-looking military uniforms, they farted away on euphoniums and piffled their piccolos, while pedalling around on bikes. This was mildly diverting for about twenty to thirty seconds, as I made my way from catering to our truck, clutching a hot coffee to hedge against the damp. But ultimately it was not great art, nor did it do much to fill the burgeoning existential void bubbling up within me, alongside the actual bubbling that was bubbling up within me.

'Silly Dutch bicycle band,' I muttered to myself. Which was a pretty accurate barometer of the mood I was in. I made a prediction that I would probably get to see Bicycle Spectacular Crescendo again the following year at the Grand Départ in Utrecht.

News filtered back from the race that Andy Schleck had climbed off and abandoned, presumably after overhearing Rod Ellingworth talking about him on a cross-Channel ferry. But, of rather more concern for the race, the pre-Tour favourite and 2013 winner Chris Froome, along with Bauke Mollema, had taken a fall in the first few kilometres of the day. It had seemed like nothing much at the time, but he'd hit the tarmac hard. Then it appeared to gain in significance by the hour.

In fact, by the time, much later, when he made his way up the steps of a mobile X-ray unit in front of a wall of fascinated onlookers in Lille, and then reappeared half an hour later to give an awkward thumbs up sign, his injury had become a definite 'thing'. And it was a 'thing' that would have consequences.

The race shuffled towards its conclusion: an extremely probable third-stage win for Kittel. There was an hour to go before they were expected in. Feeling worse than I had felt ever since we had left Leeds, I crawled back to the car, opened the door, climbed in, reclined the seat, and, in the damp dark of a multi-storey car park, fell sound asleep, slobbering into my collar. While I lost consciousness, my colleagues in the commentary box had to continue unabated. Chris Boardman later told me he was convinced that at one point Paul Sherwen succumbed to that most parlous of Tour de France commentator's ailments, 'chateau lag'; consistently talking about the castles as and when they popped up on the TV coverage, but always one palace behind where they should be.

Thomas Voeckler was in the breakaway, but to nobody's particular excitement. Was Voeckler suffering from something similar? Was he displaying 'Voeckler lag'? Were we thinking and talking about the last Voeckler, the one who rode so brilliantly in 2011, when he regained and re-held the yellow jersey over many of the same climbs over which he had suffered in 2004, while what we were actually watching was a different Voeckler, a new one?

The modern version seemed lacking in proper intent and genuine race-winning menace. It seemed, too often, that Voeckler had become a parody of himself; the gurning, bobbing, cheeky-chappy schtick was starting to wear thin. At what point, I wondered, had his charm begun to curdle? Now, his presence in a breakaway was treated no longer with delight and wonder and excitement. Rather it was met with a tut and rolling of eyes. It was perhaps hard on him. But he needed to change the tune, or rather, stop playing the song altogether, as whenever he now stuck his tongue out, he licked away another layer of his cherished reputation.

I had admired him greatly a decade ago. Yet something had changed.

Even when he spoke, some of the shine had gone. Now, to look at him closely was to see a man tired of playing the game whose rules he had invented. Sure, he'd slap a smile on his chops when he knew he was on air, as soon as the red light went on. But once he was done, as soon as he had stopped talking, his mouth shut, he dropped his grin and his eyes de-twinkled in a flash. There are, I guess, only so many years . . .

So many fine details were displaying the same subtle shift. The Tour I had grown to know, and which had become so familiar to me, had started to feel alien again. It wasn't just the Voeckler-lag. And neither was it simply the absence of Millar, Cavendish and Wiggins. Much more seriously, Pelicab, the long-standing purveyors of hired toilets to the Tour de France, were no longer on the race. This was grave news.

Pelicab had been responsible for the placing and daily

emptying of the iconic upturned green 'mushroom' *pissoirs*, around which grown men could gather, indulge their micturative urges, and chew the sporting fat. Now they had gone, and had been replaced with tiny little grey variants, no 'step-up platform' and little shelter from public gaze.

The first time I was forced to use one of these miserable sub-standard affairs was at the southernmost perimeter fence of the Lille Zone Technique. I had just started to relieve myself, overcome with justifiable self-consciousness, when a neatly attired gentleman shouted at me '*Considérez les enfants, monsieur! Il y a des enfants qui passent par ici.*' He had made a reasonable point – clearly Pelicab had not 'thought of the children!' – and one which I was in no position to dispute.

Chris Boardman has, in the past, rather implausibly claimed never to have to make use of the Tour's toilet facilities, at least, not the sit-down variation.

'How do you manage that?' we severally enquired of him, in awe and jealousy.

'Method.' In the weeks leading up to our annual departure

on the race (or 'summer holidays', as he rather quaintly puts it, as if it were straight from the pages of an Arthur Ransome adventure), he trains his body, by increments, to hold out by an extra hour each day, until he is operating at the full extension of his bowel's scope. We didn't know whether or not to believe him. But, under a fug of such contemplation, Stage 4 came to a clammy close.

Had I mentioned that Marcel Kittel won the stage into Lille? Or was that the one before? Where were we before that, anyway?

The day passed. That much I know, because at some point, we lugged our sodden carcasses, cameras and cagoules back into the Espace and wordlessly set off.

It was in a small town, over the border in Belgium, that we spent the night before Stage 5, when the riders would bow their heads into the wind and the rain, and at the same time, nod with the downward force of their pedal strokes towards the gravestones, the white crosses that would line the route with their unspeakable geometry.

On our way into the town that evening before the mess of what was to come, we knew that we had driven clear into the historical heart of all that loss of life. You could not miss it. To the left and the right of the road, we passed neat walled cemeteries, fifty graves here, perhaps a few hundred in the next. I suppose they were unremarkable in the grander scheme of things. But, by being small, they were more measurably human in the scale of the lives and deaths contained within.

In the car, conversation dried up to a trickle as we made our approach to Poperinge.

A fairground was in the main square, and even though it was closing in hard on ten o'clock on a grey and dank Tuesday night, there were plenty of Poperingers (I am certain that's what the inhabitants are called) drifting cheerily among the startlingly bright lights of the duck shoot and dodgems and the chairoplane. Gaggles of teenage girls feasted on waffles and doughnuts, families with arm-tugging young children with eyes on stalks passed along the neon aisles, and lugubrious, portly men joined at the elbow to tiny bird-like wives stood patiently in line for mussels, frites and mayonnaise, as if fulfilling a local council mandate to conform to national stereotypes.

We overshot our hotel once, only spotting its discreet signage when we had already flown by. That forced us to enter a bewildering matrix of one-way streets which took us straight out of town, before eventually turning and nudging us in concentric circles and incrementally back to our starting point, which was in fact our destination: the Hotel Recour.

It was an old townhouse, wonderfully restored to expose sandblasted stone and a steep oak spiral staircase with fat mahogany handrails and ornate carvings at the foot of the steps. Into this beautifully imagined interior we started to disgorge from the rear end of our increasingly unpleasant-looking and -smelling Espace. The foyer, paved with huge stones and heaving with imposing Flemish period furniture, started to fill up with our equipment, tripods, flight cases, rucksacks.

The concierge looked on, a corpulent man with a ruddy face, oily black hair, pince-nez glasses and an ambitiously tailored black shirt whose buttons were never really going to make it all the way down to the waistline. The shirt pulled apart at strategic gaps to reveal hirsute triangles of Flemish stomach. He smiled in welcome as we huffed and puffed and dropped our unruly assembly of kit all over his beautiful hotel.

'So, here are your keys,' he offered in a version of French even more clunky than ours. We had finally unloaded, and held out our hands expectantly.

'Two of you are in the annexe a hundred metres up the

road. And the other one has an apartment maybe one kilometre away.' One kilometre!

So we picked everything up again and loaded it back into the car, inventing ever more creative ways of swearing in a manner that could never realistically be understood by a member of the indigenous Poperinge population.

Once Liam and Jim had been dropped off at their annexe, Monsieur Pince-Nez then climbed aboard the car, and navigated me back through the fairground and out the other side of town to an anonymous side street. Here, in front of a bakery, he ordered me to park up.

Wheeling my suitcase behind me, I stood watching on as he fumbled, increasingly breathlessly, with the keys to the lock of a door at the side of the bread shop. Suddenly, and to his evident surprise, the door sprang open. Sweating slightly at his brow, he ushered me in with an extravagant gesture of the unfolded arm, guiding me to the interior of an apartment I had the distinct impression he had never once before set foot in.

We climbed two flights of surprisingly steep stairs, with recessed lighting at skirting-board level. Everything smelt new, as if the laminated flooring itself had only just been unpacked from the plastic B&Q packaging. But when we reached the top, what wonders revealed themselves! There were three bedrooms (I had a choice), there were two bathrooms, one of which contained a never-before-used Jacuzzi that was big enough to hold a Ford Fiesta.

There were two staircases: the one I had climbed up behind my host, and another mysterious set of steps leading away from the main hall down to what I assumed was the bakery downstairs.

I continued my tour. I had a pool table, a chaise longue, a table football table. And a piano. It all seemed a bit daunting, bearing in mind it was now past ten o'clock and I would

have to get an early night as we would be on the road at first light. I wasn't sure how I'd be able to cram it all in, if truth be told. Perhaps I might be able to pot one striped ball and play 'Chopsticks' on the piano before bed. But that was about as much as I could realistically undertake.

'You have everything you need?' Pince-Nez handed me the keys and left me to inspect my estate. 'Well, *bonsoir.*'

'*Merci, Monsieur.*' And off he went, one unnaturally slow footstep after the next. Down the corridor he wheezed his way, pausing twice, as I listened, to steady himself against the wall. I started to unpack.

The footsteps continued, now audibly descending the stair-case off the hall, the mystery one which I imagined might lead to the bakery. I pictured him heading down the steps, frowning in concentration and placing each foot with the greatest attention to detail, then I stopped listening altogether and assumed that he had left the building.

It was only after I had plugged the laptop in, unpacked the

iron and placed my toothbrush and razor in the bathroom, that
I became aware of the same ponderous footfall, but heading
back upwards, towards me. I looked up and towards the door,
as the noise drew nearer, until, after a dozen steps along the
corridor, he was once again at my door. He pushed it open,
and stood puce-faced and aghast, mouthing a few well chosen
words of advice born of his own personal experience.

'*Monsieur*. To exit the apartment, you must not go down
those stairs. It is the wrong way out.'

I never did find out where they led, because when the time
came for me to haul my luggage down the following morning,
I opted to go out the way I came in. But I did enjoy my night
in the newest, strangest flat above a bakery in all of Flanders.
Despite the stomach cramps, I slept deeply and restoratively.

Perhaps my sense of well-being was well founded. I sub-
sequently discovered that Poperinge was home to the Talbot
House, which served as an officers' club for soldiers on a few
days' leave from the front line. It was a place for them to
drink, eat, presumably play an upright piano not dissimilar to
the one to which I had been trusted with temporary and
inadvertent custody. Talbot House was located just far enough
away from the front line to be out of the range of the German
guns: a tiny holiday from the horror.

But this summer night in 2014, and spread out all across
a very different Flanders landscape on either side of the
Franco–Belgian border, riders fell asleep in post-industrial
franchised hotel rooms, and woke to hear the rain hammering
outside. A Flanders sky, as Jacques Brel sang in 'Marieke',
'weighs too much'.

By morning, those heavy skies had not relented, not one
bit. I was warmed into wakening by the smell of freshly baked
bread from downstairs, and made my way to join the others.
Then we got going.

*

We went to Team Sky's hotel, to try and find out how much pain Froome had endured overnight from his injured wrist, and indeed to find out whether or not it was actually broken. They were staying in a particularly bleak Ibis 'Styles' hotel, the new, budget brand of a fairly budget chain of hotels. I had never before stayed in a 'Styles' hotel but, for whatever reason, it seemed that we, as well as Sky, were destined to stay in a whole string of them before we reached Paris. Therefore, they needed a nickname, which they duly got, in homage to England's toothless 1966 World Cup winner.

So we turned up at Team Sky's 'Nobby'. The trees were blowing around, dropping thin, sodden ash leaves onto the shining fleet of Jaguars parked up around the central hub of the mechanics' truck. The metal of the roofs reverberated with waves of drops falling from above, as their crew of black T-shirted *soigneurs* and fixers came and went from car to car, scampering through the rain, and hopping over puddles.

In the hotel, and around the reception desk, as people came and went, there was much talk of the wisdom of sending the race off today on the allotted course with its nine sections of cobbles. Charly Wegelius, the recently retired pro, turned *directeur sportif* with Garmin, who were also staying in Lille Nord's 'Nobby', showed me a picture he'd just been sent by Christian Vande Velde, also recently retired, and now con- tracted to American TV.

Vande Velde had done a recce with a TV crew along the route of some of the roughest cobbled sectors. The water was standing a foot deep in places, and the sides of the narrow farm tracks had turned to mud. Charly looked at me with his usual amused inscrutability, but I could tell he thought it was madness, not that it followed that he didn't want to put his riders through the madness. I think he was just delighted he'd retired. It did actually look unrideable, and much as it went against my desire to watch this much-anticipated stage rip a hole into the race, I did not query the good sense behind ASO's decision, which was suddenly announced, to scrap two of the nine sectors. I just hoped that no more would follow.

I found Dave Brailsford sitting all alone in the carnage of the breakfast room, surrounded by opened cereal boxes and bowls scraped almost bare of their yoghurty, oaty, banana-y content. A nutrition bomb had clearly been detonated in a confined space, and not many had survived. Except Brailsford.

He was picking a nut from his teeth, and thinking out loud, as our camera rolled, on the day to come, downplaying Froome's injury, but not downplaying the drama he expected to see on the race. 'You can't defend on a day like today. That's when things'll go wrong for you. You have to ride positively.' The rain battered against the window.

When we were finished with the interview, he asked me where I'd be watching the stage. It's one of the charming peculiarities of Dave Brailsford that he always expresses an interest in what you're up to. Perhaps that over-arching commitment to getting the big picture is part of what makes him what he is, with the undeniable successes that have come his way as a result. Or perhaps, more cynically, he's just figured out that it's good PR, like the transparent ploy to which some sportsmen (and politicians) resort of dropping in their interrogator's names at every possible opportunity: flattery, recognition, needy egos, he's probably just masterful at playing them all off. Or maybe he was just making conversation, like I did when I asked him what he'd had for breakfast. I think he said toast. But it might have been porridge, I can't remember. What a marvellous charade we all play every day on the Tour.

'I'll be at the finish line, Dave. Got to get ahead of the race, and wait for it to come in.'

'I'll be squinting at the screen on the bus.' He smiled ruefully.

'Good luck, then. See you later.' Let Stage 5 do its worst.

FROOME

'Perhaps we need to save the respectful nod to the
Great War for the highlights.'

It really was just an ordinary day. Had there not been a bike
race smashing through the village, what would we have seen,
had we been watching a live CCTV feed of the main road?
Perhaps a postman might have passed from door to door,
hopping in and out of his delivery van as quickly as possible
to avoid the rain. There is a chance that the white garage
doors might have opened, and a car pulled out on its way to
the Carrefour supermarket seven kilometres down the road.
One or two desultory pedestrians might have passed from
time to time, shrouded against the heavy rain, and hurrying
by. Along the road there would have passed a number of
tractors, spewing heavy Flanders mud from the deep profiles
of their tyres. It was a Wednesday afternoon in an unremarkable place, and the weather was ghastly.

We left the hotel in Lille, and made for the finish line at
Arenberg Porte du Hainaut. We drove the race route for the
final few kilometres, down a long road, flanked on both sides
by neat workers' bungalows, all spread out in the shadow of
a brick-built colliery.

The enormous inflatable arch that denotes the Flamme
Rouge (or final kilometre) had been erected right outside
someone's front door, its wobbly presence quite dwarfing the
single-storey house. There can't have been more than about
a foot of pavement left for the residents to sidle out of their
property onto. It amazes me how little choice people get in

the matter. Imagine if you really didn't like the sport and woke up to find you can't get to the shops because someone's barriered off your road and pumped up a huge bouncy castle outside your front entrance. It would present a slight perturbation, perhaps.

Mind you, the weather was not conducive to nipping out to the shops. If anything, it was gaining in miserable intensity. We unpacked and, navigating puddles and watery bogs, located the ITV truck, just in time to see the entire summer change shape.

Gary Imlach, waiting to open the show with a lengthy and carefully scripted intro, tore up his notes. 'Perhaps we need to save the respectful nod to the Great War for the highlights.'

Chris Froome crashed definitively out of the Tour de France minutes before we went on air for the live broadcast in the afternoon. He picked that precise point in time and space to topple heavily onto the pavement, slamming hard on the tarmac. He sprang up, as riders do, if they possibly can, but this time there was not the same urgency in his movements to seek out the handlebars of his bike and haul himself back into the action. It was the second time already that day that he had been down, and the cobbles had not even raised their stony backs along the path from Ypres heading south. Added to the fall the previous day when he had damaged his left wrist, the discomfort passed the threshold of the acceptable. It was over.

He staggered around meekly, head bowed, and clutching his elbow as around him a loosely assembled posse of on-lookers, photographers and other race officials variously gawped, proffered useless help, and generally got in the way. Bikes were placed in front of him in the hope that he might race. But it was done in the same way that you might place a bowl of tomato soup in front of an ailing relative and encourage them to eat. 'It'll do you good.'

Froome's mind was made up. All he needed now was a getaway car. To climb into the back and close the door, shutting out the babbling madness around him, the cameras, the humiliation. The first Sky car to arrive was full of kit. He opened a door, tried to get in, aborted, and then closed it again. The second offered him refuge. A fragile move from car to car, a painful, creaking manoeuvre, and then he could sit down and close out the world. The car pulled away. The entourage left. A few minutes later, the rest of the race had run by, and the roads opened again behind. Within an hour, the scene had returned to normal, as the heavy rain increased. Just a village, not even a village. One Wednesday afternoon.

In the days that followed Froome's abandon, Dave Brailsford put a determinedly positive spin on the race. In interview after interview he insisted that, as disappointed as they were, their appetite to attack the race remained undiminished. In Richie Porte, he contested, they had a genuine GC contender. He happily referred to Porte as his Plan B. And he even, at one point, and a little self-consciously, referred to his third option, known at Plan G (standing for Geraint Thomas), although no one was really sure what that one was supposed to look like.

But the feeling grew that much of this well-intentioned bluster was designed to throw a fire blanket over the smouldering suspicion back home that a national hero had been mistakenly left behind. It took seconds, after Froome got into the car and drove away, for the first mention of Bradley Wiggins to ping into timelines. And over the next few days, the momentum in favour of the dropped rider grew and grew.

I am consistently amazed at the popularity that Bradley Wiggins enjoys, and how no other rider, in the eyes of the broader British sporting public, comes close to the levels of adoration he inspires.

Back in the middle of June, I even started to dream about Bradley Wiggins. This I took as a sign that the Tour now occupied too much of my life, nudging everything else out to the margins. In one particularly odd dream, he and I were attending an annual dinner at Leeds City Hall, at which, instead of saying grace, everyone indulged themselves in a rumbumptious Yorkshire parody of a Bavarian folkloric dance by slapping each other around the face and cheering, for some inexplicable but perhaps hugely significant reason, 'One in four! One in four! I will get you one in four!' I had no idea what the four were, nor what the one was.

At the back of the hall, Wiggins and I, not being from Yorkshire, were tapping out a light salsa-based dance, and occasionally holding each other by the waist.

I woke up, suddenly. Then sat up and stared ahead in alarm. What could the dream mean?

For a rider whose initial engagement with the Tour de

France was so marginal, and who perpetually oscillates in and out of love with the race, Sir Bradley Wiggins of Kilburn casts a long shadow. There was more excitement about his non-participation than there was to be about Chris Froome's actual race-favourite participation.

In fact, the day he announced that he had been dropped constituted a distinct and Kennedy-esque 'where were you when . . .?' moment.

'Will you be riding the Tour de France?'

'No. As things stand I won't be.'

So, where was I? I was driving home in a clapped-out twelve-year-old Renault Scenic with squeaky windscreen wipers and an air-conditioning unit that blew out only luke-warm air, whatever the thermostat's setting. But Bradley Wiggins's words rose above the white noise of the road, and the impotent howl of the fan.

'I'm very disappointed, obviously.' And suddenly, as if from nowhere, I was very disappointed, too.

The Wiggins Abdication had been intoned by the BBC in much the same way that Kind Edward VIII had broadcast his intention to walk away from the throne. There was, of course no silly talk of the leaving office for 'the woman I love', but there was indeed the same sense of hurt and powerlessness.

For Edward VIII, read Bradley I. The words fit like a white silk glove.

'At long last I am able to say a few words of my own. I have never wanted to withhold anything, but until now it has not been constitutionally possible for me to speak.'

The Team Sky press officers, huddled around the wireless and suddenly powerless to contain the outpouring of national grief, were left wringing their hands.

'This decision has been made less difficult to me by the sure knowledge that my brother [Froome], with his long training . . . and with his fine qualities [pinch of salt], will be able to take my place forthwith without interruption or injury [God willing] to the life and progress of the empire [Team Sky].'

The Tour, at a month's distance suddenly seemed a castrated affair; its principal drama redacted. I had spent months following the nuanced ebb and flow of team Sky's two British Tour de France winners being magnetically repelled and yet drawn inexorably together for this uncomfortable shotgun wedding on the roads of France. With a little inside understanding of quite how deeply the one resented the other and the other returned his resentment, I had become increasingly fascinated by the prospect of a fragile collaboration, with the cited aim being Chris Froome's second Tour win.

With Wiggins in the Tour, each stage, as the race rocketed towards the final decisive time trial at Bergerac, took on a perilous fascination. What if Froome punctured in the first few days (as he did in 2012) and Wiggins didn't wait? What if they ended up either side of a split in the race on Stage 2, or the cobbles of Stage 5? What if Froome got sick, lost form, lost heart, lost the team? It was a richly detailed route map, alive with potential for misfortune and skulduggery. But now, without such interest, the texture suddenly receded. The line on the map, from Grenoble to Risoul, for example, suddenly looked two-dimensional; ink on paper, rather than a ridged serpent waiting to rear up off the page. I feared for the race.

The prospect of a Tour without simmering discontent? It seemed unpalatable. I struggled to see the potential human drama emerge from the race, as it was laid out in front of me. It looked suddenly like a trade show for bicycles with advertising wrapped around to fill in the boring bits.

The Wiggins story works – his guts and frailty, charm and paranoia – all of it.

I was at an event in the winter, to which I had been invited in order to host a question-and-answer session at a black-tie dinner for Bradley Wiggins. He had been flown by private jet to the venue, and was introduced to the diners with a great fanfare. 'Ladies and gentlemen,' called one of those special town crier-type MCs, 'please be upstanding for Sir Bradley Wiggins and Lady Catherine.' In they came, he at full tilt, and his wife trying to keep up, tottering on heels into the banqueting hall. He was clutching an outsize vodka tonic.

His 'people' implored me, when it came to the Q&A to steer clear of two subjects specifically: Armstrong and Froome. When it came to my first question, which was entirely bland as I recall, he managed instantly to address both the forbidden subjects with the same robust language and in the same sentence, rather making a mockery of the sanction imposed on me. Then he went on to savage the reputations of several others. When I tried to wrap things up after twenty minutes, he insisted he was having fun and invited the audience to throw some more questions at him, while he ordered up another vodka tonic.

It was a decidedly long evening. Afterwards, the people I spoke to who weren't either too horrified for words were simply slack-jawed with astonishment at what they had witnessed: a twenty-first-century sportsman with an out-of-control verbal tick. It would be hard to say that it was refreshing to witness such massively off-message behaviour. But it was different. It was most markedly different.

And now, in the Wiggo-less reality of the 2014 Tour, we faced an onslaught of tightly controlled appropriate response. I never thought I'd find myself saying this, but I missed the very idea of him.

What was happening to me? Had I finally thrown up my arms in surrender and joined the ranks of the wider British cycling fandom, with their Wiggo sideburns, homespun roundels and patriotic hashtags? Where was my sense of Continental sophistication, my writerly detachment? Where had I left my aloof?

Here I was, wilfully forgetting my own not always easy relationship with one of British sport's most difficult personalities, hoping that he would make selection for the race. As if in denial about the countless hours of my life I would waste waiting for Wiggins to either talk to us or not talk to us, I longed to be able, perhaps for the final time, to tell the story of how much these two wildly different men with their bickering partners, genuinely could not abide each other.

The TV viewer was to be denied the right to watch, free-to-air and in hour-long nightly highlights packages, an emotional nuclear bomb being detonated on the flatlands of Belgium and on the slopes of the Alps and very, very slowly exploding in high-definition across our television sets. Who, in all this push for 'performance' was thinking of the justifiable need for the idle masses to consume a nightly show of human treachery for their edification? How thoughtless of them to ignore us.

But in the end it did not come to pass. Sometime around mid-morning on 27 June, the day after Wiggins had just suffocated the life out of the opposition to clinch yet another national time-trial championship, an email thumped into my inbox, a incendiary missive of great digital heft.

It contained written confirmation that Sir Bradley Wiggins would, for once and all, definitively, not be taking part in the bicycle race to Paris.

This rather rudely worded tweet, addressed to me and to Team Sky, best summed up the reaction of the Great British Public:

I hope Froome is proper shit at the Tour, and @nedboulting nips to Lancashire to interview Wiggins, to find him pissing himself laughing.

Nastily worded, horribly prescient.

Even before the cobbled sectors of Stage 5 finally broke the race into fractured bits and pieces, even before Vincenzo Nibali's seemingly effortless assumption of a Tour winning lead, and before Lars Boom's immense attack all the way to the finish line, it had been over for Chris Froome.

I watched the live pictures, then grabbed my anorak, and headed out into the pouring rain to see if I could find the Team Sky bus, parked up in a long row of buses, just over a level crossing, past the finish line. The publicity caravan had just passed through, and was using the same stretch of road to get away. But things had ground to a halt, and nothing was moving, so that the road was completely blocked, to the left with team buses, and to the right with the absurdity of the caravan. Most of their drivers and *animateurs* had, to everyone's relief, switched off their loudspeakers and killed the inane music to which they had been subjected, and had subjected everyone else, for the previous five or six hours. Their operators sat stoically in their over-decorated cabs, exposed to the driving rain.

Alongside the Sky bus, with its blinds down and door firmly shut, there was an enormous madeleine cake, around which, in the torrential rain, a cluster of smiling youngsters, strapped into their vehicle with all sorts of safety harnesses, were still blurting along with the ear-splitting din. You could just about make out the words, sung with heavily accented gusto, straight at the blacked out windows of Sky's mobile headquarters, in which the team hierarchy were presumably still digesting the news that a year of meticulous planning for the race, and a multi-million-pound investment, had just been washed away in the gutters of northern France.

'If you're 'appy and you know it, clap your 'ands!'

I stood for a while, feeling the drip of rainwater down the

back of my neck. At one point I thought I could make out Dave Brailsford's legs through a gap in the privacy curtain, pacing up and down. But then they too disappeared into the impenetrable gloom of the interior.

'. . . and you really want to show it. If you're 'appy and you know it, clap your 'ands!'

Feeling like I was intruding on private grief, I slouched off, soaked to the skin and shivering.

Stage 5 contorted the race, the second in a series of blows that would rain down on everyone but the sublime yellow jersey. It ended with Alberto Contador detached by a couple of minutes to Nibali. It put Andrew Talansky somewhere in the middle, with Geraint Thomas and Richie Porte trying to salvage something for Team Sky. As Thomas later put it, 'I said to Richie, "Let's just smash it and see what happens."' As plans went, it wasn't subtle.

The team made hasty private arrangements to smuggle Chris Froome off the race and get him home to Monaco as soon as they could. It became my job for the evening to try and make sure that they were less than private, and to see if he would talk to us, at least briefly, about the crash.

So, with subterfuge and camouflage on our minds, we made our way back, with heavy hearts, to that same Ibis hotel in Lille, and set about the onerous business of waiting, watching and listening for signs of a Tour de France champion about to be whisked away under our noses. I went into tracker mode, reading the signs of movement in the lobby with all the instinctive expertise of a hunter-gatherer in a pair of soggy jeans and even more sodden trainers. Outside, it continued to rain, unabated.

There was a group of Dutch corporate guests of the team, all dressed in matching Sky-branded clothing, propping up the bar. They were well into their stride in terms of their beer consumption and were gaining steadily in volume and excitability. Every time anyone of any note from the team appeared in the lobby, they had to endure a round of selfies with their VIP guests before they could proceed. But the prize selfie, the one with Froome, had so far eluded them. The man had not been spotted by anyone.

Lurking near the emergency exit at the back of the lobby, I overheard a conversation between one of Sky's support staff and someone from the hotel. They were discussing the best route out of the back of the hotel. Affecting an air of casual enquiry, I wandered off round the back of the hotel, just at the point when Dario Cioni, Froome's personal minder, drove his team-issue Jaguar round the back. Something was clearly about to happen. We set the trap. Liam and Jim took up a position behind a bush, the camera poised. Then Dario moved the car. Now Liam and Jim stood under a tree. Dario moved the car again, this time parking it round the front of the hotel. Liam and Jim had no option now but to stand in plain view of everyone right at the front of the hotel, with all our laugh-able pretence of discretion abandoned.

We had drawn the attention, too, of a couple of print

journalists who shadowed our moves, having picked up on the same scent. And then, with a sudden instinctive rush, and without any obvious cue, we all simply walked back to where we had started in the hotel lobby and out of the rain, completing our absurd itinerary.

And right at that moment, Chris Froome appeared, coming from the breakfast room where I had sat with Dave Brailsford at the beginning of the day. He was wheeling his own suitcase, as if he were about to set off on a school exchange trip. He walked up to us and started to talk.

In the middle of his dignified, measured words, there was a sudden, thunderous crashing noise from just to our left. One of the Dutch guests, in order to get a better view of the rider for his selfie collection, had managed to send flying one of those information stands which proliferate in hotel foyers. It fell, and then he fell, drunkenly. The metallic clatter and human howls that accompanied this act of almost total clumsiness were enough to stop Chris Froome in his tracks. He paused, mid-sentence, and looked over with great concern at the fallen drinker as the man lay on the ground, his legs wrapped around a whiteboard. Only when he was sure that the man was not in any mortal danger did he continue. Then he made his way out of the hotel, and out of the race. The remaining Dutch drinkers watched him go, suddenly much quieter.

Two falls in one day then. But with varying degrees of significance.

VERDUN

'Men will have learnt how to suffer. Their energy,
their tenacity, their stoicism will all have grown.'

They were markedly sombre, the next days on the roads
through the Pas de Calais, across into the Somme and down
through the Departement du Nord. As if ordered on command,
a grey shroud was drawn over the landscape along from the
Channel coast, and inland. It looked like November, it felt
like April, but it was in fact July.

I doubt the riders thought about the Great War. I should
imagine it was the last thing on their minds. But that was
not the point, the remembrance was not for them. They were
the actors moved into position against a scrolling backdrop,
and pushed briefly into the foreground as the race scythed
through the landscape.

We parked haphazardly, and without much due care and
attention, right outside the simple facade of the Faubourg-
d'Amiens Cemetery in Arras. The skies were still heavy, and
it was still raining, which did not surprise us in the least.
From there, we walked to the Village Départ, housed within
the austere confines of the ancient Quartier Turenne barracks,
whose central courtyard had been turned into a mudbath by
the unrelenting wet.

On our way there, we passed a new addition to the publicity
caravan, a car converted to carry a huge display promoting
the town of Arras. A sudden ray of sunshine caught the display:
'Ville de Mémoire, Terre de Remembrance.' That certainly
made a change from men in latex baguette costumes, and

entire plastic cheeseboards. Arras was marketing itself, as does Ypres and so many of the towns near the Somme, on its historical association with the Great War.

The Tour de France had quite deliberately chosen this centenary year of the outbreak of hostilities to retrace much of that terrible, immobile front line, and three stages in particular, heading from Ypres to Nancy. While Ypres, overshadowed by the immense mass of the Menin Gate, drew the focus for British remembrance of the war, the further the race weaved south and east, the more it stirred French sensibilities, as it edged close to Verdun, the site of colossal loss of life. Germany's generals had promised to 'bleed the French army white'. They nearly succeeded.

I did not know, until this year, what a resonance the name of that epic siege has in French national life.

The closer we drew to Verdun, the more imagery of fallen riders and fallen soldiers was mixed into the race footage by the host broadcasters of France Télévisions. It was unusual for the Tour to spend so much time in this part of France. The Somme, the Aisne and the Ardennes: these are departments that do not usually enjoy much limelight as the race tends to skip over them in a hurry to reach the Alps. But now, as the weather continued to provide a melancholic backdrop, it was this land we gazed at on our screens during sleepy phases of the race. It was not easy to imagine what had happened here.

It was, obviously, not the first time there'd been a bicycle race over these battlefields. The first one, right after the war, had been one of the nastiest ever ridden.

Scarcely six months after the victorious Marshal Ferdinand Foch, flanked by senior allies from the British armed forces, sat opposite Count Alfred von Oberndorff in a railway carriage in the middle of the forest near Compiègne to sign the Armistice, somebody suggested the marginally less atrocious idea of a bike race.

Once more a newspaper was to blame for inventing voluntary cruelty for public entertainment. The Parisian daily *Le Petit Journal* put up the not insubstantial prize fund of 8,500 francs. The newspaper was the brains behind the legendary suffer fest Paris–Brest–Paris, a race that took over seventy-one hours to ride on its first edition, and involved the riders carrying all their food and supplies with them, and falling asleep in ditches en route.

But this time they delved still further into their limitless capacity for cruelty, when they came up with the concept of the Circuit des Champs de Bataille, one of the toughest in history, and a race described brilliantly by Tom Isitt in *Rouleur* magazine. It was, according to Isitt, conceived as an attempt to 'reinvigorate bicycle racing in France, Belgium and Luxembourg after World War One, to honour those who had died on the battlefield . . . thumbing its metaphorical nose at the vanquished foe on the other side of the new border' of Alsace-Lorraine.

There were seven stages, each one more than 300 kilometres, looping through a shattered landscape. 'Month upon month of shelling and terrible weather turned the Somme into a featureless morass of chalky mud as far as the eye could see. For mile after mile, the previously charming countryside had been replaced with a stinking primordial swamp of mud, corpses and metal. The trees were reduced to blasted stumps; belts of wire and duckboards zigzagged crazily in all directions. There was no colour, no respite, no comfort.'

The eighty-seven starting riders were equipped with wholly inadequate maps, which failed at the first instance in the face of roads and junctions that simply no longer existed. The weather was unseasonably cold. The pavé iced up. Riders got lost, sheltered overnight in battle trenches, and those that did make it to the finish line, like the great Belgian champion Charles Deruyter, almost perished from the cold.

By Stage 6, as the race headed along the Voie Sacrée, the key front line that had saved Verdun at great cost, there were only twenty riders left. Over the Ballon d'Alsace, snow started to fall. The race passed not far from Douaumont. Back then, the 130,000 skeletons of fallen soldiers, which are now gathered and laid to rest in the vast ossuary, simply lay scattered and exposed to the sun and the rain, the wind and the frost.

I could go on. But you get the picture. The race was a disaster, really.

Deruyter won it, amid allegations of cheating (how unusual for cycling!) and he trousered the substantial prize money. The next year it was reduced to a one-day race. And then it never came back, having been miserably ill-conceived in the first place.

But the fact of its brief existence said something at least about the time and the place.

To compare attitudes and inclinations, as well as character across generations is of course, almost inevitably, brutally unkind to the present day. By comparison, it is tempting to

rubbish one's own age. It is also something of an anthropo-
logical cul-de-sac.

But precisely that comparison was unavoidable, as the 2014
Tour de France entourage of air-conditioned buses started to
unload its millionaire cargo onto the roads of the Flanders
and the Ardennes for Stages 5, 6 and 7.

By simply turning up, with its risible battalions of oversized
Haribo sweets attached to the roofs of cars, fleets of police
outriders and squadrons of helicopters, to chase along the
route of so much bloody history one hundred years before,
the Tour invited a reflection on the changing nature of human
endeavour and values, in war and in peace. And while real,
awful and contemporary battles raged half a world away in
Ukraine, Iraq, Gaza, Syria and elsewhere, bringing about an
updated and brutal new version of misery, Western European
eyes could address their gaze back to their own horrors and
view them afresh, through the filter of their shared common
history. To ask oneself: what were we then, as men?

Sixty-seven professional riders died in the Great War. Some
were better known than others. Some are less well remembered. Two brothers in law, Léon Comès and Léon Hourlier,
who was a three-time national champion of France, both died
in the same aeroplane accident in 1915. Hourlier had been
on the track, ready to start a pursuit race at the World
Championships in Copenhagen, the previous year, on 28 July,
when the starter had walked onto the track, and advised
everyone in a number of different languages, that as France
and Germany were now at war, it would be best for all the
riders to go back to their hotels with immediate effect.

Fifty riders from the ranks of the Tour de France, an event
that was just eleven years old at the outbreak of the First
World War fell to their deaths under the wave of hostility
that swept across France towards Paris. The German front
lines advanced, were pushed back, and then stagnated. That

was when it all became incomprehensible. The war swallowed whole lives, and a landscape, without discrimination.

It wasn't just Lucien Petit-Breton (whose real name was Mazan), among former winners, who perished. The man who succeeded him as the 1909 Tour de France champion, the Luxemburg-born François Faber, died on the front line at Artois at the age of twenty-eight. The military powers had tried to persuade him to join up as a cyclist (a relatively safer occupation, predominantly involving running messages behind lines), but he had instead chosen to fight for the Foreign Legion, which was exposed to the greatest dangers of all. As an almost inevitable consequence, he was shot dead on 9 May 1915, after the whistle had gone up for an assault from the trenches at Mont-Saint-Éloi. He'd barely advanced much more than a few metres, before crying out, 'I've been hit.' He was not the first, nor the last, to die in such a way and with those words.

Octave Lapize, who won the Tour in 1910 was another casualty. It was he who had assailed Henri Desgranges, the man who had invented the Tour and who had come up with the arduous course, with the famous words, 'Vous êtes des assassins! Oui, des assassins!' Despite the savagery of Desgranges's early Tours, those words now read with empty bathos, when set alongside the fate that was to befall him. On 14 July 1917, engaged in a dogfight with a German biplane, his aircraft was hit by enemy machine-gun fire at close range. Instinctively he put the plane into a dive, but after descending a few hundred metres, one of his wings detached and he plummeted towards the ground eight kilometres behind enemy lines.

'When peace finally comes, cycling will know a brilliant, happy period'. Lucien Petit-Breton, who won the Tour de France in 1907 and 1908, before both Faber and Lapize, believed fiercely in the purgative effect of the war. At thirty-four years of age, Petit-Breton was already an experienced man, with the voice of an elder statesman. But he had great faith.

'Men will have learnt how to suffer. Their energy, their tenacity, their stoicism will all have grown. At the moment at which their morale demands of them to "let go", they will recall the suffering of the trenches and will rediscover new reserves.' He was killed in a vehicle accident as he drove in the dark, twenty kilometres behind the besieged front line at Verdun. He collided with a horse-drawn cart, and was killed instantly. It's uncertain exactly where this happened, but as the 2014 peloton crossed through Charny-sur-Meuse and kicked north of Verdun, it might well have ridden over the very spot where the two-time champion perished.

Petit-Breton's prediction about the world of cycling being peopled by battled-hardened, morally straightened men of great honour has admittedly taken a bit of a knocking. What happened to those men who, having plumbed the depths of human despair, would rise again and march towards a happier, bolder future?

I am fairly certain that when he penned those words (just a few months before his death) for a column he was writing for *L'Auto* newspaper, he would have been dismayed, for example (and it is only one of many), to have encountered a duplicitous and incredible attempt to win the Tour exactly one century after Petit-Breton's first win, in 1907.

In 2007, the Danish rider Michael Rasmussen was forced by the weight of public opinion to disappear in ignominy in the middle of a race he was dominating, after he failed to put to rest well-founded rumours of wrong-doing. He became a standard-bearer for the moral swill that cycling had found itself stirring. Rasmussen's career, at a century's distance, sits at the opposite extreme of the moral see-saw from the handlebar-moustachioed, middle-parted gallantry of the 1907 winner.

Or perhaps it's not so simple.

Maybe Petit-Breton might have admired Rasmussen's bulletproof ability to tough it out in the face of universal disapproval. Who knows what kinship these two men might have enjoyed? It is possible that they were both able to focus on a target, both knowing what it felt like, via foul means or fair, to lead the Tour de France. They were both winners (except in Rasmussen's case, whose yellow jersey was handed to Alberto Contador, who in turn, two years later handed his 'win' to Andy Schleck).

I fail to see the connection between them and us. I refuse to group our two generations together, call it sentimentality, call it what you will. I fail now, looking down at my fingers, tapping away at the plastic keys of my computer, to believe that I am the descendant of these men and women who endured and died, and just a few years later had it all to do again.

I have been glad for this diversion through history, along the A4 from Verdun to Metz, and then south onto the A21 to Nancy. The Tour de France has coexisted neatly, and appropriately, with the march of modernity, called into being because of the seemingly simple bicycle, that beloved symbol of progressive humanists, poets, vagabonds, criminals, visionaries, surrealists, futurists, communists, fascists, butchers and bakers; all the everyday protagonists of the incendiary century that lies smouldering in our rear-view mirrors as we head south and away from the past.

The cataclysm of the Great War left its mark on the Tour as if the race were a blasted tree trunk on which the bark grows over the scar, adding ring after ring of annual regeneration until not much trace is left, save for a misshapen outline of something traumatic beneath the surface.

SAGAN

'Every stage is a Peter Sagan stage.'

Things had started normally enough for Peter Sagan. In Leeds, he had been on exemplary Peter Sagan form.

That day he had been one of the final riders to sign on. He climbed up the steps of the podium outside the City Hall, to be greeted enthusiastically by a man with a microphone.

'Peter Sagan,' said the man, correctly. 'Can you give me a sense of how it feels to be here at the Grand Départ in Yorkshire? What's the atmosphere like ahead of the race? And how do you think it's being received in Leeds?' He thrust the microphone in front of the deadpan young Slovakian.

Sagan took a second or two to gaze out on the massive crowds packed up against the barriers, and stretching up Headrow and away from the city centre. They waited for him to deliver his verdict. And when it came, it was devastating.

'Hello,' he said, and walked away.

But after a few days, I had started to worry about the Green Jersey. There was no need for me to worry about him, of course, since Peter Sagan is as solid a piece of flesh and as tough a competitor as you are likely to find on the Tour de France. But still, he didn't seem quite himself.

First there had been his baffling appearance at the Rider Presentation (or 'Opening Ceremony' as the Tour was trying to rebrand it) back in Leeds. I am led to understand that it was in homage to Wolverine, of whom I know very little, save for the name. Sagan had spray-painted his bike and his helmet with the trappings and iconography of this fictional character, and that all looked highly professional. But I couldn't help feeling that his haircut, in its sheer complexity and botched execution, had been more homespun. It suggested a degree of improvisation, to say the least, and possibly the use of scissors and a mirror.

For he had appeared on stage sporting a head of hair that can fairly be described as very surprising.

It was as if he'd washed his hair and then been hung upside down with a battery of hairdryers blasting downward thrust at his locks. Then, once he had been righted again, the central plateau at the top of his cranium was ironed flat and dipped in the same phosphoric green stuff that you use to make things glow in the dark, so that a ridge of unruly and upstanding hair now fringed his head like the trimmings of a thick-crust pizza.

But, despite my best efforts, I am not doing it justice. It was far more complex than that. The fact of the matter was that the World's Most Exciting Cyclist had taken to the stage with a barnet so extravagantly daft that it almost defied belief. It was, at least in part, vertical, which hair should obviously never be. And it had been highlighted light green, which is also a thing that it is probably better not to do with hair. The result was that he looked as if his head had been dunked in copper carbonate solution and then passed under a magnet from a breaker's yard.

The presentation team, including the unflappable Jill Douglas, working on the stage that evening did well to stick to the script. Once he had made his way across to them, they asked him something appropriate and generic, along the lines of 'So, Peter. What are your ambitions for this year's Tour?' But, as Matt Rendell pointed out to me, there was really only one question that should have been asked, only one question that was really relevant, and everyone at home was thinking the same thing at the same time.

'Peter! What in the name of God has gone wrong with your hair?'

'My hair is like this because I am Peter Sagan.' That's what he would have said, I am certain of it.

He is, or maybe was a year or two ago, the closest thing that cycling could boast to a real life superhero. Young (in 2014 he was still only twenty-four, which is nothing for a cyclist), and incorrigibly fun-loving, he started off life as a mountain biker and all-round eccentric, turning up to races in a pair of gym shoes instead of proper cycling footwear.

When he made the switch to professional road-racing, he had an instant impact, winning major races almost effortlessly, and putting the fear of God into the rest of the peloton. His unique selling point was, and still is, his versatility. He can climb, he can ride fast over a sustained period, he can descend quite fearlessly, and he can sprint. That means that there are a number of different ways in which he can win races.

There was a time, long ago, when riders who could do everything flourished on the Grand Tours, and not just on the one day Classics. Riders who won in the mountains, and in the long-form time trials, would also contest bunch sprints for fun, and set Hour Records on the track. And there was none greater than Eddy Merckx.

That is why, as in football, with its endless search for the 'new Best', or the 'new Maradona' there are occasional riders who are saddled with the unwanted moniker of 'the new Merckx', in an era when the cycling landscape has become so specialised and stratified that there can never be another all-conquering all-rounder. But that doesn't stop the yearning. And nor has it stopped people from comparing Sagan to the great Belgian, an accolade that at times he has seemed to justify. His first two Tours were triumphant. He won three stages in 2012, and the green jersey. Then he won another stage in 2013, and once more finished the race in green.

The Green Bouffant of 2014 was just typical Sagan. The Tours he has ridden have all been royally exploited by his insatiable desire to promote his own highly individualised brand of weirdly teenaged self-aggrandisement. There were his notable celebrations, from Running Man (legs pumping, arms pumping, in homage to Forrest Gump) to the Chicken (legs pumping, arms a-flapping). As he won plenty of stages in plenty of other races too, there were plenty of Saganesque variations on offer. Often he would round things off with some roguish, borderline reprehensible behaviour, such as signing the breasts of a female fan, or pinching the bottom of a podium girl, as he did after the 2013 Tour of Flanders.

This, you might think, is unremarkable behaviour, especially when you put it alongside the self-indulgence of footballers who are simply unable to celebrate a goal without variously pointing to their names on their back, kissing the badge, raising their fingers to the sky in homage to a recently deceased relative, swinging their arms in a cradling motion to pay tribute to their own ability to procreate or, in Robbie Fowler's case, dropping to their knees and pretending to snort up a line of cocaine.

But celebrating stupidly simply isn't very cycling.

In the field of athletic self-love (dressed up as 'charisma'), cycling has lagged woefully behind other sports. Perhaps this is because of the prerogative for zipping up and showing off the sponsor's name, the one fundamental of winning which oils the rusty, misshapen wheels of commerce in this highly dysfunctional sport.

Or maybe it's because of the sheer difficulty of doing anything other than sitting upright and shouting with your arms spread-eagled when you are coasting over the line at forty miles an hour. Have you ever tried it? I have, I am ashamed to say. I can manage nothing much more than a wobbly three or four metres before I am lurching, hands-first, back to the comforting feel of the handlebars beneath my palms, separating me from certain pain. In short, it isn't that easy to show off much on a bike, unless you are able to pull a wheelie up a mountain, as the more extrovert members of the *gruppetto* are wont to do on mountain stages, for the edification of the patient masses.

But Sagan's exuberance is a game changer. Not since Mario Cipollini's inexplicable cult status as 'something of a character' (predicated on his insatiable attention-seeking outfits, which ran the full gamut from tacky to gawdy to Blackpool-on-a-Friday-night) had cycling known an expanding violet quite like Peter Sagan.

He started to turn up to races with a different theme each year, pimping his bike and spray-painting the frame and his helmet with another action hero/fantasy monster, in broadly the same aesthetic style with which heavy metal-admiring German truck drivers like to adorn their HGVs. Sagan needed bling, cycling needed bling, ergo cycling needed Sagan, every bit as much as Sagan needed cycling. A virtuous circle had been closed, one that everybody could enjoy.

But what saves Sagan, what makes him better than the sum of his marketing, is the unbending, non-pliable, unreconstructed Sagan-ness of his every expression, his every utterance. Now, Sagan-ness is a hard term to define, as well as to spell. It is occasionally monosyllabic, but it can be expansive at times. Mostly it is downbeat, but has been known to stray into the realm of pure bravado. It is, as I was to find during this Tour, endearing, and enduringly fascinating. This is largely because it is not artificial. There is no spin with Sagan, save for the poster-on-the-bedroom-wall superhero branding. When he speaks, he is unable to hide behind any amount of hair gel. For the Sagan-ness of Peter Sagan will out, as sure as eggs are eggs and hair is hair.

But this year was proving to be a bit of a tester, to say the least. Everything was in place for another show of strength from the Terminator, as he has on occasion been known. Everything, that is, except for the missing top 5 per cent of form; that extra bit, which wins you bike races in a sprint.

Not that 95 per cent of Peter Sagan was entirely pointless. It was easily enough to win the green jersey for the third consecutive year. On the first seven stages of the race, he did not finish outside of the top five, but, equally, he did not win any. This was almost impossible to achieve, it almost flouted the law of averages. Time and time again, he'd get everything into place, and then misread the race by refusing to chase down riders on his own, or he would get edged out of a group kick. This was where his problem lay, this was the heart of 'Sagan syndrome', as we dubbed it; the terrible burden of being brilliant. An outstanding sprinter, but not quite the best, a powerful climber, but not the best, a powerful time triallist, but no Tony Martin: he was just too good at too many things, and perhaps not quite the best at any of them. And wherever he went, whatever he did, he was a marked man. The peloton simply never took their eyes off him.

Every day, after the race, dressed in the green jersey that he'd virtually won before we'd crossed the Channel, he would enter the interview area with a reluctant shuffle, knowing what questions to expect.

On Stage 5, in the rain and over the cobbles, and riding over the pavé at one point with such consummate ease that he carried his shades in his mouth and was breathing through his nose, he'd managed fourth place, heading a group of riders that included Fabian Cancellara.

After that effort, he confided to me, 'This is not the winning Peter Sagan.' He looked mightily confused by this rare turn of events that involved him regularly getting beaten by other cyclists, who didn't have the humility to finish behind the taciturn Terminator. Then he added, 'I do not know what to do.' And it was clear that he didn't.

The sparkle had gone, the twinkle had deserted him. Even the infectious nervous giggle with which he often rounded off his enigmatic pronouncements had gone back into its hutch to lick its fur. Seven consecutive top-five finishes was, by any normal yardstick, exceptional. But if you have banked up a series of extravagant celebrations ready to be unleashed on the waiting world, then third place or even second barely registers.

On Stage 6, and not for the first time on the race, he fell. Yet, despite cuts to his elbow and his legs, he still managed to contest the bunch sprint that was won by André Greipel from Alexander Kristoff. Sagan came fifth.

That day the media minders who chaperoned the riders from the podium to the waiting press had a warning. 'Only one question today for Sagan. He fell, and he is very angry.'

We are often instructed to ask 'just one question', something that we never do. For a start, there is a risk that, with Sagan being Sagan and extremely steeped in Sagan-ness, the one answer might be as short as 'Yes.' Or maybe 'Maybe.' Or 'No.'

But also, and more pertinently, I like to think of my interviews as a conversation, along the lines of something you might engage in during the course of normal human interaction. Here is an example of a conversation:

'Good morning.'

'Good morning.'

'How are you?'

'Fine, thanks.'

'Good.'

If the one-question-only rule applies, restricting the conversation simply to an exchange of 'Good mornings', then it is of no merit, it is simply like passing someone in the corridor.

However, allowed to breathe and develop, it can release a gem like 'Fine, thanks.' At this point it has become a full-blown conversation, an exchange of information with content and context. It is, in fact, a story. You could run this on the highlights show, or even write it up as a written race report, under the headline:

RIDER X DECLARES HIMSELF CONTENT

Rider X today described himself as feeling well, and thanked the waiting media for their concern. It was in answer to questions that had arisen as to his exact state of contentment that he finally confronted the issue head on. 'I'm fine,' he said, before expressing his gratitude for the attention being paid and the concern expressed as to the levels of well-being he was currently enjoying. 'Thanks,' he said to the assembled members of the press, who had asked him how he was feeling.

So my rule of thumb is never to allow myself to be restricted to just one question. Especially not by Peter Sagan, who now paced, with the weary reluctance of a condemned man, to where I stood. I was busily exuding what I hoped looked like a consoling beam of admiration and sympathy, although I now accept may well have just looked like an irritating simpleton hanging over a barrier with a microphone in his hand and a daft grin across his features.

'Peter, I am worried about you. Are you enjoying this Tour de France?'

A Saganesque pause. 'You know. It is hard when every day you are close but not winning.' Then there was the giggle. It had been a long time since it had come out to play, a winning chuckle that sounded like it came from an old-fashioned talking toy with a drawstring. It made me smile, and it almost, almost, made him smile too.

'Keep smiling though,' I implored. He looked at me quite intensely, so I went on to explain myself. 'The Tour de France needs you smiling.' It was meant as a compliment. But it came across differently. It must have sounded to him like the words of an idiot.

'I would like to see you smiling if you had crashed three times.'

The simple, undeniable logic of what he said left me nowhere to go, except to say, 'Fair point. That's a fair point.'

And with that, he walked away, and straight towards the clutch of shaven-headed security personnel with earpieces and muscles rippling under sharply tailored suits who had appeared from nowhere, to indicate the presence of the President François Hollande. They parted to let Sagan through. The Slovakian, dressed from head to toe in green, stomped sullenly back to where he'd left his bike, leaning up at the back of the podium, hopped on it, and rode off with his head bowed. The guards watched him go, and then returned to checking Facebook on their iPhones, unable to hide their boredom at the patent lack of clear and present danger, save for the slightly glowering mood of a young Eastern European Wolverine impersonator on a bicycle.

The next morning, at the start line, I decided to seek him out again. The profile listed in the road book for Stage 7 looked decidedly Saganian. That word denoted a certain type of stage which suited his characteristics: punchy climbing and recklessly fast descending. It had the requisite Saganian short sharp climbs in the closing kilometres that should have presented no great obstacle for him, but, in theory, might have been sufficiently difficult to drop the massive bulk of both the big German sprinters, and, with luck, the huge frame of Katusha's increasingly threatening-looking Norwegian Alexander Kristoff.

'Good morning, Peter.'

He had emerged from his lime-green Cannondale team bus into the watery sunlight of Épernay, blinking and shy when confronted with the standard gaggle of gawkers, autograph hunters and selfie junkies who had gathered around his themed bike that bore the number 51.

Then there was me. I assailed him with some questioning. 'How are you?'

'I am still alive.' (The man could write his own headlines.)

'Today's stage is a Peter Sagan stage.' I decided that, since he often referred to himself in the third person, I would too. That way we cut out any need for either first or second persons to intrude on the conversation.

'Every stage is a Peter Sagan stage.'

He lost the stage. But he lost it by an impossibly small margin to Matteo Trentin. The photo-finish revealed that after 245.5 kilometres there was no more than the width of an outer tube between first and second place. And it was no surprise whose wheel was the wrong side of that split.

That day, I simply didn't know what to say to him. So I think I kept it brief.

'Peter. Bad luck.'

'Always I have unluck.'

'Unluck': a word he had invented on the 2013 Tour when he suffered from a fair amount of it in the early stages of the race. Now it had descended on him and smothered his every effort to break free of such a remarkable losing sequence.

'Unluck' was the perfect word for where he was right now.

CARAVAN

'Do you have a whole load of different thumbs for
different degrees of tan, John?'

Meanwhile the race meandered on. The opening phase drew
to a close. It now had a definite shape from which the fat
had been chiselled away. I was telling anyone who would
listen (there weren't many) that it was perfectly set up now.
Yes, Chris Froome may have gone home. But the time gap
between Nibali and Contador was almost tailor-made to
produce a race. I was still working on the (not unreasonable),
assumption that Contador could and would out-climb the
yellow jersey whenever they drew a finish line on top of a
hill, and even more so when the hill was a mountain.

It was only a matter of time, literally: how often, and how
much time could the Spaniard take? Because I saw no
possibility that Nibali could take more. By the time the
Pyrenees were surmounted, I foresaw a slide-rule final time
trial, with the entire outcome of the race in the balance until
the final rider had crossed the finish line in Bergerac. It
looked that good.

I was starting to feel better and, recalled to health, suddenly
became mildly unbearable for my fellow travellers: vigorous,
engaged, energetic, boring. I had begun to get up early every
day and go running for the first time since I had broken a
toe back in June when trying to play football in my socks.
Running is always good for my mental health, even if the
pace at which I now practise it probably has precious little
impact on my physical health. My appetite was back, for the

Tour de France as well as for food. I was hugely looking forward to what remained of the race. And to lunch.

Nevertheless, I had gradually started to become aware of a disconcerting slackening of interest back at home. The regular phone calls I received in the opening week from British radio stations started to dry up, and when they did happen they often contained tell-tale phrases such as 'the Italian rider in the lead'. Much as I had absorbed the initial shocks of the big-name departures and adjusted my expectations, this was not the case for more passing British interest back at home. Cavendish had crashed, and now Froome, too. There were only Geraint Thomas and young Simon Yates left on the race with British passports to carry around in their back pockets and present to the French gendarmerie, if challenged. It was thin soup indeed.

While the TV ratings continued to carry with them the momentum of the Grand Départ, still consistently outscoring the previous two years, I was aware that British newspapers were pulling back their correspondents. The redtops were the first to leave, as we bid goodbye to the writers from the *Sun* and the *Mirror*. The big-hitter from the *Daily Mail* who was due to come out on the race now that the World Cup had finished decided to give it a miss, and while the *Guardian* still had their people on the ground, the *Telegraph*'s correspondent, covering the race for the first time, wasn't sure how much longer it would be before he, too, got the hook.

Other than that, the race was starting to take on a very familiar feel, as after a week or so on the road, I began to renew acquaintances and greet old friends.

'Isn't that Jacques?' Liam asked me.

We looked ahead at the figure dressed as a baguette, handing out slices of bread made with yellow food dye to the crowd waiting at the finish line. Jacques had been the Bannette Baguette on the 2013 Tour, during which we had often exchanged bread-related pleasantries, which I am sure amused him greatly. But, now that I looked at him, I wasn't totally convinced that this baguette was actually our friend Jacques.

'Are you sure that's him?'

'I don't know, but I think it's him.' We squinted again at him as he performed a sprightly jig in his bread costume. 'It looks like him.'

This was indeed true, since he looked, for all the world, like a giant baguette. Unmistakably.

There are many functions on the Tour that are so specialised that the numbers of people capable of executing them, even if you were to draw on a globalised labour market, would not amount to many more than there are riders capable of winning the race; a handful at best.

Most of these noble, disparate, desperate, brilliant,

battle-hardened oddities go unnoticed as the race trundles like a crusade across Europe. The Tour entourage is a twelfth-century army picking up and dropping off staff, acquiring secondary, tertiary, and whatever the word for four-fold is, industries as it passes: The caterers, the lawyers, the mercenaries, the shrink-wrappers, the armourers, the blacksmiths and laminators, the IT engineers, the wheelwrights and the speakers.

Among their merry number are the *animateurs*. Jacques, in his baguette, was an *animateur*.

They are special people, often festooned with bizarre wigs and clad in orange jumpsuits and blessed (or cursed) with relentless enthusiasm for powdered drinks or detergents. They are able to keep up a day-long hyper-animated diatribe of impassioned spiel about whatever mundane household product they are charged with the obligation to hawk. They are also extremely irritating people, obviously, but at the same time deeply admirable professionals whose trade makes the Tour de France tick.

Their work pays the bills. And their trade is surprisingly ancient. Advertising is even more interwoven into the fabric of the race than doping.

The origins of the Tour de France are by now well versed (a need to boost the flagging circulation of *L'Auto* newspaper, the forerunner of *L'Équipe*). But it is perhaps less well known that from the very start the race attracted a bunch of other barnacle brands attaching themselves to the hull of the peloton across the oceanic expanses of *La France profonde*. In 1903, when the race was first held, its passage was sponsored in part by two brothers. They were confectioners from Angers, Adolphe and Édouard Cointreau, whose clear orangey liqueur features quite frequently in my everyday life, much to my colleagues' derision. The Cointreau brothers had an eye for publicity, and were in fact the first company in France to produce a filmed commercial, as far back as 1898, of which sadly no copies still remain.

In fact, booze in various forms was for a long time the mainstay of Tour sponsorship, as Europe laboured under the convenient misapprehension that regular self-dosing with reasonably strong fortified wine and spirits was somehow beneficial for health and well-being. Most of France's bewildering array of flowery aperitifs and digestifs have at one time or another been branded as 'toniques' and have featured on the Tour de France's publicity caravan, from St. Raphaël to the almost undrinkable Suze, of which I am particularly fond.

The same pretensions towards healthiness applied to chocolate, most of which in the 1930s was sold through pharmacies, as it was considered of such high medicinal value. Jean-Antoine Menier's eponymous chocolate brand was for a long time closely associated with the race, and some even say played a role in the decision to make the leader's jersey yellow to match their tissue wrappers. Menier started his professional life as a pharmacologist. When he first delved into the world of chocolate, he came up with the ground-breaking idea (which persists to this day) of dividing his chocolate bars into six breakable sections; one for every day of the week, except Sunday.

The addition to the entourage of one or two liveried vehicles throwing out goodies (500,000 paper hats and almost as many sample bars of Menier chocolate) was a piecemeal affair until it was formalised in 1930. Henri Desgrange was forever railing against the influence of the commercial teams, and wanted to do away with what he saw as a manipulation of the result for commercial ends.

So the following year he began his thirty-year experiment with running national teams, all equipped with the same standardised bike, yellow in colour, and marked with an 'A' for 'Auto'. The problem was that now the Tour would have to fund all this extra expense out of its own pocket. And that's how the idea of the publicity caravan was born. With that, France, or at least that bit of it that shrieks with scarcely comprehensible delight when a free paper hat gets thrown through the air towards it, would never be the same again.

Not everyone thought this idea was quite as splendid as did Henri. In fact, the communist L'Humanité newspaper lambasted Desgrange for exploiting the common foot soldiers of the peloton while drawing a fat salary from his whoring of the race: 'The old alligator has derisorily draped the men in the imperialist colours of the five nations.'

But the idea persisted, and gained traction year on year. By the post-war years, the design of the vehicles became more and more flamboyant, a particular highlight being the Bic supercar, an elongated rocket-shaped thing 'powered' by two 'nuclear reactors'. Now, in the roaring fifties, everything took off, and the caravan started to acquire its recognisable modern identity. The crowds by the side of the road cheered wildly at the sight of huge bottles of fizzy drinks, bags of coffee, cans of tinned mushrooms, shopping trolleys groaning with oversized fibreglass painted fruit and veg all perched on top of specially modified vehicles.

Celebrities jumped on board. France's foremost accordion player Yvette Horner once stood in a Perspex display case on a car not dissimilar to a Popemobile and played the squeezebox for five hours at a go while smiling and trying not to throw up all over the driver. There was a replica of this car on the 2014 race, which, rather disappointingly, featured neither Yvette Horner nor anyone playing the accordion.

In 1988 the concept of the Village Départ was called into existence by the already legendary Tour de France marketeer Yves Arnal; a man who would go on to oversee nearly forty years of the caravan. Essentially, this is a gated community established for one day only at the start line, in which the chosen few are plied with locally produced wine, cheese, fruit and bread. The start town must undertake to deliver 1,500 items of bread and pastry by the early morning. In 2013, Arnal, whose love affair with marketing was as baffling as it was enduring, wrote wistfully of the Village Départ. 'My one big regret? Never having been able to install a real bakery in the Tour de France village. I dreamed of the fine smell of freshly baked bread and hot croissants.'

As big regrets go, this one is probably acceptable.

These days the procession of the caravan starts with a specially adapted vehicle carrying on its back a huge mobile cyclist hunched into an aero-tuck and wearing a yellow skin-suit. Then there follows a vast lion, much like a scarily big version of the cuter cousins that riders clutch on the podium. This one hurtles toward the waiting masses at thirty miles an hour with its hairy lion's arms outstretched in exuberant embrace, an idiot grin across its furry maw. These two icons are the vanguard, and represent the Tour's principal sponsor Crédit Lyonnais. And after them, the deluge.

Prizes are accorded for certain categories. For example, in 2012, Saint-Michel walked away with the Prix de l'Objet Publicitaire, for their ground-breaking sachets of individual madeleine cakes, of which I must have eaten half a dozen a day. The year before that, Bic won the gong for their 'ecological ashtray'. No, me neither.

And in 2011, the Prix de l'Animation went, rather controversially in my humble opinion, to 'X-Tra' for the stripteases performed over and over again by two *animateuses*.

And it is to these good folk, whose incessant din makes our lives such a perennial misery, that I must doff my free Carrefour casquette, the staff who work the microphones or hang suspended on a highwire over a float or sit for hours in a harness yelling about crisps. To them the glory of the race!

*

The great Gérard Holtz would have made a tremendous *animateur*. Indeed, it would not surprise me at all if he had started out his professional life dressed in a giant chicken costume, working on the caravan for Le Coq Sportif in the early 1970s. Holtz has been the tidy face of French TV's coverage of the Tour de France for nearly thirty years, a small man, almost seventy years of age, with blow-dried hair and sparkling teeth. He presents from the start village at the beginning of each day, and then arrives breathlessly but still tooth-sparklingly behind the podium to interview riders and present the rest of the show, both the Avant Tour and the Après Tour. And often his day does not end there.

Our hotel in Arras displayed a poster for *The Forced Marriage* by Molière, performed by (you've guessed it) Gérard Holtz. He was due on stage that very evening, only a matter of hours after the race had finished. There he was, dressed

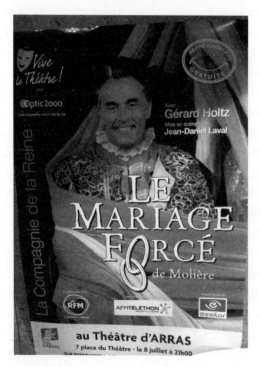

in seventeenth-century costume, the whiteness of his teeth offset by the whiteness of his neck ruff. No wonder Nicolas Sarkozy made him a Chevalier of the Ordre National du Mérite in 2010. Like L'Oréal, the man is worth it.

I have never actually spoken to him. The closest we ever came was in 2013, when he kept Chris Froome all to himself on the Champs-Élysées for an unreasonable length of time, leaving me to fill endlessly until he was finally ready. So part of me was tempted to go along to the Molière evening and heckle.

But most conversations on the Tour, especially those conducted face to face, rather than face to baguette, begin with a smile, and a handshake and then the time-honoured question, 'How many Tours is it for you, now?'

That was the question I put to the great iconic Danish commentator Jørgen Leth, as we stood side by side at the urinals (it's normally after a week that inhibitions around urinating and conversing tend to break down completely).

'Thirty-one Tours now.'

'Wow.'

'The people still like to hear me commentate.' He chuckled. 'I don't know why.'

For Jørgen, the month of July is the indulgence of a passionate hobby, rather than anything else, for this is not his day job. He is in fact one of Denmark's greatest avant-garde film-makers, with a colossal reputation back home, as well as overseas. If you want a flavour of his work, you would do well to watch the 1967 short film *Det perfekte menneske*, which opens with a long shot of a man in a tuxedo stuffing a pipe and then lighting it, over which a clipped voice narrates, 'Here is a perfect human. Here is a perfect human. Here is a perfect human functioning.'

In 1976, he made a brilliantly evocative film about Paris–Roubaix, called *A Sunday in Hell*, which is probably the best film ever made about cycling, even though it is nearly forty years old.

Jørgen is deeply tanned, tall, beautifully dressed and tousled. If someone pointed at him on the street, and invited you to guess at his profession, you would probably come up with 'surrealist film-maker and cycling commentator'.

He emigrated a long time ago to Haiti, lost everything in the earthquake, and now, at the age of seventy-seven, has rebuilt his life and continues to make arthouse films, the most recent of which, *The Erotic Man*, has tarnished his reputation to some extent, since it details with astonishing honesty his sexual predilection for surprisingly young women from a range of third-world countries. Undaunted by the public's response to the frankness of his approach, he continues to make films.

'I am always making a film,' he told me, as we washed our hands in two wholly inadequate adjacent sinks.

'What are you working on right now?'

'A film about a baseball match . . .' He looked at me with a look of pure artistic mystery, as much as that is possible while using a hand-dryer in a mobile toilet unit. '. . . in Bilbao,' he added, enigmatically. And with that, he was off, scurrying back to the commentary box to deliver more existential *bon mots* to the viewing Danish public.

But even if Danish television still stuck rigidly with such a tried and tested formula, they were, on other levels, formidable innovators. Their fine cameraman Troels Sørensen was the first of the pack to come to the Tour with an ergonomically designed back-saving suspension device which fitted around your waist and shot a huge crane over your shoulder from which you could hang your camera, meaning that the extraordinary weight of the kit was lifted from your upper back. The only problem with these devices was the way they looked, which was, to say the least, cumbersome and affected. Cameramen being cameramen, and almost to a man unnecessarily macho, not one of them could bring themselves to look that daft. In fact, it turned out, not even Troels opted to persevere, and he quietly dropped his winch after a couple of years of ridicule, and then simply didn't come back to the Tour, only briefly to resurface in 2014, as he was assigned to making a fly-on-the-wall documentary about Jorgen Leth.

It seems that it's a small world, Denmark, as Hamlet tried to point out.

You can generally recognise cameramen who have a certain number of miles on the clock by the way they hold themselves without a camera on their shoulder: distinctly off-balance. Their right shoulders slope down with a worrying gradient, and end a good few inches south of where their left shoulders are. But they do not complain.

In 2013, one of ITV's two Tour cameramen, a stocky, taciturn Western Australian named John Tinetti, enhanced his well-earned reputation for heroic stoicism still further when he turned up in Corsica for the start of the 2013 race missing a thumb and an index finger. Turned out he'd accidentally cut them both off a few weeks previously with a circular saw. 'It never even hurt.'

Instantly he became known on our crew as 'Kit-Kat', a nickname that almost works, but not quite, since Kit-Kats actually have no thumb and four fingers, not three. Still, the name stuck, and to this day it elicits a cheap laugh every time it gets an airing, which is almost every day.

Kit-Kat's principal innovation on the Tour de France coverage on ITV came about a good few years ago, when he became an early adopter of the Segway, those weird electrically powered platforms with two rubbery wheels that whizz along, seemingly with a mind of their own. Controlling the Segway with only his stocky, taciturn and hairy Western Australian knees, John was thus able to travel alongside Chris Boardman as he rode his bike and film him talking to camera, describing, for example, the final kilometre of a stage. He was the envy of the finish line.

This was a brilliant idea, which gave ITV great kudos, and enhanced Kit-Kat's reputation in the closed world of the Tour de France TV circus until 2014, when the Danes caught up.

We were somewhere near Reims when we first spotted him, a hitherto unknown Danish cameraman, tall, blond, and perhaps twenty years younger than John. He scooted along with consummate skill and grace on a brand-new Segway, and he was enveloped in the highly specialised hydraulic exo-skeleton of a steady-cam. We all gazed at him in muted wonder as he riffled past us, noiselessly, perfectly. Even John dropped what he was doing, and stared as the Dane glided past.

'He's faster than you, John,' someone offered.

'He's younger, too. And better-looking,' added another, perhaps unnecessary, voice.

There was a long pause, as John shrugged and started to walk away.

'And he's still got both his thumbs.'

This was particularly unfair, since John had arrived in Yorkshire complete with the full set of two thumbs. The fact that one of them was plastic and pink and had a habit of falling off was neither here nor there. It was John's fake thumb, and he was very proud of it. He had to answer dozens of questions about his thumb, as there seemed no end to our curiosity.

'Do you have a whole load of different thumbs for different degrees of tan, John?'

'No. Just this one.'

By the time we eventually got to the South of France, and the sun started to get to work on the rest of John's anatomy, his thumb remained resolutely Action Man pink. It looked like an old-fashioned uncooked banger next to a row of well-grilled sausages.

'When your thumb was delivered, did it come with a nice case, John? Like a glasses case, with velvet on the inside and a nice hinge that snaps shut?'

'No. They just handed it over like this.'

'So what do you keep it in?'

'My pocket.' He thought about it for a moment. 'Or my rucksack.'

On several occasions though, and often at comically inopportune moments, the rogue prosthetic went AWOL, and fell away from the rest of John's hand. A tape exists, which for obvious reasons was never broadcast, in which Gary Imlach stops mid-piece to camera, and says to the cameraman behind the lens, 'John. You've dropped your thumb.' This was followed by a typically dry Imlach aside, in which he comments, quite correctly, that this was one phrase he never thought he'd utter.

And one phrase I never thought I'd utter was 'Greg LeMond sang for me.' But again, on this most unpredictable of Tours, it was true.

My birthday coincided with Stage 7. I was not expecting much. This was born from the experience of eleven previous occasions on which the eleventh of July has failed to impress anyone, least of all me. I haven't been at home on my birthday since 2003, so my youngest daughter, Edie, has never once witnessed at first hand the irrepressible bundle of over-excitement I become on My Big Day, leaping out of bed in my pyjamas and tearing into the big stack of presents waiting for me downstairs. This rather heavy use of irony is designed to reveal the bare-faced reality of what has become a depressing annual routine. It matters little, and increasingly (decreasingly?) so as I pass unwittingly into my unremarkable mid-forties. I don't mean to sound overly gloomy, but a decade of not wearing party hats on Tour has made me think that the entire institution of the birthday speaks more of loss than celebration.

Sometimes I will get a card. Indeed, when I actually did turn forty, I think I got two. One year Kath, my wife, even made me a ginger cake, a family recipe, which, wrapped in foil, and maturing slowly at the bottom of my suitcase, seemed to get better and better with each passing stage until, by Paris, it had become a culinary masterpiece. And every year, except for the (very frequent) years in which they forget, the production company will raid the petty cash and send Matt Rendell to the 'Boutique Officielle' to buy me a wickedly overpriced Tour de France mug or baseball cap. That's the choice: a mug or a baseball cap.

I told Matt this year, a few days before the big day, that if he presented me with a seven-euro mug this year, I would smash it on the tarmac in front of him, and, picking up one of the shards of pottery, grab him by the neck, hold the jagged edge to his throat and drag him off backwards, shouting, 'One false move and Rendell gets it.'

I'd actually like a key-ring. That's the truth of it. But certainly, no more mugs.

This year, I turned forty-five in Reims. Over breakfast, which, to my unreasonable delight, featured a debut appearance after twelve Tours of lychees, Liam presented me with another slab of that family ginger cake which my family had smuggled to him back in Yorkshire. He'd been lugging its not negligible heft all the way to the Hotel Porte Mars on the Place de la République, where, to his great relief, he was able to hand it over to me.

'Bet you can't guess what that is.'

'Cake.'

I was pleased to have been remembered after all. Funny how, actually, it never ceases entirely to matter. I went back to the brown gloom of my hotel room, which looked a bit like Bobby Ewing's office in *Dallas*, to pack and prepare for another day on the road, but this time a year older.

That evening, we spent the night in La Bresse, close to the next day's finish line in Gérardmer. Arriving just in time to persuade the pizzeria opposite the hotel (it was another Nobby) that it might be worth their while staying open for an hour longer while an impromptu party got underway.

What made this one particularly special was the fact that we were joined, entirely at random, since the chances of bumping into colleagues scattered over a few hundred square kilometres is surprisingly remote, by the team from Eurosport. In particular, Greg and Kathy LeMond, who both seemed to be loving the experience of touring with the TV production after a prolonged absence from the race. Greg had been booked by Eurosport to co-host a pre- and post-race show with the incomparable Stefano Bernabino, the most Italian man I am ever likely to meet.

Now, here they sat, unwitting guests at my birthday party, enjoying the evening, and chatting amiably to all and sundry. Suddenly the lights went out, and I became, for the first time

in my life, that person to whom everyone in the restaurant turns and tunelessly drones 'Happy Birthday'. From the direction of the kitchens came not so much a cake as a pizza, drizzled with chocolate sauce, bedecked with dollops of vanilla ice cream and bejewelled with as many vaguely festive things as the kitchen staff could find lying around. That included a few wedding-bell trinkets, four glow-in-the-dark bracelets and a lit candle that declared unequivocally that it was my twentieth birthday.

'You're twenty?!' roared Greg LeMond throatily. 'You're kidding me!'

'I've had a hard life, Greg.'

And with that, the three-time winner of the Tour de France shook my hand vigorously, and slapped me hard on the shoulder with one unclenched palm of an immense leathery hand. And that, I contest, was one of the best things that has ever happened to me on my birthday.

And the so the Tour family continues to wax and wane, adding some guests each year, shedding others. The riders would not know it, and why should they, but there's a parallel world locked into their same Parisian orbit. One to which I have always felt both honoured and dispirited to be a part of. Unequivocally, after all these years, I belong.

VOSGES

'If everyone wore the same thing, or drove the same car,
well, it wouldn't be much of a life, would it?'

'As we steadily headed eastward I realised that I was, very
slowly, being injected into the Germanic lands which . . . at
the time seemed a sodden, dull part of the world, but which
had been fought over by the French and Germans for centuries
and in which hardly a field had not been the arena for some
awful war.'

It's a little unkind to the Alsace, perhaps. But I like Simon
Winder's description in *Germania*, his excellent history of
Germany, of passing from 'real' France (the easily likeable
version with olive groves and boules) into a part of the country
where olives are replaced by gherkins and no one feels well
disposed enough to play boules.

There's enough truth in his assessment for me to work
with, and so I think of it every time I enter the land in which
mountains are known as *ballons*, and dogs are properly scary,
rather than just handbag accessories. When the Tour period-
ically kinks off to the left, as it did now, and dashes south
towards the Alps, it sometimes, and rather dutifully, passes
through the Alsace. Here the weather and the topography
conspire with the general oddness of the language to cast a
spell of weirdness over the race for the day or two of its visit.
It is either glaringly bright sunshine, which makes the shadows
underneath the lush, heavy foliage even darker, or it is a
deluge. Normally, it is a deluge. Sometimes you will get both
climatic extremes in the same day, or even in one hour. Or

even, as happened to me at the finish line in Gérardmer, in the space of one thought.

At around about midday on Saturday 12 July, I felt a hot sun peeping through the cloud cover for the first time since we had left Dover. Five straight days of watery gloom had left me craving both light and warmth, like a troglodyte at the end of winter. In an instant I had peeled off my jumper and thrown down my coat, gazing skyward in the same shameless manner that Muscovites do at the first hint of spring.

But a passing Belgian reporter rebuked me in forcible terms, scolding me for such naivety.

'Don't go too early. You are too optimistic. The rain is coming back, hard.' He pointed, and at that precise moment, the sun was extinguished behind a black cloud. 'Look!'

A crash of thunder. Then it started to teem with rain.

Meanwhile, out on the race as the bunch ambled through the valley, loosening their legs for a triptych of climbs in the final thirty kilometres (hills that I had foolishly decided to ride over that morning with Chris Boardman, but that's another story), the sun shone brightly. As they passed through a small town called Baccarat, they flew past a roundabout that featured a fountain, out of which gushed yellow-dyed water. Marcel Kittel even had the time to point it out, and smile as he passed by. It was all very happy-splashy, unlike the dull grey-out that we were enduring at higher altitude.

Up in the hills, and in particular on the punchy little climb to the finish line just outside Gérardmer, it was throwing it down. By the time the diminutive Blel Kadri had dropped Sylvain Chavanel and Simon Yates (or 'See-Moan Yatt-Ezz', as Kadri bafflingly referred to him in his barely comprehensible post-race interview) to take Stage 8, it had dried out somewhat. But the weather gods of the Vosges were in no rush to change things too dramatically from their well-established groove of penetrating damp.

When the rain does decide to fall in this part of the world, it falls with a particular contempt for anything caught beneath it.

When it rains in the Alsace, the rain actually tries to destroy the Alsace, and all its confused inhabitants.

On the afternoon in 2009 that a sort-of Australian called Heinrich Haussler raced to a famous solo win into Colmar, nothing remained dry; the skies simply dropped onto the Alsace and wrapped the whole land in a watery embrace till air and rain and earth were no longer distinguishable. The only other element missing from this list was fire, but the matches wouldn't catch, and even the Zippo had given up. The water penetrated through everybody's physiology to the level of mitochondria, and it wasn't until the Tour reached Paris a week later that our water-logged cells' pH levels had osmosed back to something approaching normal. To this day, I have heard it told, if you touch Haussler on the cheek, buttocks or feet, he feels cold and clammy. I cannot confirm this, as his press officer expressly forbids it.

It was fitting that Haussler won in the Alsace as well, given the ancestry of his family name (he spent the first fourteen years of his life in his father's homeland of Germany) and the indeterminate, trans-cultural nature of its pronunciation. It is a name that always presents me with something of a problem, since I never know how much authentic Germanic heft to lend my articulation of the 'r' and 'ich' in Heinrich. He is, after all, basically an Australian, so I should probably stick to the anglicised 'Hein-Rick Howzzler.' It's a good question though, and one that recurs in this German corner of France with a pleasingly appropriate frequency: how foreign-sounding is too foreign-sounding? How German is too German? Here's a conundrum that faces me on the Tour on an almost daily basis: the yellow jersey in 2005, on the last occasion when the race finished in Mulhouse, was a certain

Jens Voigt (or 'Big' Jens Voigt, to give him his full, and almost obligatory, moniker).

Now, how should you pronounce his surname? The accepted version that's crept into the English-speaking cycling world is 'Voyt'. In fact, it's become so accepted, that I suspect 'Big' Jens even thinks of himself as Jens 'Voyt', and probably even 'Big' Jens 'Voyt' at that. Or even 'Big' 'Jens' Voyt', with each separate word intoned hugely and boomingly.

And yet, that's not his name. It is simply a garbled mis-interpretation that has somehow become common commentator currency. And now no one wants to rock the boat for the sake of anything as trivial as accuracy. 'Voyt' should be pronounced more like 'Focht', in which the 'ch' is soft, a sound which doesn't actually exist in English. There's clear linguistic blue water between 'Voyt' and 'Focht', which makes any attempt to lend his name its correct articulation sound either pretentious, or simply wrong. So, rather than standing up for what is true and correct, most of us, down the years, have simply opted for a falsehood designed to make our parochial Anglophone lives easier. Until, that is, this year. Overcome by the desire to do this great rider justice on his final race around France, I decided to start calling him by his name, although, admittedly, I switched streams midway through, so that during his Stage 1 breakaway, he was 'Voyt', but by the time he joined the break into Bergerac, he had become 'Focht'.

The same rules apply equally to the Danish rider Michael Mørkøv, whose Russian-looking name should actually sound something like 'Merk-oh-euh' and Michał Gołaś, the Polish sprinter who is actually 'Me-How Go-Wash', but thankfully he doesn't win often enough for us to mangle his surname.

And, of course, we have not even mentioned Thomas Voeckler, who was born and raised in the little town of Schiltigheim, for which there are three acceptable pronunci-ations, none of which actually involve an obscenity but all of which run the gauntlet. Voeckler is 'VeurClair' according to the French, 'Furklair' for the Germans and, inexplicably, 'Little Tommy Voyckler' for Phil Liggett, who is demonstrably neither French, German nor Alsatian, but from the Wirral or somewhere like that.

So the Alsace is a minefield, both metaphorically and literally. Here we are, dodging the concrete horrors of the Maginot Line, not far from the birthplace of the culturally ambiguous Arsène Wenger, surrounded by a hard-to-fathom fusion of France and Germany, reflected in the esoteric culture of the land, and even in its place names.

From Gérardmer, we struck off the next day towards Mulhouse, a town which changed hands as often as it changed names. It is pronounced 'Milloose', and not how you think it should be given the way it looks. If it were simply 'Mul-house', it would have been better placed as a climb on Stage 2, somewhere after the second categorised climb of the day, on the road to Sheffield and not far from Blubberhouses.

Perhaps it's because the two opposing European cultures (the Franco–German dichotomy) are so wildly irreconcilable, that there is no such thing as a seamless cross-seeding of one into the other. They don't knit together easily, it's like trying to mix egg white and toothpaste, where pockets of one and the other remain, but they never dissolve into a solution. In Mulhouse the half-timbered houses look obdurately Germanic, and the town features one of France's only major Protestant churches. The residents borrow heavily from Germany's unambiguously ghastly Karneval tradition. This culminates, at least for the women of the town, in 'Bibalafrittig', (literally 'chicken Friday' in Alsatian dialect) in which ladies go to great trouble to dress in huge stuffed chicken costumes and drink heavily in the name of fun. No one remembers why they do this.

But alcohol-based celebration of near-flightless birds is not something you will see in the rest of France, and there will be those who feel that its restriction to the wooded hillside towns of the Alsace is fit and proper. This is a part of France that, with its strangely named grape varieties in tall, thin green wine bottles, is less than perfectly understood in the rest of the Republic.

Fittingly, the most famous son of Mulhouse, gained his monumental and yet unfortunate fame for being misunderstood and maligned. Alfred Dreyfus was a Yiddish-speaking Jew from the Alsace who, rising through the ranks of the French army in the late nineteenth century, was accused repeatedly, convicted of, and imprisoned for spying for the Prussians. He was completely innocent, of course, but all that Germanic/Jewish sounding stuff just made him appear dodgy in those days of unchecked anti-Semitism. He was just a little bit too obviously 'other' and so therefore fitted the bill.

All this injustice is rather at odds with the recent history of the Tour de France in this part of the world. The last winner of a stage into Mulhouse itself was Michael Rasmussen in 2005, who was not quite as innocent and persecuted as Alfred Dreyfus. And before that, in 2000, it was Lance Armstrong, who also scores zero on the Dreyfus-ometer. Except, of course, it wasn't Armstrong who won that stage, because the record books now show that he never won anything. Everyone knows that.

So it was high time Mulhouse got to celebrate a worthy winner, and weather that did not make you long for Morocco. On the 2014 Tour, they got one of those. The skies glowered and spat, ruffled and blew all day, threatening at any moment to get all Old Testament on us, but the man who crossed the line in first place was very much a New Testament man. Tony Martin wins races in the simplest way imaginable. He just rides faster than everyone else, and gets to the end of the race before them all. It's that straightforward with him.

But between the German and his stirring victory lay six categorised climbs, most of which bore tellingly Germanic names: the Col de la Schlucht, Col du Wettstein, Côte de Gueberschwihr. And then there was the final mountain of the day, the simply titled Grand Ballon.

My day started badly. Before breakfast I had ventured out of our hotel at the start village in Gérardmer for a run. After turning left, instead of right, and ending up running for a quarter of an hour through the most charmless part of town, whose primary feature is the vast Linvosges bed linen factory, I finally hit fortuitously on Gérardmer's main claim to fame, its picturesque lake. An hour or so later, after I had completed a lap of the water, past German campers stumbling blearily towards the rocky bank and flinging themselves with penetrating shrieks into its icy depth, I made it back to the town square and our hotel.

It was there that I discovered, to my horror, that our car

had been besieged. When I parked it up the night before, it had been one of a row of vehicles innocently lined up in a side street. But during the night, every other car, except for mine had been moved in order to make way for the Tour de France. The race started at the exact spot I had chosen to jettison our battle-weary Espace, and as I found it again, it was fenced in by barriers and stood awkwardly next to the very arch that marked the stage start. It was the very definition of 'in the way': my own low-key tribute to the Orica Green Edge bus of 2013 which had crashed into the finishing arch.

There followed a sprint up three flights of stairs to retrieve the car keys, a treacherous descent, and a sprint back to the car, where an impressively ill-tempered row ensued with a Tour official, who had it within his power to throw me summarily off the race.

'Where have you been? We've been trying to telephone you for three hours!'

'Running. And before that, sleeping.'

He didn't seem to like the tone of that answer, so he cut to the chase. 'Why did you park here?'

'Because there was a sign which said I should park here.' It was true. The car was right next to a large 'Hors Course' Parking sign, which I had spotted and obeyed the previous evening.

'But this is the race route.'

'But you put a sign there.'

'No, we didn't.'

'Yes, you did.'

This argument was getting nowhere. But he blinked first.

'This was an error of the local organisation.'

'Well, there you go then.' I flung my arms up in what I hoped was a gesture which might be internationally understood to mean something like 'Well, there you go, then'.

And with that, I drove off in search of a more legal parking space. The argument had been strangely exhilarating, and certainly testing, since it had all taken place in French. I had never before had cause to be narky, sarcastic, furious, indignant or supercilious in French before. But that morning, I got an opportunity to practise all of the above, and I think I got away with it. To my astonishment, later that day, our production manager received an apology on behalf of the race organisation. Such contrition on their part was completely unprecedented. For a while, I became something of a minor celebrity on the race, someone who people would point out to each other and refer to in hushed and awed tones. (This happened in my mind, and not in the actual world.)

'He's the guy they said sorry to.'

'Who?'

'Him, over there.'

'Oh, him. Yeah, he looks a bit smug.'

Once we had regrouped, we went off in search of interviewees before Stage 9 got underway. Many of the team hotels were close to the start line, and so the riders left their rooms, picked up their bikes and rode down there themselves. I spotted the tiny figure of AG2R's Blel Kadri posing for a selfie with a pack of schoolkids. He had been stalking the bars of Gérardmer until close to midnight the previous evening, privately celebrating his stage win, and passing almost unnoticed through the crowd; the centre of everyone's attention just a few hours earlier but already receding into partial, if not total, anonymity.

Garmin Sharp's American team leader Andrew Talansky, battered and bruised from repeatedly hitting the tarmac, was in deep consultation with a mechanic. They were recounting the events of the previous day, when Talansky had lost control of his bike on a corner, as he descended from the Col de Grosse Pierre. What had been remarkable about that crash was not so much that he had gone down, but what happened afterwards. The TV cameras, which had missed the actual

moment, caught only the aftermath. Talansky, who had sprung back to his feet, was fiddling with the bike, making sure that the front wheel was turning without impediment. He was being helped in a highly unusual way.

Through the rain-spattered lens, it was possible to make out a disconcertingly tall figure with flowing blond locks, a skirt and an outrageously tall and wobbly Dr Seuss-like hat. The figure was grappling with the bike, trying in any way possible to help the stricken American. They were a decidedly odd couple, alone in each other's company on the side of a Vosges mountain in the pouring rain.

'And you know what was the weirdest thing? That lady trying to help me!' Talansky had obviously experienced the unusual encounter with exactly the same amused bewilderment as most of the viewing public.

Later that morning, I met the lady in the hat and the skirt, who turned out not to be a lady at all. Dominic Debarreix was actually a sixty-year-old former HGV driver from Mâcon, enjoying the first year of his retirement by pursuing the Tour

de France all the way from Leeds to Paris in the company of his wife.

Talansky had crashed right into their patch by the side of the road, cartwheeling over a little Union Jack camping chair they'd acquired in London. 'We were so frightened for the rider. I hope he is OK.' Dominic said to me. 'Who was he?'

I told him about Andrew Talansky's serial misfortune, and he sympathised.

The skirt was in fact a kilt, bought in slightly misconstrued homage to the Yorkshire Grand Départ. His outfit was rounded off not only by his towering, padded Tour de France top hat teetering atop his hair, tied back in a long ponytail, but also by his footwear; the kind of ornate gothic boots you'd more readily associate with the bass player from Whitesnake. It was a striking sight, if truth be told, and I am not going to pretend that I don't have some sympathy for how spooked Andrew Talansky must have been by his unexpectedly flamboyant mechanic.

'If everyone wore the same thing,' said Dominic, tossing back his ponytail of unevenly henna-dyed hair and allowing me to appreciate his row of discreet earlobe studs, 'or drove the same car, well, it wouldn't be much of a life, would it?'

His wife nodded in agreement. 'Dominic likes to be different,' she offered, by way of elaboration. Then she returned her gaze to the as yet empty start line, where, in just a few short minutes, she would get to glimpse fleetingly the same pack of riders she'd fleetingly glimpsed every day for the previous nine days.

We got on our way, as did the race. As they wiggled over mountain passes, the favourites (and by that I mean Nibali and Contador) marked each other, and a breakaway was allowed to go clear. That in turn disintegrated, under the grinding weight of Tony Martin's singular ability to hurt himself, and as he motored towards victory, a Frenchman, Tony Gallopin, suddenly saw the opportunity arise to snatch for himself a temporary yellow jersey. Not only that, but since the following day was 14 July, it meant that he'd be wearing yellow on Bastille Day. That, obviously, is a bit like winning the lottery on your birthday, if you're a French cyclist.

Meanwhile, we continued our stolid journey towards the finish line by car, rumbling through uninspiring towns whose houses bore the trademark cladding of diamond-shaped downward-pointing concrete tiles on their flanks. We passed timber yards and potassium factories, and stopped for lunch at a patisserie that sold a two-metre-long loaf of grey bread. In the hillsides all around us, the endless, thick forests kept their dark and dripping counsel.

At the finish line there was a distinct lack of atmosphere. The Tour had plonked itself down on the approach road to a huge car park between the bus depot, the municipal cemetery and the exhibition hall. There was nothing of note to stir the soul for as far as the eye could see, save for an expanse of tarmac so endlessly broad and featureless that it swallowed the Tour de France with room to spare. As a result, the whole area had a curious, decompressed, unimportant feel to it. The race, ideally, needs narrow, tight avenues, hemmed in on either side by rows of townhouses, from whose balconies flags catch on the breeze, as the noise of the Tour clatters around the artificial gully. There would be one or two finishes like that still to come, but we would have to wait until Nîmes and Bergerac to experience them.

Martin, whose pendant lower lip appeared to have expanded in the humidity, blasted across the finish line after a ninety-kilometre solo effort. He looked so attuned to his effort that I wondered, for a fleeting moment, whether he was going to bother to stop at all. He looked like he had no intention of relenting, as he arrowed straight towards the huge attendant press pack. But miraculously, he pulled up just short of calamity and started to talk.

'I think I have invented a new time trial.' Indeed. Why bother with the other riders if you can just do it on your own?

Then, at a gap of two minutes and forty-five seconds, a group of seventeen riders, headed by Fabian Cancellara, dragged the virtual yellow jersey of Tony Gallopin over the line. He too was engulfed.

Behind him, Vincenzo Nibali's Astana team were not chasing to keep the jersey. They had bigger fish to fry the following day. As their occasionally dastardly team manager Alexander Vinokourov so patronisngly put it, this was to be considered 'a present for France'.

So, exactly how grateful was France? Quite grateful is about as strongly as I could put it. But not very grateful.

For a start, Tony Gallopin was riding for the Belgian national team, which was a bit irritating. And, equally, because the French understand cycling, they knew how brief this yellow jersey would be, and, in their hearts, they understood that Vinokourov was correct, which made it even worse. This was a crumb from the table.

Of course, the intrusion of reality into the proceedings didn't stop the moment from being very special for Tony Gallopin. As he stood on the podium, dressed in yellow and holding in the air a cuddly lion, a group of half a dozen riders, who had become detached, crossed the line right in front of the podium. Often the Tour de France does not wait for everyone to finish before it salutes its winners, so this was nothing unusual. Among those riders were a number of Frenchmen, who glanced up at the podium as they free-wheeled by. I should imagine that national pride might well have played second fiddle to other, more base, sentiments, which would have been quite understandable. Professional jealousy might have figured.

If he can do it, then why not me?

We took our leave of Mulhouse, though we had seen barely any of it, and set off for Belfort, whose architecture is as it sounds: glum, militaristic and a bit bizarre.

BELLES FILLES

'The Swede contemplated the young girl,
struck dumb in wonder. With one look, in that instant,
they fell truly in love.'

It was the next big day on the race. After the cobbles, this was the stage which most pundits, riders and spectators had circled in their road books. And it was to take place against a familiar backdrop.

I pulled on my running kit, laced up my shoes, and set off up the hill from Plancher-les-Mines, a desultory sort of a place with a few clapped-out factories and sweet-smelling sawmills. As I eased my Espace-bound legs into some sort of passable rhythm, I lumbered ponderously through the streets, nodding a quick hello to the descendants of Ines the Beautiful, the

town's legendary martyred virgin. They were preparing for the passage of the Tour by hanging polka-dot jerseys from their garden fences, or slapping a Carrefour cap on a taxidermically arranged dog sitting in a state of ossified attendance in a window.

I ran slowly, dragging in nosefuls of good mountain air, past houses from which there was a sporadic trickle of inhabitants spilling onto the street. Someone had made lovingly executed hand-painted portraits of riders and mounted them on ply-board banners placed at regular intervals as the race route meandered through the village. Armstrong was there, recognisable in his US Postal livery, as if nothing bad had ever happened to diminish his appeal. Then there was a grimacing Jan Ullrich, with T-Mobile epaulettes, then Froome, winning on Mont Ventoux.

Some children were lighting bangers and dropping them in letterboxes as I ran past trying to look all parental and censorious. They saw me and simply guffawed.

And in the middle of the town, at the crossroads, there stood a Norman-looking church that would not have been out of place in Wiltshire, whose bells suddenly swung into noisy life. It struck nine as I jogged by and headed for the climb. After an awkward thirty seconds during which I had to suffer the indignity of being barracked by a group of very avant-garde drunks hanging around a vacant stage on which, presumably, some local rock band was scheduled to perform several hours later, I turned right and started to climb steeply uphill. The mossy, fern-packed sides of the road ran with deep channels of fast-flowing streams. The Vosges mountains, finally warming up and coming to life, were trying to shake a week of rainwater off their backs.

In only its second visit here, the Tour had already created an iconic climb. The first time had been genuinely historic.

I had waited a long time to see a yellow jersey worn by a Briton on the Tour de France. But, in that regard, I was hardly unique. Whole generations of cyclists had been born, ridden and gone to their grave without so much as an inkling that it might ever become a possibility. So my wait was far from long. But ten consecutive Julys still amounted to a couple of hundred bike races without even the remotest prospect of genuine GC success. I had waited an equally long time to see a British rider even placing themselves in the position to win, or threaten to win, a mountain stage. It was true that Bradley Wiggins had finished in a surprisingly high placing on a few climbs in 2009, but before that? Well, Robert Millar was before my day. And between Millar and Wiggins there was absolutely no one, if you exclude the one day Chris Boardman finished in the GC group with Miguel Indurain on the climb to La Toussuire ('My GC career lasted exactly forty five minutes').

As dusk fell on that day in 2012 I found myself riding up and down the final ramp on this very distinctive climb. The final few hundred metres of the stage to La Planche des Belles Filles are brutal. You round a sharp right-handed hairpin and suddenly the road rears up at an utterly unreasonable 22 per cent which feels more like 30.

The air smelt of pine, the sun was still hot, though low in the sky, as all around me the Tour was being dismantled. An hour or two previously, this wall of forest had been the fairy-tale background to a remarkable event.

Chris Froome had won the stage (his first ever on the Tour) and Bradley Wiggins had ridden into a race lead that he never relinquished. The two riders crossed the line separated only by Cadel Evans. Froome sat up and extended his ludicrous arms (twiglets) towards the tops of the pine trees. At a few seconds' distance, Wiggins was a more inscrutable figure, hunched against the killer gradient, and then coasting to the line. And then came the textbook bony embrace between skinny leader and his skeletal lieutenant, between the new race leader and the stage winner, teammates.

A casual observer could easily have been duped into thinking that all was gloriously well in Sky's firmament, their two
British stars achieving a perfect mountain duet. It was a
remarkable occasion, and it nestled down into my memory
neatly, packaged up in a yellow bow-tie and marked 'Reasonably
Special. Unpack on Miserable Days'.

And yet, for some reason I had never been able to remember
the name of the location where it all took place. So many
other events become synonymous with their place that the
two sit together, perfectly aligned. Beloki's crash in 2003 was
in Gap. Vinokourov's ignominious exit in 2006 came about
in Pau. Cavendish winning in 2008 happened in Chateauroux.
Armstrong gapping Contador in 2009 was on the road to La
Grande Motte. They roll off the tongue. Froome's re-called
attack in 2012? La Toussuire.

But this one, the day the first ever British Tour de France
winner took the yellow jersey? Where on earth was that? It
had a silly name, that's one thing I can remember.

La Planche des Belles Filles! The (Wooden) Board of the
Beautiful Girls! Bonkers. This is not a place name. This is
like Ashby-de-la-Zouch; it is in fact a loose and ill-fitting
assembly of oddly matched words flung together and stuck
on the wrong road sign in the wrong place. Now, happily,
with the Tour de France returning once again (2012 was its
debut on the race) I have been handed a second chance to
get my head round this rather puzzling place name.

It got its name in 1635, some say, during the Thirty Years'
War, when pretty much all of Central Europe was being
overrun by a Swedish army intent on expressing its principled
opposition to the doctrines of Catholicism by beheading children, disembowelling and raping – or raping and then
disembowelling – their parents.

So 1635 it is then. Or, if we simply can't really be bothered to give the illusion of historical veracity to this legend, then we could go with the official tourist board, who date the story as '*Il y a bien longtemps...*', or 'A long, long time ago...'

So now that we know it's almost certainly utter nonsense, we can sit back and enjoy it in the knowledge that it never really happened.

This has always been my problem with all that pseudo-documented Arthurian stuff, or most of the stories involving Boadicea (including the wholly unnecessary late-twentieth-century revision of her name), or anything involving Dick Turpin. It's all a load of hokum dressed up as something historical. I would much prefer to read about burning bushes, resurrection and transubstantiation, all of which fall into the category of 'a little improbable' than to be force fed, as evidenced fact, the nineteenth-century inventions of hired fantasists and professional yarn-spinners looking to rebrand their local town.

So, anyway, here is it: the Legend of the (Wooden) Board of the Beautiful Girls (In as Much as It Relates to Stage 10 of the 2014 Tour de France).

One day (probably around about then . . .) the inhabitants of Plancher-les-Mines, going about their dutiful, if slightly miserable, Alsatian business of mining gold and lead from deep subterranean caverns, were in for a rude awakening. They got wind, probably literally given seventeenth-century hygiene standards, of a marauding Swedish army, just a day's march away from their pretty and distinctly non-militant mining community.

Now it just so happened that a local farmer had a breathtakingly beautiful daughter. This kind of thing often happened to farmers, so no one was very surprised. In fact, the villagers rather routinely, and with a distinct lack of

*imagination, ascribed to Ines the 'appearance of a queen'
and the 'virtues of a saint'. So far, so good. The problem
was that the Swedes were doing a lot of rape and murder,
and the more saintly the victim, the more 'Grrrr!' they got
about the whole thing, and then things never ended well.*

*There was only one thing for it. Ines (for that was the
lady's name) gathered up all the other maidens of the village,
even though not one of them was really a match for the
stunning Ines, who really was remarkable in her virtue and
beauty. The rest were fine, you know, but no more than
that. Together, and dressed in their most precious Festival
Day white robes (you can probably see what's coming) they
made their way, chanting choral incantations, to a secret
lake high up on the hillside. This spot, which on the day
of Stage 10 of the 2014 Tour de France was respectfully
marked by a line of makeshift urinals and chemical toilets
erected by the commune, was a place of perfect seclusion.
There was no way that the Swedes would find them there.*

*Oh yes they would! The girls, combing each other's hair,
singing gentle lamentations and pressing flowers all the
while, listened in increasing horror to the shrieks and cries
of their at-that-very-moment-being-horribly-murdered breth-
ren echoing up from the valley, as the Swedes vented their
awful bloodlust (this was, you see, a long time before Volvo,
with its concern for health and safety, came to define the
spirit of the Swede). They were drawing ever closer. But
nothing, legend has it, stopped the girls from continuing
their crochet work. And nor should it have done. Brave girls.*

*Suddenly, in a clearing in the woods there appeared a
Swedish officer astride a mighty white steed (nowhere in
the accounts of this legend does it actually say this, but I
don't think we'll find anyone who would object to this
slight embroidery on my part. At least no one from the
local tourist board).*

Run, Ines, run, you might think. Make for the safety of the woods! Flee, and take your dear petrified singing sisters with you!

Except head-in-the-clouds Ines doesn't do that at all. Instead, and not especially usefully, she falls in love. Instantly. There and then. And do you know what the noble Swede (possibly astride a mighty white steed) does? Exactly the same thing as Ines. Let's go back to the historical source:

'Le Suédois contemplait la jeune fille, muet d'émerveillement. Dans un regard, l'espace d'un instant, ils s'aimèrent vraiment.' *The Swede contemplated the young girl, struck dumb in wonder. With one look, in that instant, they fell truly in love.*

So how will this end? Will he spare her, marry her, and call a truce to all this frightful bloodshed? Will the Thirty Years' War be prematurely ended after only seventeen years, saving millions of innocent lives?

No. The other Swedes attack the girls, who run into the lake and drown. The main Swedish chap tries feebly to stop them, lifts Ines out of the water, lays her out on a mossy bank, tries a bit of fruitless CPR, and then gives up. Before moving on to the next massacre, he inscribes an epitaph to her onto a (wooden) board, and that's your lot.

Or:

Les Belles Filles is not Les Belles Filles at all, but Les Belles Fahys, which means 'beech tree' in an old Alsation dialect.

There are lots of beech trees on the lower slopes. It might be that, let's be honest.

And here we were, two years on, back for more. As I continued to run up the crazily oscillating gradient, I passed a steady stream of picnic-schlepping spectators, trudging heavily uphill in their rain capes. I heard only French being spoken. At one point, close to the final kilometre, a couple of skinny Belgian kids in the colours of their local cycling team rode past me, chatting impressively calmly in Flemish, but otherwise I could only conclude that this was not a stage for the visiting wider world. Most visitors from overseas had opted instead to keep themselves warm and dry and out of the Vosges deluge.

The top of the mountain, when I finally reached it (at the end of that brutally steep ramp inside the final 200 metres), was a scene of great disorder. The huge convoy of heavy TV trucks, including our own, piloted by the heroic Richard Gaines, had tried to park up in their allotted places in the very small hours of the morning, only to find themselves sinking deeply into the mud, or scoring the summit with cavernous furrows, which soon filled up with rainwater. Within the space of a few minutes, the game was up, and with most of the vehicles stranded axle deep in mud and immobile, the rest were pulled into place by an almighty tractor. One by one, they were cajoled into position by the giant grunting engine. It took all night and most of what remained of the morning to get them into place. And then it continued to rain, sometimes with great ferocity. That didn't help much either.

This was to be our place of work as we hopped to and from the various trucks, trying hard not to slip into the worst of the mud where entire TV crews could be lost for ever. French TV riggers led the way by putting bin bags over their shoes and up their legs, taping them up with gaffer tape just below the knee, as if they were aping medieval ironmongers. Everyone else, who didn't have access to bin bags and gaffer tape just minced around the carnage and hoped for the best.

I couldn't help wondering what the environmentalists who express such concern over the prospect of a few hundred cycling fans trampling down some wildflowers on Box Hill every now and again would have made of this devastation on top of La Planche des Belles Filles. Not even King Gustavus Adolphus's marauding Swedish army had done that much damage. In fact, 400 years from now, they might have renamed the place altogether and written an entirely new legend about how the mountainside was torn apart one day by an army of growling diesel-powered long-wheel-based haulage plants. La Planche des Camions.

So, for the sunshine of 2012, now read the mud and gloom of 2014. It did brighten up eventually, but the sunshine burst through way too late for Alberto Contador.

His crash, a long way from the finish, occurred mostly without witnesses, and spelt the end for him, but only in agonised stages of decline. And those were played out very publically. For us, watching at the other end of a television feed, there had firstly been the sudden shock of seeing him down. Like Nibali, and unlike the perpetually tipping over Chris Froome, Andrew Talansky or Geraint Thomas whose perfectly executed comedy head-over-the-handlebars dismount over a straw bale had been his latest variation, Contador was not a rider who fell often.

Then there was the agony of watching Contador trying to chase back on up a climb, and accompanied by a band of teammates who had to slow themselves considerably in order to make sure they didn't inadvertently drop him. At some point, maddened by what he felt, or rather, couldn't feel, he tried to push himself back into contention, and stood up in the saddle on his rebellious (and, it turned out, broken) legs to accelerate up the Col du Platzerwasel.

Then, pretty much the next time we saw him, he was thanking his teammate Mick Rogers by placing a hand on his back. After that, he slowed, pulled over to the side, and climbed off. Another year's work, wasted.

And then there was one.

No one dared to say it, but at that moment, Vincenzo Nibali won the Tour de France. So, you can stop reading here, if you wish.

Nibali's attack on the final climb came earlier than most people were expecting. And it looked almost effortless. Behind him on the mountain, huge damage was being done, not just to the legs and hearts and morale of those vanquished GC riders, for whom it spelt the end of any lingering sense that they might be able to challenge the Sicilian (or it should have done, if there had been even a modicum of realism in their public utterances), but also in the projected advertising coffers of commercial broadcasters across the world. This might prove to be a hard race to sell, with its leader so impervious to harm.

I had no language in common with Nibali who, from now until the end of the bike race, would be presented to me if not on a plate then at least on a stool, at the end of every stage for interview.

Not being able to understand Italian, at least no more than the gist of it, had not previously proved too much of a problem. Faced with an Italian stage winner on previous editions of the race, I had always been able to resort to the simple phrase: *'Una bella vittoria!'* And then I'd thrust my microphone in their general direction, in the hope that they would go through the usual checklist of thanking their teammates and sponsors, which we could then get translated in time for the highlights show. Whether it was Alessandro Petacchi or Rinaldo Nocentini, they seldom disappointed in that regard.

But with Nibbles (the rather puerile nickname, which became common currency, swerved the endlessly boring debate about whether it should be pronounced NIBali, or niBALi), I could no longer restrict myself to such a narrow line of enquiry. If we were going to get through two more weeks of this together, we had to move the debate on from 'Una bella vittoria'. There was more to this race than that, wasn't there?

So, I spoke to him in English, instead. Barking at him like a late-afternoon drinker in a Marbella bar. He understood enough of my questions to answer in Italian. And then, rather riskily, since I often had only understood maybe 5 per cent of his first answer, I would ask him a follow-up question, which I hoped he had not addressed in his first answer. But then again, even if he did answer my second question with the Italian equivalent of 'I just told you that, you big-nosed shambles of a man,' at least I wouldn't have been able to understand the insult, so we would happily have gone through the ritual of signing off our minute of mutual incomprehension with our daily, almost liturgical:

'*Grazie*, Vincenzo.'

'You're welcome.'

We became so good at our nonsensical exchanges, that, towards the end of the Tour, we even started to interrupt each other, like an over-familiar couple might. I started to warm to him, in as much as you can warm to a man who talks in code like a Latin robot. Even when his deeply foreign words were translated back to me, they hardly ever surprised me. They weren't very revealing.

Nevertheless, listening to Vincenzo Nibali speak was a constant source of joy to Matt Rendell, a fluent Italian speaker, even more fluent cycling speaker, and the world's leading authority on Marco Pantani, the last Italian to win the Tour. He delighted in the sheer poetry of Nibali's win, embraced with commendable passion its sheer Italianness, and fell quite obviously and profoundly in love with the Sicilian and everything that the Sicilian said about bicycles. It must have driven him mad that he had to translate my inept interviews every day.

Often I'd find him slaving away in the truck, an hour after the end of the stage, transcribing into English my Nibali interview.

'What did he say, Matt?'

'Oh!' He would lift off his headphones and look at me with wonder in his eyes. 'You, know, just stuff... but he's bloody wonderful!'

'Yes, but what actually did he say?'

'Ah. He's fantastic. Vincenzo. What a bloody rider.'

Then I'd be forced to look over his shoulder at what he'd typed.

Today, my team were very strong, and I had good legs for the climb. But it is only one day. We still have a long way to go... etc. etc. etc.

The quotes were never much more elucidating than that. 'Is that it, Matt?' I'd ask. 'Is that all he says?'

'Yeah,' he'd grin back at me from ear to ear. 'Wonderful.'

But I half knew what he meant, even through my linguistic fog. Nibali looked sublime, and serene, on a bike and off it. My workplace, standing at such close physical proximity to riders after they have just endured a stage and dug as deep as only they know how to, can be very revealing. That magnification is increased when the rider is wearing the yellow jersey. They have all had their tics, down the years.

Michael Rasmussen, Floyd Landis (and though I would not want to bracket any of these names together for obvious, and possibly legal, reasons) Andy Schleck, Carlos Sastre, Bradley Wiggins, Chris Froome and most definitely Cadel Evans all brought a certain edginess into play. In Froome's case, for example, it was expressed by the immense effort he underwent to appear in complete control. With others, like Evans and Wiggins, there was either tension or a fragility that might at any point spill over into bouts of paranoia. Even Lance Armstrong's considered belligerence and his almost daily habit of playing to the gallery were the by-products of a mind constantly trying to work out how to toy with the race. But Nibali had none of that about him.

He slipped through July, and met with the world insouciantly, dealing with each set of circumstances on its merits and simply getting on with it. He was neither effusive nor tight-lipped, he was respectful, but without over-playing it. And that was just how he rode the Tour de France.

Watch his face. Pain piles in on all those around him. Does he hurt? His expression is vacant. He concentrates, but there is no tension.

When he crested the ridge of the Planche des Belles Filles, you could almost see, if you tried hard enough, the bobbing form of Chris Froome, and the dancing jig of Contador alongside his imperious upright posture in the saddle; the two ghost riders of the race that never was.

It was gone ten o'clock and it was cold by the time we reclaimed our car at the foot of the mountain, in a car park in Plancher-les-Mines. The descendants of Ines the Beautiful (or they would have been if she'd lived long enough to procreate, or if she'd even lived at all) littered the dusky streets, some staggering across the road.

We stopped at a pizzeria which had no pizzas, since the family running the establishment had given up, and settled instead to getting noisily pissed. From them we picked up a bottle of undrinkable bootleg Côtes de Provence, which we drank, and we bartered for the cooling remains of their almost extinguished barbecue.

Dinner was one and a half cold Merguez sausages and a three-hour drive.

But who's complaining? It's how young Ines would have wanted us to remember the scene of her martyrdom.

PART 3

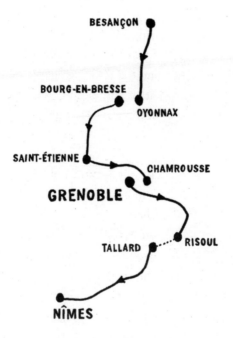

BESANÇON

'Band of Brothers. The whole box set.'

The sun came out in Besançon, and the race fell asleep. Shortly before midnight the night before, we arrived in a Campanile hotel, inevitably situated in an industrial estate six kilometres from the city centre. There is a certain comforting familiarity in the Campanile range of hotels, born from the fact that the rooms are architecturally identical wherever you are, in just the same way that a Big Mac is a pasty mess of a meal whether it's ingested in Prague, Preston or Port Stanley.

The gherkin in the bun of a Campanile hotel room is undoubtedly, as Chris Boardman astutely noted over breakfast the next day, the stool, which is provided in each guest's identical cell. It is circular, backless and made of moulded plastic, and gets marvellously in the way as you try to navigate the thin aisle between the bed and the window, or the bed and the wall. It is not only ugly and uncomfortable, it is also utterly pointless. The notion that you would opt to sit on it, instead of the bed, to rest and admire your surroundings is quite fanciful, and exists only in the imaginations of whichever firm of architects won the multi-million-pound contract to revamp the Campanile franchise, a job which must have taken them most of the afternoon to complete.

But they're simple, wholesome places, and there is something profoundly reassuring about the twisty pole mechanism which brings down the shutters, and reduces the light in the room to the exact same grey, indistinguishable murk, entirely uniform whether you find yourself in the middle of a burning hot Provençale afternoon, or a stormy Tuesday morning in Rouen. You tend to sleep well in them.

Waking to sunshine for the first time since we left Cambridge and ratcheting up the squeaky blind, I gazed out at a scene of calm renewal. The Tour was licking its wounds.

Riders wandered aimlessly down outdoor staircases from elevated walkways, or rather, they slouched. Families, complete with bald-headed pre-school children had mysteriously appeared on the hotel premises overnight, their kids' pale scalps like button mushrooms blinking at the morning. Riders' wives nursed coffees on the hotel's modest terrace, half their attention turned to the button mushrooms, the other half trying to listen to the sotto voce mumblings of their gaunt, weary husbands or boyfriends, ten days into a torture that knew no end.

I went downstairs too. I opened my laptop in the welcome, bright sunshine of the terrace, and tried to establish what the day had in store. The riders would ride their bikes, slowly, and not for very long. I would interview riders slowly, and also not for very long, with any luck.

Suddenly I became aware that Jean-Marc Bideau, the very rider who had been overtaken by his honourable breakaway companion Jan Bárta on the way into London on Stage 3, was staring at me, intently. He was there with his wife, and they were sitting at the table next to me, drinking a juice. Now, I have to admit that I never get riders staring at me, as I normally stare at them. So this was unusual, and a little unnerving.

'Bonjour.'

'Le wifi. Vous avez une bonne connexion?'

It was a very odd thing to be asked. But, since he had raised the subject, I tried to tell him that I had experienced a fair few problems logging on. But then, to be honest, I thought there were bigger issues hanging in the air. Like, for example, the Tour de France. It was the first Tour Bideau had ever ridden, after a notable but largely unrewarded career trawling the less well-known teams of Northern Europe, like Roubaix Lille Métropole and the forgettably named Unibet.com.

And here he was, at thirty years of age, not only riding a Tour de France, but featuring heavily in one. Good on him. I was feeling tremendously well disposed towards both him and his team, and I wanted him to know that all his efforts were acknowledged and appreciated. He was a Tour rider. That still commanded huge respect.

'Le wifi est de la merde ici.'

Two teams were in the same hotel. The catchily named Bretagne-Séché Environnement occupied the prime spot near the reception area, and a little further back up the access road, a fleet of red-white-and-blue Katusha vehicles made sure that should there be a fire, almost no one would be saved as the fire engines would have had to shoot the water over the top of their two (TWO!) team buses from a distance of a hundred metres or so.

Culturally, the two teams were at opposite extremes. Katusha, with their millionaire climber Purito Rodríguez and their loosely assembled international potpourri of *domestiques*, were financially pimped by some seriously minted sponsors. In fact, in common with the race leaders Astana, who drew on the entire mineral wealth of Kazakhstan to pay for their energy gels and bicycle pumps, Katusha's liveries bore witness to major corporate investment. One of the world's richest companies Gazprom had their name on the side of the bus, as well as a host of other Russian monoliths who'd chipped seven-figure sums into the team from the petty cash tin.

'Here, look over there.' Matt pointed at some bloke, rather obviously, with a fork. 'You remember him?'

I looked at the guy. He was in a Katusha tracksuit and was standing at the Campanile breakfast buffet, trying to unstick two slices of Emmenthal from one another using only a fork. This was not something that could easily be achieved. But he was in no rush, and neither were we. It was a rest day.

'No.' With a teaspoon, I swilled the plain yoghurt around in its pot. 'No idea.'

'Ha.' Matt stuffed almost an entire croissant in his mouth. 'But you're about to tell me, am I right?'

I watched him chewing, and about a minute later I was still watching him chew. Finally, he took a sip of orange juice, and then spoke. 'That's Uwe Peschel.'

I looked at Uwe Peschel again, a trim chap, with mostly receded grey hair.

'Right.'

The name meant very little to me, and at that precise moment even less than the plain yoghurt into which I had poured a small hotel miniature pot of honey. And believe me, after a week on the road in French hotels, the yoghurt did not amount to very much, meaning-wise.

'Peschel.'

'You interviewed him in 2004, through a side window of his campervan.'

'Did I?'

'He'd posted the best time in the time trial, and was waiting to see if it would hold. He was very patient with you, as you patronised him. Because you had absolutely no idea that he was a really bloody good time triallist.'

'Did I? I mean, was he?'

'Peschel? Bronze medallist at the Worlds in 2003, behind Mick Rogers and David Millar. That's pretty good.' It was a result that got even better in 2004, when Millar was stripped of his title, bumping him up to second place.

Peschel had separated the cheese slices, and was now

eating them stuffed awkwardly into an overly hard baguette end. Matt, meanwhile, was chuckling to himself, seemingly still amused by my ignorance, ten years on. I finished my yoghurt and left him to it.

Later that day, I made sure that I spoke to Uwe Peschel face to face. This time we met not at the side of a campervan but over a coffee dispenser in the lobby. I'd wanted to apologise for my lack of preparedness of a decade ago. But in the end, all I could muster was, 'Wie schmeckt der Kaffee?'

I knew exactly how the coffee tasted, so I wasn't actually interested in his reply. Nevertheless, I went through with the enquiry.

'Gut, danke.' This was our second, and possibly final, conversation.

The rest of the rest day was far from restful.

Team Sky (remember them?) were still, technically, in the race. In fact, Richie Porte, despite losing time to all the other GC riders on the Planche des Belles Filles, was still in second place overall and being talked up by Dave Brailsford, whose wave of positivity showed no signs of ebbing. Rather, it continued to crash over any ears or microphones or cameras that stood before it. The message, reduced to its essence, was this: there were longer, more gradual climbs to come that would suit Porte in a way that the less malleable Vosges *ballons* had not.

But when we got to their team hotel, it transpired that Porte's principle concern was not for the Alps, but for the laptop (I reckon, if we're being honest, it was probably a MacBook) he'd left in his hotel room in Mulhouse.

'I was going to watch a few videos.'

'Which ones, Richie?' I asked him.

'*Band of Brothers*. The whole box set.' The leader of team Sky, on their ill-fated rampage through eastern France wanted to watch a series about Easy Company and their ill-fated rampage through eastern France, it seemed.

A Team Sky helicopter would almost certainly have been scrambled to try and retrieve it so that it could be carried on a black merino cushion, with a blue stripe down the middle to the hotel bedroom of their official Plan B. In fact, Dario Cioni had just phoned the hotel. 'They're fetching it, Richie.'

Meanwhile the rest of the British and assorted international press cortège was gently asking Porte about his race, and egging him on to make bullish predictions about what he might be able to achieve in the coming week. When they were done with their interviews, Dave Brailsford called them all together and asked them, informally, where all the doping questions had gone. This time last year, as he reminded them, Chris Froome was being besieged.

There was just a moment's awkwardness while the journalists shuffled in their seats and waited to see who would speak first, like a class of schoolchildren being held back from play until someone owned up. Then, one by one, they replied.

'It's the difference between first and second place, I guess. The yellow jersey.'

'Chris still had a largely unexplained rise to account for.'

'He'd come from nowhere, basically.'

'With Nibali, you can see the progression of a career. His progress has been slow and visible.'

And off they all went to the Vincenzo Nibali press conference, with Brailsford's cleverly inserted words perhaps already forming an unconscious question in their minds.

For the remainder of the day, after we had edited our package about Sky and sent the rest-day programme back to London for later broadcast, we had some free time. So, inevitably, Liam, Jim and I trawled lamely through the most enormous branch of Carrefour that I had ever seen. We bought some wine and a bag of pistachios.

'We've been here before, haven't we?' said Liam. This struck me as being a hilarious assertion, like being shown a picture of a tree in a wood, or a grain of sand on a beach, and suggesting that you'd 'seen it before'. But again, I was struck by my wildly conflicted feelings towards these monolithic French hypermarkets. I should, in principle, get great pleasure from the wonderful arrays of fresh fruit and vegetables, their fish and charcuterie, but instead I invariably find myself gawping at the endless aisles of tinned carrots and haricots. And then I get stuck in the clothes aisles, trying to establish why, even here, everything smells strongly of Camembert. We drank an awful coffee in one of those strange outlets on the way in and out of the supermarket, and left.

That evening we struck out into Besançon, a town I have visited on many occasions, but never had cause to take in the city centre. It turns out that it is quite a marvel; the kind of place that, were it in England, would be marketed to within an inch of its life as an architectural and historical gem. White stone townhouses, with arcades at ground level for cafes,

flank a deep-looking meandering river that cuts through the old town. We sat down at a restaurant. I ate a beef Carpaccio, followed by beef chasseur, having chosen, I guess, from the beef menu. And as we ate, the sun burst out, and the temperature rose instantly to high summer. It was suddenly sweltering.

When we returned to the hotel, long after dark, Katusha's heavily bearded maverick Italian Luca Paolini was still up, swigging beer from bottles and singing bawdily with a crew of his mechanics as if they were all extras from *Pirates of the Caribbean*. It was fair to say that he was taking a relaxed approach to the Tour de France. During the first week, he'd been snapped by a photographer checking his iPhone, midstage. That had prompted the organisers to remind riders that 'the use of telephones during the race is expressly forbidden'. Paolini must have been like that kid at school who everyone knows will get sent out of the dinner hall at lunchtime for flicking mashed potato at the deputy head. Part of you likes him, but another part of you is scared of him. In fact, the whole of the Katusha team struck me as a bit like that; a supercharged, slightly roguish bunch of riders with no particular plan but loads of unbridled aggression and talent.

In the morning, I overheard a discussion in English between two of Katusha's senior management team, one of whom was Russian, and the other possibly Dutch. They were talking in secretive tones about the arrival of a new sponsor. I was straining to catch the details.

'Mumble, mumble, mumble...significant investment.'

'Mumble, mumble, mumble...by autumn at the latest.'

'Mumble, mumble, mumble...can you pass me the butter.'

'Mumble, mumble, mumble...different targets for next year.'

'Mumble, mumble, mumble...twenty-five million.'

'Mumble, mumble, mumble…bloke listening to us over there.'

Quite hurriedly I picked up my stuff and left the breakfast room, bumping, literally, into Brice Feillu on the way out. He greeted me, mistakenly, like an old friend. True, I had spoken to him once or twice, most notably when he won a famous stage to Andorra on the 2009 Tour, but our relationship didn't extend much beyond that. He was about to join his older brother, Romain, for breakfast. The Feillu brothers, one a stocky sprinter, and Brice a beanpole-thin climber, did not much resemble one another. But for a while, they had been quite big news in French cycling. Brice had even been talked up (like Pierre Rolland and others after him) as a potential Tour winner. Now they were riding for the Breton team with the lowest budget of any squad in the race, whose team bus was plastered with the names of sponsors such as Ventura socks and Lucien Georgelin confectioners. The Feillus themselves were having largely invisible races, and that in a team that was noticeable for squeezing a rider into almost every breakaway. Anyway, I greeted him equally warmly back, and we shook hands. There was a split second of doubt that passed between us, though. I could observe it clouding his expression as he withdrew his hand, when it must have crossed his mind that he did not really have the faintest idea who I was. And we both moved on.

But where the Feillu brothers had dared to tread a few years previously, more French riders were queuing up. In fact, down at the start line of Stage 11 in Besançon, under a long, pleasantly sun-dappled avenue shaded by a line of plane trees, there was quite a hubbub of excitement. For the first time that I could recall since 2003, I went off to interview one of the Française des Jeux riders at his team bus. There was a small crowd, mostly there to catch a glimpse of the young rising star Thibaut Pinot.

Pinot had shown himself strongly on Stage 10, finishing just fifteen seconds behind Nibali, and he now found himself up to sixth in the overall standings, with plenty of potential to improve in the higher mountains. He was tall, elegant, well spoken, humble. There was a lot to like about him, not least the fact that he was French. To get close to him, I had to (politely) push my way through a crowd of onlookers. One of them, kindly recognising that I perhaps had a professional duty to discharge, allowed me through and engaged me in conversation. A long-standing cycling fan since childhood, he had started to lose interest in the race over recent years. Now, suddenly, he was watching again with a keener interest.

'*Le Tour est intéressant pour les Francais pour une fois.*' He seemed eager to share his reinvigorated excitement with anyone who might listen. As I stood waiting for Pinot to emerge into the sunlight, I remembered Rod Ellingworth's assertion, way back on that pitching and yawing cross-Channel ferry that Pinot was the One. Of the current crop of French riders, he had it in him to win the race one day.

That same day *L'Équipe* newspaper had published an interview with Dave Brailsford, in which he had been asked about the prospect of winning the Tour with a French rider. Yes, he had replied, that would be a fantastic achievement. Did he see it as his next objective? Yes, he had answered.

What a firestorm that simple assertion had unleashed!

Brailsford had felt duty-bound to pour buckets of cold British water on it during the rest-day press conference, claiming that it had been taken out of context, that Team Sky was still, at heart a British project, and gently reminding everyone of what he'd achieved on behalf of British Cycling.

The reason, I was beginning to understand, for his very obvious courting of the French cycling public, might well have had its roots in the previous year's Tour. During Chris Froome's three-week stranglehold on the race, and the constant swirling of doping rumours, it is fair to say that large sections of French supporters made their mind up about Sky. And then they made their feelings felt.

Peter Kennaugh, who had been such a key part of the 2013 Tour, once told me about the stage to Alpe d'Huez, which they rode up twice on the same day.

'The first time we went up was just incredible. I wasn't really thinking about much there: the crowd, the atmosphere. I took the whole thing in. I didn't even feel my legs. It was one big roar. It gave me a totally new vision of the sport. I couldn't believe how big the Tour was. I'd never seen cycling that way before, the amount of people . . . it was off the scale really.'

Then, when the race came around there for the last time, everything had changed. Kennaugh had done his job, and was alone on the climb.

'The second time round I rode up it on my own. It wasn't as fun as the first time, put it that way. All the abuse. That was the worst part of the Tour. I had people swearing at me, people who had no idea about my history in the sport calling me a doper. And it was all the way up. It was horrendous, a mob environment. On that final climb we just went through a wall of abuse.'

That, according to Kennaugh, was the default position of the French fans. 'The whole Tour was like that. It was bad. It's amazing how Team Sky get it and Contador and people like that are all loved.'

'I suppose they're just jealous.'

It had stung the team, more deeply than you might imagine. Perhaps that was why Dave Brailsford had appeared eager to appeal to their French hearts and minds, *leurs esprits et leurs cœurs*.

Pinot appeared, to a barrage of cheers. He fiddled with his bike computer, strapped his helmet on, dropped his shades, and then answered my questions. I found myself interviewing French cycling's biggest star, in French, in front of a sizeable crowd of French people, in France. This was like the GCSE oral exam from hell.

'Thibaut. Sir David Brailsford', I intoned with a heavy French accent, adding in his knighthood just for good measure, '*a dit que c'est son prochain objectif de gagner le Tour de France avec un coureur français.*' As I told him about Brailsford's stated aim of winning the Tour with a French rider, he started to smile. He knew very well what was coming. And so did the crowd.

'*C'est, peut-être, vous!*' I used that 'I put it to you, Mr Pinot, that he meant you!' voice that barristers use during cross-examination.

'*Non.*' Laughter and relief all round.

Apparently Pinot liked fishing with his family in the mountains of the Haute-Saône and was perfectly happy where he was, thank you. Anyway, he had a bicycle to race. I scraped a pass in my exam, and left for the stage finish at Oyonnax before I misconjugated a verb in public.

FRENCH

'I remember sitting on the pavement, trying to see if my head was broken, and when everyone told me that my head wasn't broken, I said, "Fine. Then it'll be OK."'

As we traced a more direct route south, and the weather turned distinctly more Tour-de-Francey, I wondered about how to pronounce the name of the next finishing line. It sounded like a character from an *Asterix* adventure. But when we got there, it actually appeared more like a backdrop for some gritty social-realism drama set in the Parisian suburbs. Wet clothing was draped over balconies in the estate that dominated the scene, unhappy-looking dogs trotted briskly around every corner in search of a fight.

And yet, it was a special place. For the otherwise unremarkable town of Oyonnax saw fit, in November 1960, to yield up to the world the great Éric Barone.

Even at the moment that he first inhaled the mountain air and screamed his infant lungs hoarse, destiny was tapping him on the shoulder. It was no surprise to anyone that he would go on to achieve fame and sponsorship in equal measure. After all, he was already equipped with a name that could easily be adapted to a highly marketable, if a little well-worn, soubriquet: the Red Baron.

But unlike his illustrious, and a little murderous, aristocratic German predecessor, Éric's particular predilection was for plummeting earthwards, rather than escaping its bounds. And instead of a triplane, he chose a bike with an equally odd-looking design.

An early career as a stunt double for the likes of Sylvester Stallone and Jean-Claude Van Damme, in some films that were presumably too bad to endure, was only a warm-up for the main event. Between 1994 and 2000, and already in his mid-to-late thirties, this chiselled son of Oyannax (he has a marvellously understated stud in his left ear, and a De Niro-esque mole on his right cheek, both of which add detail and charisma to his already handsome smile) decided that a man of his age should dedicate himself not to gardening or golf, but to riding as fast as possible down a mountain.

Obviously, if you want to do this really fast (which the Red Baron most decidedly did) you should choose a snowy mountain, with ice involved. Here there is less friction, you see, and maybe also more survivability if you happen to fall off. Also, you should encase yourself in a shiny bright red Kevlar skinsuit that leaves little room for testicles and their accoutrements, and place an extremely silly-looking 360-degree flared transparent helmet atop your head. Then you are good to go. The rest is presumably just about staying upright and avoiding dying.

His top speed was reached on 21 April 2000 at Les Arcs. He hit an utterly improbable 222 kilometres an hour; the kind of velocity which even on the autobahns of Germany might attract some serious attention from the polizei. Remember, because this is important, he did this speed on a pushbike. I once topped out at thirty-five miles an hour on the big downhill bit in Greenwich Park and endured a few seconds when I knew not whether I would live or die.

Monsieur Barone eats thirty-five miles an hour for his *petit dejeuner*.

For the past decade, he has left behind him the icy slopes of the Alps, as they are decidedly old hat, and headed for the volcanoes, specifically, although not exclusively, of Nicaragua. He took his bike with him, and guess what? After a few adaptations, including knobbly tyres and a flame-proof saddle, he started to ride it down them, thereby establishing a whole new genre of extreme sport, with its own equipment, etiquette and records (all of which the Red Baron probably holds). While there is no imminent prospect of Volcano-Descent Biking being included in the Olympic programme for the Tokyo Games, it is a burgeoning sport, now practised by at least one or two people annually, although one of these is the Baron. In fact, frankly, whichever volcano you're thinking of riding down in a bespoke figure-hugging aerosuit, the middle-aged man from Oyonnax has almost certainly beaten you to it. And yes, that includes Mounts Fuji and Etna, since you ask.

He's not easily put off. In 2002, hurtling down a volcano in Hawaii, and just after his computer had registered 172 kilometres per hour, the forks broke on his bike and he ended up doing the rest of the descent on his arse. And his wrists and ribs and hands and elbows and then head. And, finally, his arse again.

And this spring, fourteen years after his record on snow was set, he announced that he would attempt to beat it. This time, instead of Les Arcs, he chose the steepest, baddest run of them all: the legendary slope at Chabrières, with its 98 per cent gradient close to the summit.

Information about this attempt is sketchy. There is no trace of his breaking the record. And the last update on his own website makes no mention of it. Instead, he's opened a Pilates studio in his home town on Oyonnax, which seems far more appropriate for a man in his mid-fifties.

There is also only a single reference that I can find to doping in the world of Wildly Uncontrollable Bike Hurtling (or whatever it's called). And it is rather sweet. It seems that the Red Baron's performance-enhancing drug of choice is, as he puts it, his sheer, colossal *joie de vivre*.

In his words: 'Voilà mon carburant, mon énergie, voilà ce qui dope mon dynamisme.' That's my fuel, my energy. That's what dopes my dynamism.

Although why he chose Oyonnax to be so dynamic in is anyone's guess. On the evidence of the little bit of it I saw, there was as much dynamism in the place as you expect to find in an oil painting by John Major.

On Stage 12, as is often the case, languor started to afflict the travelling circus of the Tour. People started to fall asleep on the job, off the job, at the table, in chairs, mid-sentence. It was as if an invisible hand were passing through the compound closing eyes and whispering 'Sleep!' into ears, like some supernatural, talking, amputated Paul McKenna body part. Tiredness, and its cumulatively acquired cousin, knackered-ness, had become a contagion, something that could no longer be contained nor controlled.

And the guitars came out. With the sudden onrush of hot,

sunny weather after so much Stygian gloom, came the unwelcome proliferation of the guitars. It was not so much the
instruments themselves, which were largely blameless, it was
more the grisly sight of their practitioners. To play the guitar
in the middle of the afternoon, waiting for a race to hit town,
there are certain rules that need to be observed. It is important
to be stripped to the waist, male, in your mid-forties, normally
either Dutch or French, and unable to remember all the
verses to 'Hotel California'.

Deep in the middle eight of the Tour de France, stages
come and go without much fanfare. And so it was that
Oyonnax passed into memory (and, for most people apart
from for Tony Gallopin and his family) straight back out again,
in the time it took Éric Barone to nip out to the get the
papers.

It was, though, another opportunity for the great bewildered
Peter Sagan to air his soul-searching. He had been part of a
group of four or five riders who had got away on a descent,
and had ended up contesting the stage. Gallopin, by dint of
being massively underestimated by all the others, attacked
and stayed away. The rest were too busy watching Sagan, who
was too busy watching the rest. This was the very essence of
Sagan Syndrome, or Being Too Good For Your Own Good.
He was confused that no one had seemed willing to work
with him to bring back Gallopin.

'I would have beaten Gallopin. But I cannot beat all of
them.' He came ninth.

To add to his general malaise, it was only after he had
spoken to me on camera that his attentive press officer noticed
a bogey clinging to the outside of his right nostril. He was
handed a handkerchief, and took an age trying to remove it,
as he stood in front of banks of patiently waiting media, who
had lowered their cameras out of respect for his difficult
moment.

There was a curious echo of that momentary embarrassment the following morning at the start line in Bourg-en-Bresse, when Garmin's sports director Charly Wegelius came out to explain that Andrew Talansky had left the race. He delivered interviews first in French, then Italian, in which he recounted the previous day's traumatic events for Talansky, and how his repeated falls had finally taken their toll on the young rider. All the while he talked, though, no one told him that his flies were undone. Once his press officer, Marya, was informed of Charly's less-than-ideal zip alignment, she waited for him to finish his Italian interview, and before he turned towards our camera, she whispered into his ear the terrible truth. Charly looked down in sudden shock.

'Oh shit,' he grinned. 'What do you want to know, Ned?'

And we did the Talansky interview, in his third language of the day. There was no one there from Finland, otherwise he could easily have made it four. But I got the only interview that Charly Wegelius did that morning with his flies done up; a scoop of sorts, but in a 'Dog Bites Man' sort of a way, rather than 'Man Bites Dog.'

Even before that, the day had started weirdly. I had gone for a run and, for the first time ever, had been joined by Liam. Liam is not given to running, in the same way that cats are not given to giggling. Nevertheless, I commended him for his effort and we set off, ambling up a long avenue out of town towards our destination, the Royal Monastery of Brou with its crazy coloured tiled roof. There Liam turned around and yomped back to the latest 'Nobby' we were staying in, getting thoroughly lost on the way and picking up extensive inner-thigh chafing from the gusset of the swimming shorts he had pulled on for the exercise.

I ran on and found a beautiful empty woodland park, which I had all to myself, soft underfoot, and deep green above me. The quietness took me by surprise. Although I was just a few

kilometres away from the city centre and the Tour de France, I might as well have been on the moon, if the moon had an atmosphere and trees. I found myself wondering how long it would take anyone to find me if I just keeled over and packed up. It wouldn't have been the worst way to go.

We were bound for Saint-Étienne, the scene of a few horrors down many years of the Tour de France.

'I could draw you a map,' Bernard Hinault had told me, the day before. 'I think I can remember every single spot. We were eight hundred metres from the line.'

It was 1985. Bernard Hinault was in a group of GC riders that had got away on the descent into town. They were chasing hard to gain time on opponents, as Lucho Herrera (who had also crashed horribly) rode out the stage win a minute or so ahead of them. Then it all went wrong. The sprint was a mess, and a sudden touch of the wheels dumped five of them on the ground. Hinault, in the yellow jersey, planted his face onto his bike so hard that the frame of his glasses broke his nose.

'But it was a really horrible fall.' I was a master of stating the obvious, even in a foreign language, in fact particularly in a foreign language. '*Non?*'

'Well, I had others, too,' Hinault shrugged. 'I remember sitting on the pavement, trying to see if my head was broken, and when everyone told me that my head wasn't broken, I said, "Fine. Then it'll be OK."'

'And how did you get to the finish line?' Again, a stupid question. Because as anyone knows, who has seen the footage, Hinault remounts and rides on, his face awash with blood. Once over the line, he almost falls off the bike, and a policeman hands him a towel, which turns crimson within seconds.

'You never thought about abandoning?' The stupid questions were piling up. This one he treated with utter contempt.

'Never, never. Even though I suffered enormously for the following two days. But I never thought about abandoning.'

'And you won the Tour de France that year.'

'There you go.' And with that he swooshed off, to the accompaniment of a lot of people whose task it is to accompany Bernard Hinault from one place to another.

I suspect that being Bernard Hinault is actually an enormously simple exercise. You wake up in the morning completely sure of the way the world works, and at night, as you go to bed, you probably reflect on how the world proved you completely correct, before sleeping the sleep of the utterly certain.

What was the last-ever French Tour winner making of the national hysteria that was bubbling all around him? I have my suspicions.

I would guess that he did not take much time to read the papers. But if he had on the day of Stage 12, he would have been confronted by a wave of excitable hyperbole. Under a tremendous picture of Tony Gallopin celebrating the previous

day's win, as the bunch closed in on him, heads down and blurrily out of focus in the background, *L'Équipe* was just warming up its 'Marseillaise'.

'The majestic success of Tony Gallopin is a symbol of this Tour which is being lit up by the French every day and on all fronts. What a splendid revolution!' And that's a word they don't use lightly in the Republic of France.

It was as if Marcel Kittel, Tony Martin and Vincenzo Nibali were on a different race and therefore didn't count. Which in a way they were, and so they didn't.

But it was hard to begrudge the French a certain amount of pleasure at what they were witnessing. They had the sublime symmetry of the Gallopin story, with his podium girl, bike-racing girlfriend Marion Rousse who kissed him after his stage win, and was then contractually obliged to go and kiss a bunch of other men. But they also had three other riders in the top ten: Romain Bardet, Jean-Christophe Péraud and Thibaut Pinot.

There was even some rather hesitant talk of the advent of a golden generation for French cycling. Now that really was rather previous. France, after all, used to be a conveyor belt for champions.

Towards the latter half of his career, Bernard Hinault had to put up with the emergence of the irritatingly good, irritatingly popular Laurent Fignon as his spur, contemporary, rival and nemesis. But that clutch of French talent that emerged after the domination of Eddy Merckx was as nothing compared to the situation the nation enjoyed in the late 1950s and early '60s. They could pick a winner, in those days, by playing a game of cards. Mostly, of course it was the great Jacques Anquetil who drew the winning joker from the pack, and on whom fortune shone most favourably. But there had been perhaps half a dozen others who also could have walked away with a string of French Tour victories, had it not been for the fact that there was so many stonkingly good French riders to compete with.

Which brings us neatly to Raymond Poulidor, the itinerant hairdresser turned cyclist, who became known as the Eternal Second, because, like an early adopter of Sagan Syndrome, he just couldn't win the damn race.

'Poulidor!' One of us will point him out. It happens every year.

'Where?'

'Over there.' By the coffee stand, surrounded by a few women in the canary yellow of Crédit Lyonnais, his employer: our first glimpse of him on the race. It will be the first of many. And there he is again, craggy, barrel-chested, with a fulsome, fleshy nose and a thick thatch of snow-white hair. Pou-pou.

On the first occasion this year, in Leeds, the great man was eating a pork pie, surrounded by beautiful women, and generally being ignored by everyone else.

The first sighting of Raymond Poulidor on any given Tour

de France is like touching the over-polished granite-sculpted foot of a saint in some familiar cathedral. It is an act of affirmation, a seeking-out of the comforting thought that all is well in the universe: gravity still works, night will become day, and a sponsored Poulidor will always be on hand to talk about never having won the Tour de France, with his famous grammatical lapses and his pronounced nasal whine.

He is now seventy-eight years old and, despite occasional flushes of impatience, shows signs of neither slowing up nor clamming up and refusing to discuss his status as France's most revered runner-up. It is a thing of great wonder how much the French love him.

Not one rider, I suspect, has enjoyed such a long and uninterrupted relationship with the Tour de France. Eddy Merckx is a common enough sight on the modern Tour, but he was only an occasional visitor when I first started to cover the event in 2003. And besides, I am never sure under whose auspices he is there. The list of those willing and able to extend him an invite is long and shows no sign of receding. But Merckx, nevertheless, retains a unique air of mystery. Now you see him, now you see only his backside getting into a Skoda and being driven off.

For eleven months of the year Bernard Hinault eats lunches at the expense of local authorities bidding to win the Tour, and for one month only he emerges, butterfly-like from his hospitality chrysalis and reminds the home nation how long it has been since they have won their race. This he does simply by standing still, smiling and ageing.

Like counting the concentric rings inside a tree, this national sporting failure is measured in the holes Hinault employs to buckle his belt. But even his association is considerably younger than that of Monsieur Poulidor.

For a start, Poulidor rode the Tour fourteen times, finishing second on three occasions and only to the likes of Jacques

Anquetil and Eddy Merckx. He won eleven stages. And he won every other bike race on earth, pretty much, just not the big one. In fact, never did he wear the *maillot jaune*, not once, not even fleetingly. In the Prologue of the 1973 Tour he failed by just eight-hundredths of a second, and in 1974, on the Puy de Dôme, he famously missed out by fourteen seconds.

I have always found it pleasingly contradictory, then, that the very sponsor whose colours and logo are so inextricably bound up with the iconography of the *maillot jaune* should choose the very man who never pulled it on to be their brand ambassador. For that is the honourable, remunerated function which *L'Éternel Second* now diligently fulfils. Daily he wears not a yellow jersey but a yellow shirt, collared, and embroidered over the right breast pocket with the LCL logo. His lack of belonging to the club of those who have worn the actual leader's jersey of the Tour de France is made explicit by this rare choice of clothing. It is a shortcoming he willingly celebrates by his daily attire. So either Poulidor has a particularly nuanced sense of irony coupled with the patience of a saint, or he's being subtly humiliated, patted on the head and asked to pose for photos unworthy of his marvellous career. Or, thirdly, and perhaps most probably, he's simply getting a proportionate sum of money for his troubles, and couldn't care less what people like me write.

Still, he's a generous-spirited man. I've asked him all sorts of daft questions down the years. Back in the days when the barbershop in the Village Départ still existed, I asked him how often he cut his hair. And six or seven times I have asked him to describe his rivalry with Jacques Anquetil. This is like banging on to Steve Ovett about Seb Coe incessantly. You can do it once, perhaps. But not every other year. So, in the full knowledge that you will never read this, Raymond: thanks. I'll bring you a copy out to the 2015 Tour.

Anyway, back in Leeds, I sat him down briefly, and asked him to describe his relationship with Jacques Anquetil.

He sighed. 'There wasn't just me and him, you know. There were two other riders who were just as good. Roger Rivière was one...'

'Wait a minute please, Monsieur Poulidor.' I wanted to record this, so that I would remember what he said. I extracted from a pocket my Dictaphone, and pressed the record button.

'As I said, Roger Rivière was one, and the other was...'

My battery went dead.

RIVIÈRE

'He carried within him the absolutism of cycling.
Everything was easy to him. The turn of the pedal,
and the terrible mortification.'

Once again, that wonderful, disconcerting feeling of memory being stirred. This happens often on the Tour, as I cross and re-cross the tyre marks and footsteps and diesel spills of previous years.

Sometimes these are false memories, generated by a capricious trick of the synapses, but sometimes they are genuine: an event experienced with extreme clarity, and then, as soon as it has passed, locked away. A certain trigger will call it back to life; a shop sign, a bridge, the way a slip road onto a dual carriageway passes over a factory at chimney height.

Roger Rivière was born in Saint-Étienne. And he died here, too.

It is a workmanlike town, by which I mean to say that it works hard at being a town, and does not rely on having a Gothic masterpiece at its heart like Chartres or a Roman amphitheatre in which to stage Verdi operas and Son et Lumière shows, like Orange. Instead, it boasts a distinct and certain identity, much of which revolves around its iconic football club, but also draws deeply on the industrial production of the bicycle. In fact, it has, in the past, been known as the City of Cycles. Mercier bikes, for example, are from Saint-Étienne.

A century ago, Saint-Étienne was also home to the manufacturing and retail giant Manufacture Française d'Armes et Cycles, which later became Manufrance. Their Hirondelle brand became as famous as Raleigh was in Britain, and was the bike of choice for everyday use, ridden by millions of French cyclists for decades. They are still celebrated by enthusiasts who mourn their demise. Website forums are dedicated to the restoration of Hirondelle frames. A cursory browse through their postings will leave you with several more methods for buffing rusted chrome callipers than you had ever imagined you might need. These pages have one image in common: the slender, pretty image of a swallow, diving three-quarters towards the earth, the 'Hirondelle'.

That, for many years, must have been a visual shorthand for Saint-Étienne, and might have been a passable metaphor for Rivière himself.

But that was not all that Manufacture Française d'Armes et Cycles had to offer, not by a long way. This industrial giant was a kind of *fin de siècle* Argos. Their amazing catalogue, now highly collectable, regularly ran to over seven hundred ornately illustrated pages and was widely distributed throughout the French Empire and beyond. In fact, the introduction to their 1905 catalogue was translated into Arabic, Mandarin and Sanskrit, as well as every European language. It included, according to an English translation which stands up well alongside Google Translate, '750 pages, 4500 engravings, a great number of coloured pictures and a great deal of informations of every kind, needful to Hunters, Cyclists, Fishers, Tourists, Sportsmen etc.' Mercifully, given its great heft and beauty, as well as its substantial weight, it would be 'posted gratuitously and free on free application'.

This, then, was much more than a sum of its parts, more than simply a mail-order company. It was a self-contained industrial revolution, way ahead of its time, and vast in its scope. From its base in Saint-Étienne, it turned out huge amounts of hardware relating principally to hunting, shooting and bicycling.

Sometimes, given the bewildering range of items in stock, the lines between these various categories inevitably blurred. There was, for instance, a miniature pistol available for purchase designed with the security-conscious cyclist in mind. It was small enough to fit into a rear pocket, and would discharge half a dozen tiny little bullets more or less safely, and more or less in the direction of the angry assailant. The need to fire from your bicycle may seem far-fetched nowadays, but when you put it in the context of the 1904 Tour de France then it seems less paranoid.

It was on the Col de la République, on the outskirts of Saint-Étienne that a mob gathered near the top, ostensibly to support the local rider Antoine Fauré. This they did, pushing him over the summit by fair means and foul. But they were also there to assault the winner of the first-ever Tour, Maurice Garin. They caught his jersey, and dragged him from his bike, beating him with sticks and then hurling stones at him as he tried to escape. It was only when warning shots were fired in the air that the crowd dispersed. Fauré, incidentally, was disqualified.

If you browse through a copy of the 1905 Manufrance catalogue, you might be surprised to learn that the gun went by the name of VeloDog. Already, it seemed, and long before Froome-Dog was called forth onto the pages of L'Équipe, the French were wise to the broader, English-speaking world, and its infantile dependence on puns and nicknames.

Sadly, this venerable company fell into terminal decline in the late 1960s, failing to compete with the demands of a modern, global trading environment. They'd started to make crap mopeds, and the Japanese were much better at it, it seems. A decade later they were still submitting largely hand-written accounts, even though any self-respecting office vibrated with the clacking of Olivetti typewriters. And in 1979 they went into liquidation.

The great institution still exists, in name, of course. Manufrance is a mail-order catalogue, but it is mostly online, and it no longer sells pistols for cyclists. Watering cans and lengths of garden hose are more its thing. And it has one sole remaining high-street branch, on the Rue de Lodi, the slightly run-down main shopping street in Saint-Étienne, not far in fact from where Rivière once owned a bar.

Sadly the 'M' has fallen off the sign at the front of the shop, and some spray-can funsters have inserted the letter 'S' between the 'U' and the 'F'.

ANUSFRANCE doesn't have quite the same ring to it.

At the finish line, near the football ground, there are a large number of Stéphanois. This is the name given to anyone from Saint-Étienne, and in particular, their football fans, who, dressed in the green kit, throng the barriers. They watched Alexander Kristoff beat Guess Who into second place in a sprint finish, although the organisers, not having yet seen the

photo finish, try to tell him that he's won. They ask us if we want to interview Peter Sagan, the winner of Stage 12. It is an awkward moment for everyone.

But the main business of the day for me is the appearance of photocopied A4 posters, sellotaped to lampposts all the way up the finishing straight, advertising a book called *Roger Rivière: Le vélo c'était sa vie*, by a chap called André Piat. The author himself, I suspected, had stuck them up overnight, perhaps capitalising on the influx of cycling fans into town, and hopeful that some of them might care to read up on Saint-Étienne's most famous cycling son. He left his contact details; a mobile number which I rang.

And rang. And rang.

Eventually I left him a garbled message. 'Monsieur, if you are here in Saint-Étienne, then please call me. I would like to buy a book.'

He never replied, so I never did get hold of his book. But, nevertheless Rivière has a story worth telling.

In 1976, and on national television, a grave-faced French presenter looked to the camera and introduced an obituary.

'Terrible news has reached us. In Saint-Étienne, Roger Rivière has just died. I would like to present to you some of the images from the career of an exceptional champion: a champion who, right to the very end, was pursued by pitiless ill fortune.'

Then, as if to prove his point about Rivière's bad luck, the film gets stuck and doesn't roll. The presenter holds his grave stare at the camera, looks down, shuffles a paper, looks back up again and lifts his left hand to his chin with a mixture of appropriate grief and understandable panic breaking over his features. Finally, after an uncomfortable ten seconds or so, the film runs.

It is beautiful.

The wonderful, sanguine Jean-Paul Ollivier narrates, his voice is dark and betrays a hint of hurt. Over an image of Rivière winning a time trail on the 1959 Tour, he intones, 'He carried within him the absolutism of cycling. Everything was easy to him. The turn of the pedal, and the terrible mortification.'

You wouldn't get a phrase like that on *Grandstand*.

Perhaps because he lived, because he survived, his name has not fared well.

Rivière's fall was sudden, literal, inexplicable and severe, and his injuries, both psychological and physical were profound. But he didn't die, and so his character flaws and human weaknesses remained open to public scrutiny. This state of partial dissection was the fate that Tom Simpson escaped.

Instead of dying (and he later confided in a journalist that what he endured was 'so awful that I would rather have been killed on the spot'), Rivière was taken by helicopter to hospital, where he neither fully recovered nor succumbed completely to his condition. There's a phrase in German, which translated means 'too little for life, too much for death'. It fits the final years of Roger Rivière like a glove.

Next to the feted, tragic heroes who have ridden the race and come to grief, from Simpson to Pantani and Fabio Casartelli, the name of Roger Rivière does not mean much. Even in France, he is remembered dimly and infrequently. And this despite the evidence that suggests that, had he continued to race, he would have sat snugly at the heart of a great generation of French riders, and would have fought Jacques Anquetil tooth and nail for every one of those four consecutive wins from 1961 to 1964. Rivière was that good.

So I plead forgiveness for the fact that I knew little about him until I happened upon a picture of him. It is a misleading image. I suspect that the original, taken on Sunday 10 July 1960, had been in black and white and that the version I have seen in print has been retouched into colour, in keeping with the fashion of the age. But that scarcely matters.

The picture, at first glance exudes an air of pastoral tranquillity. It shows a man asleep. He is lying on his left side on a bed of summery leaves. Dappled sunlight spreads over the scene. His right hand supports his head. He is wearing a short-sleeved jersey of red, white and blue. There is some writing on the front, but what it spells is hard to discern. There is a sheen of sweat on his forearms and his temples.

Only on closer inspection does it hint at a different and awful reality. There is a tiny rip in the fabric of his jersey, just below his right shoulder blade. And, while his right eye is shut, his left eye is slightly open. The eyeball has rolled back. In fact, Roger Rivière is in excruciating pain, and worse than that, he thinks that he is paralysed. So his fear is even greater.

It was as a track rider that he made his mark. In 1957, and in his first season as a pro, he took the world pursuit title when he beat Albert Bouvet, another Frenchman. Later that year, he added the French national pursuit title by taking the scalp of Anquetil, two years his senior. After that, he never looked back. In September, at the Vigorelli track in Milan, he set a new World Hour Record, and repeated the feat a year later at the same venue, when he became the first man to break the forty-seven kilometre mark for the hour. 'Le Recordman' had come from nowhere and blown everyone away.

The Hour Record has, for certain cycling purists, long been held as the ultimate and most exacting test of greatness. Its purity (let's put to one side the confusion over bike design which Boardman and Obree unearthed) and simplicity appeal to those who seek to answer this: who is the fastest?

Well, on this evidence, Rivière was.

But, though track riding had its place in the French psyche, it did not compare with the attention accorded those star riders who competed and won on the grandest stage of all: the Tour de France. And so, fifty years before Bradley Wiggins attempted to make the same transition, Rivière set about reinventing himself as a stage racer, and with instant success.

These were wonderful times for the French cycling fan. In the tricolour of the French team, they were enjoying something like dominance. Louison Bobet won three consecutive editions in the mid-fifties and, when he stopped winning, Anquetil was widely expected to pick up where Bobet left off, which he duly did, winning his debut Tour in 1957. In addition to these two colossal riders, they also boasted Henry Anglade and Raphaël Géminiani (who would, by a very circuitous route, end up lending his nickname to the clothing brand now worn by Team Sky). Both of these men were deemed capable of winning the Tour themselves. Even when this stellar French team made a tactical mess of the race, as they did in 1956, it was still won by a Frenchman, the much derided, but also much cherished, Roger Walkowiak (think a popular Oscar Pereiro). And it would be wrong to omit from this list the world's best sprinter, André Darrigade, who went on to amass twenty-two stage wins on the Tour de France. It was like having Wiggins, Froome, Nibali, Contador and Cavendish all on the same team. Into this extraordinary pool of talent, the precocious Rivière announced his presence with a metaphorical dive-bomb into the deep end. He would ride, and maybe even win, the 1959 Tour.

Managing all that talent, and the egos that went along with it, was fraught with complication. The French national team manager was a man called Marcel Bidot, who, by and large, worried and vacillated and got things wrong. But he was first on the scene, a year later, when Rivière lay under a tree, sliding in and out of consciousness and fighting to stay alive. He had cradled him in his arms.

The acknowledged stars, Bobet and Anquetil, did not much take to the idea of Rivière joining the team. Bobet admitted that he was a 'classy rider', but that 'the Tour was something different'. And Anquetil was even more dismissive of his new teammate by removing any doubt that he could envisage himself in a supporting role for Rivière. 'I'm not going to change my behaviour. I remain his implacable adversary.'

Rivière simply replied, 'Anquetil doesn't know me. He doesn't know my character, my methods, my ideas. So how can he judge me and refuse to work with me?'

But the uncomfortable truth was that Rivière, unlike the elegant Anquetil, was not well liked. He had a reputation for arrogance, solitariness and ruthless ambition. And more than that, he was a colossal, and unabashed, pharmaceutical nightmare. In an age when, even by Anquetil's famous admission, there was no such thing as clean rider, Rivière set new standards in chemical enhancement. His *soigneur*, Raymond le Bert, who had worked with Bobet for thirteen years, walked out on Rivière mid-Tour after spotting needlemarks on his thighs and stumbling across a cardboard box in which Rivière kept his illicit stash of uppers, downers and everything-in-betweeners. Leaving his rider on the massage table he left the room, pausing only to say to him, 'You're going to lose your health and possibly your life. Maybe you'll win the Tour, but one day something bad is going to happen to you.'

Rivière shrugged off the criticism. Unabashed, he declared to the press, 'People have called me a "Laboratory Rider", and that my performances have been enhanced by a very precise preparation. I take that as a compliment, since it proves that I know what I want and how I can get it.'

It is worth noting that at this time the word 'doping' had

not yet entered the vocabulary, but that is not to say that there wasn't considerable public concern about riders' nefarious and widespread habits. And what was apparent with Rivière was that, for all his protestations, this was not so much a scientific aggregation of marginal gains as an outrageously bloated cocktail of amphetamines and opiates. People didn't like that.

Either way, a combination of his natural talent and the extra leg-up that his medication afforded him was having its effect on the race. He won both the flat time trials, beating Anquetil in the process and, capable of defending in the mountains, he was riding in fourth place as the Tour entered its final week. Ahead of him was Anquetil, and, in second place, the autocratic Henry Anglade, who was not liked by Rivière, Anquetil and Bobet, all of whom contrived to allow the Catalan Federico Bahamontes to win the race, rather than working for Anglade.

It was a disastrous mess, and the French crowd, who had seen through the self-serving charade, booed them all roundly when they attempted a lap of honour in the Parc des Princes. Such was the feeling of disgust across the nation that Marcel Bidot, the manager responsible for this shambles, returned the day after the Tour finished to his home town of Troyes in disguise, wearing a scarf, cap and hooded anorak to avoid recognition, despite the July heat. If there had been a French Sports Personality of the Year for 1959, none of them would have won it.

This did little to enhance Rivière's reputation either in the peloton, or with the public. But he had made his mark. That autumn he married Hugoette, his childhood sweetheart, and bought a villa on the banks of the Loire. So life was all right.

The following summer, after a disappointing early season campaign, he lined up for his second Tour as the notional leader of the French team. Bobet was fast becoming superannuated and timid in the face of opposition, Géminiani was no longer considered strong enough, Anglade had had his chance and Anquetil was simply absent, having ridden and won the Giro d'Italia.

When Bahamontes, the winner of the previous year, climbed off after Stage 2, this only strengthened Rivière's pre-eminent position. By the final week of the race, he had won three stages already, and was handily placed behind the Italian Gastone Nencini, (think Vicenzo Nibali, and you're close enough, except that Nencini also liked chain-smoking and oil painting, as well as descending like a man possessed) who had gained time in an early move. Rivière, though, knew he had a time trial still to come before Paris. A Tour win was within touching distance, and so, with not inconsiderable hubris, he instructed his wife to buy a pretty dress for the celebration.

The doping continued. In fact, the closer Rivière came to glory, the more he sought comfort in its altered states, both psychological and chemical. Nencini, in truth, spooked him. Everything about the Italian's strength genuinely terrified him. With this fear beating in his heart, he enlisted his new, and ethically edgy, *soigneur* Julien Schramm to help him. On the second rest day, Schramm opened up his entire armoury, and put it at the disposal of his rider. Team manager Marcel Bidot even walked in on them as they were preparing for the following day's racing.

He took in the scene: Rivière injecting himself in the groin with an amphetamine preparation. And then he slowly closed the door behind him, and left them to it.

On the morning of Stage 15, a photographer captured the moment when, in the early kilometres, Rivière spotted his young wife by the side of the road and wheeled over to greet her. In the snapshot he is pulling away from her, his arm outstretched as she leans towards him, smiling at a joke he has shouted in her direction. He too is smiling. This would, he thought, be the day he might win the Tour.

The next photo of Hugoette Rivière that exists was taken a few hours later. She is striding, ashen-faced, across the car park of the Clinique Saint-Charles in Montpellier.

Stage 15 was a mountainous affair through the Massif Central. Rivière had been keeping pace with Nencini over the top of the Col du Perjuret (which, amazingly, translates as 'Perjury Mountain') but, on the descent, he made the grave mistake of trying to stay with the Italian, and, if the chance arose, attack him. When he spoke about it later, he claimed that he'd believed Nencini to be in distress on the climb. The whole move was unwise. Rounding a tight corner, with the group spread out, Rivière misjudged the angle and left the road, somersaulting over a parapet and dropping fifteen metres into a ravine.

The race flew away from him and then there was total silence in the valley. No one had the slightest idea where Roger Rivière had gone. There had been no witnesses. The following day, *L'Équipe* reported that 'For five minutes, we believed that he'd been vaporised.'

Film pictures of the race tell only some of the story. You can see nothing, really, as the camera searches wildly down the ravine. Then there is a cut, and we are up close alongside him, his head cradled in the arms of rescuers, and his expression tells you all the need to know about the terrible pain he is in. He has broken six ribs, massively damaged his kidneys and smashed two vertebrae. But his spinal cord, by extraordinary chance, is intact.

He is taken, eventually, by ambulance to a waiting helicopter, which has only been able to land two kilometres away. There is a momentary scene of farce as a farmer, distraught at seeing so many onlookers and photographers trampling down his crop of beans, brandishes a gun and threatens to shoot them.

Then the helicopter takes off and Rivière begins the second half of his life. As an invalid. And as a liar.

His first instinct was to blame the mechanic for the accident, telling the media that he had pulled on the brake levers to no avail. But they found the bike perfectly intact, and the brakes were fully operational. Then the truth slowly emerged. Rivière was almost insensate after taking a huge dose of a drug called Palfium, whose properties are similar to morphine. It grossly affected his reactions. The truth was, he'd done nothing to prevent the accident, because he was incapable, almost stupefied by what he'd taken. He'd done it to himself, in other words. Sympathy slowly melted away.

He never recovered fully. He had lost about 20 per cent of the motor skills on both legs, and though it could appear as if he were unaffected, it meant that he would never ride competitively again.

Film exists, shot only a few months later, of Rivière riding alongside Louison Bobet across a cold, muddy landscape. Both are wearing woolly winter clothing, with Rivière clad especially esoterically in black slacks tucked into checked golfing socks, and a white 'Rapha' (the original version) jumper (yes, jumper).

As they trundle along, they are interviewed by a French TV reporter on the back of a motorbike. He buzzes around them, throwing in questions and then stretching out his microphone. At one point he shows them the speedometer on the bike that indicates that they've hit thirty kilometres an hour. 'Not bad', he quips, unamusingly.

Yet, even though in this short clip Rivière is full of bullish optimism, it is clear that he is not moving in the same way. He looks off-balance, cumbersome. The crash had left him unable to flex his ankles to the full extent, and his pedal-stroke, compensating, looks heavy. At one point Bobet places a hand on his shoulder in a chummy way and leans on him as they ride. You almost want to scream with referred pain.

But by 1961, he'd given up.

There's another funereal television interview with him, conducted by a lugubrious fellow by the name of Léon Zitrone who sits alongside him on a balcony overlooking his garden near Saint-Étienne. This is Rivière's public acknowledgement that he can no longer chase his dream. With a polite, if pained, expression, he is sitting cross-legged, in a tremendously natty Italian suit, waiting for the first question to come his way. After an interminably long introduction, in which he lists the significant landmarks in Rivière's career, Zitrone then opens his account.

'Roger Rivière. When you were a rider you didn't smoke. Now, you smoke.'

Rivière glances wistfully down at the cigarette elegantly clasped in his manicured left hand.

'Does this mean that you are lost to active sporting endeavour?'

'Yes. Practically.' And then he quips, almost able to smile, 'Maybe fishing.'

'Excuse me for asking. But is the mortgage paid off on your beautiful house?' This is Zitrone's brusque style, it seems.

'The bike was his life.' His wife is heard to say, later in the film, (perhaps, many years later, inspiring the title for the biography I was unable to buy in Saint-Étienne). Our inter-rogator now looms over her in his oversized suit, as she swings her legs and perches casually on a garden table, trying to look relaxed.

'Do you think that he can re-forge another form of happi-ness in his life, madame?' She looks temporarily terrified by his question. And she had good reason to be. Their marriage would soon end, and Rivière's life would unravel.

He sold the villa to buy a bar in Saint-Étienne, which he called Le Vigorelli, named after the Milanese track which had been the scene of his greatest triumph. It folded. He bought a holiday park in the Loire valley. It failed. He tried to become a rally driver and failed. He bought a night club and disappeared into a life of nocturnal addiction.

Palfium. The very same drug which they had found in the pockets of his racing jersey on the day he had crashed, the very same drug with which they had treated him in hospital for his chronic pain, had completely taken over his life. During a court appearance at which he was charged, alongside three separate doctors, with falsifying prescription procedures, it was established that he had consumed 32,000 pills over a three-year period.

It wasn't his only brush with the law. He was arrested, held overnight, and ultimately released when he was named as a getaway driver by the leader of a gang who had carried out an armed robbery in Arles. Although the case was never satisfactorily resolved, his reputation was, by now, in tatters.

In 1975 he was diagnosed with throat cancer. Six months later, on 1 April 1976 and a few weeks after his fortieth birthday, he died, after complaining that he'd rather 'they cut his legs off than let him die of suffocation'.

It was a desperate end to a desperately unhappy life. And it is hard to look at pictures of him in those final years, thick-set, swarthy and largely unsmiling. He has the menacing intensity of Miguel Indurain. But unlike Indurain he will be remembered only loosely, and occasionally, when people like me stumble across his story and want to know more. For the most part, I sense, he will be wilfully forgotten, airbrushed from the annals of French cycling history.

Or, as *L'Équipe* put it, when he disappeared over the parapet, 'eradicated purely and simply from the map of the world, from this immense and chaotic landscape'.

CB

'That'll be in your next book.'

This is the third book I have written, and in every single one of them, there is a section about Chris Boardman.

For a man whose clothes and character are as purposefully practical and devoid of frippery as those worn and lived in by Chris, it is remarkable that I still have things I want to tell you about him.

For example, I discovered during a recent trip to the Lake District, on which we were joined by his wife Sally, that he doesn't order his own food in restaurants. She does it for him. He doesn't even glance at the menu, because it all happens without his involvement. You might find that this denial of his freedom of choice (being treated, frankly, like a big grown-up baby) would be something against which such a formidable competitor might rail. But actually, it's an arrangement with which he is particularly pleased. 'It's efficient. There's no wasted time. Sally gets two orders in, in the time it would normally take to order one. And she knows what I want better than I do.' That evening he ate a giant bowl of pork scratchings.

Anyway, my point is this: I really, honestly didn't want to write about him again. But then he said something that forced me into an involuntary about-face. He had just been shown a photograph.

'That'll be in your next book,' he told me.

I wasn't sure whether that was a prediction or an instruction, so here it is anyway. The explanation as to what is going

on in this picture is too tiresome to put down in black and white, but suffice to say, that's CB on the left, I'm on the right and the giant rabbit in the middle belongs to his daughter Aggie. Let's move on.

We rode together on a few occasions during this year's Tour. And even before the Tour started, we had spent time in the Lake District, filming some inserts about climbing and descending. Our budgets didn't stretch to the Alps, so Ambleside it was. On Wry Nose and Hard Knot passes, we pretended we were on the Galibier. Most of the time we were there, Chris was on the phone, busily selling his bike company to Halfords. The multi-million-pound deal went through the following day, which was fortunate for him, as he managed to avoid having to buy all the crew dinner, which the crew most certainly would have suggested. Probably quite vocally.

*

During the Tour itself, the first time we got out on our bikes together was in the rainy Vosges mountains, a dismal ride over three steep climbs, on the second of which we had ambushed Didi Senft, aka the Devil, before he'd been able to get his vocal chords working for the day's gargling.

'Morning, Didi!' I accosted him cheerfully, as he stepped out of his campervan, unfortunately for him at just the moment we were riding past. Chris chipped in with, 'Hello.' I wondered whether he'd ever actually spoken to him, or just caught a glimpse of him flashing by as he laboured hideously uphill in the heat of an actual race.

The Devil looked momentarily bewildered, as if he were suddenly caught out by a terrible self-awareness. Who am I? Who are they? Why am I wearing this hat, and this scarlet leotard? Come to that, Chris seemed bewildered too.

Didi, it must be said, is slowing up a little, as the years and the Tours catch up with him, and our sightings have become commensurately rarer. But he is a delightfully benign man, who, sometime in the mid-to-late twentieth century, as he was entering middle age and for some reason known exclusively to Didi, decided that he could only fulfil what remained of his ambition by growing a fulsome and unkempt beard, pulling on red tights, fashioning a homespun devil's trident and blurting incomprehensible nonsense in a made-up language into the ears of riders as they rode past.

Dieter (for that is his real name) is, of course, widely celebrated. He is a fan royale, known and affectionately respected for his efforts to promote Satanist cycling culture. His ownership of the status of Tour Eccentric and the place conferred upon him as a result within the firmament of the Tour's greatest stars has never really been in doubt, not from the moment he first appeared at the 1993 Tour on a tandem of his own construction (he rode it with his wife Margitta in the rear seat, facing backwards).

Sure, he has deep-seated otherness which separates him from a good deal of the world's population who would think twice about spending July in scarlet tights bouncing from foot to foot and warbling. But Didi is smart. He is in fact a gifted engineer capable of building absurdly large and also absurdly small, as well as absurdly absurd, bicycle inventions. He curates a museum in which he displays over 120 examples of his greatest work, including the largest mobile guitar in the world that also happens to be a working bicycle. And guitar.

That morning, as Chris looked on in mild distrust, Didi tried to emit devil noises, but they fell flat. Instead of the full-throated crazed nonsense he usually hollers, a mere trickle of unconvincing madness passed his lips and fell soggily to the ground in the damp morning air. It was so un-mad that almost intelligible words very nearly crept into his diatribe. This wouldn't do at all. Fortunately, by the time we met him on the climb to Chamrousse, he was back to form, springing out towards us and babbling wildly in his strange hybrid warble.

It wasn't just Didi that had picked up by the time we swapped the Vosges for the Alps. Everything was that bit brighter and more finely tuned. I was a touch fitter, and could keep pace with Chris for that much longer (except until the final four kilometres where I tried to attack him and he made me cry). But it wasn't just about our ability on the bike. Our showering proficiency had improved tenfold as we tried to get ourselves used to the changed look and feel of the shower block (yes, they too had been downgraded in the Great Pelicab Shakeup).

Our first attempt to use them was at Gérardmer, where I'd forgotten a towel, and both Chris and I had forgotten shower gel. We miscalculated almost everything, from the angle of trajectory of the showerhead to the length of time you'd need to figure out where you could possibly hang everything so that it didn't fall down into the three inches of standing water at the base of the unit.

Just when we thought we'd cracked it, and were struggling with the finishing touches of getting dressed again, I heard a thunderous crash from Chris's cubicle, followed by a torrential gushing of water and an uncharacteristic string of profanities. Apparently, trying one-handed to pull his pants on, he'd lost balance and fallen backwards onto the push stud. That, in turn, activated the shower jet, and within seconds he was soaked again, and now so were his clothes. And, when he did finally manage to get dry-ish and dressed, he realised that his two Superman socks were from different pairs, and didn't match. You can only imagine the effect this had on him.

That was followed, a few days later, by another genuinely horrible day's showering on the Planche des Belles Filles, when the boiler had packed in, and instead, we were attacked by a jet of glacial water. My abiding memory of that traumatic session was of a giant Dutch truck driver screaming in his shower cubicle, and then jumping out of the shower stark naked to show his equally rugged Dutch truck driving mates the extent of the cold. This he did by pointing at his genitals and roaring with laughter. I got my stuff together and scarpered.

By the time the race finally reached the Alps, though, the sun had started to get to work, and there was no need for any further Dutch exhibitionism to illustrate a point about the cold.

Chris and I decided to film another brave assault on a mountain on a long but surprisingly even climb up to the first proper summit finish of the Tour, at Chamrousse. I can't pretend it was much fun. Riding up mountains isn't, until you stop. But we were doing it for the telly, and had to try to appear witty, informative and engaging, which is next to impossible. And so it proved.

The climb to the summit of Stage 13 had started with an hour or so of standing around in the car park of a Kyriad hotel to the north of Grenoble, watching Chris fettling the bikes. I've learned over the years that it's best not to ask what he's doing, as he flicks out another Allen key and tuts over some minute adjustment to a bit of innocent-looking metal that does something significant to your gears. I sometimes think the name Alan would have suited him better than Chris, in recognition of his affection for the Allen key. Alan Boardman. And if he asks if your tyre pressure is OK, it's best to shrug your shoulders sulkily and wander off, since he'll only test them again, no matter what you might say in response.

Once the fettling was finally over, we set off in the blazing sun. Within five minutes we'd found the race route out of Grenoble and started to ride up a steadily rising valley road towards the foot of the big climb. After seven kilometres we reached the sulphurous stench of the spa town Uriage-les-Bains, where Alan amusingly asked me if I had farted.

When the race came through here at a quarter to five in the afternoon, the main contenders were all together. The team of Vincenzo Nibali was driving hard. They were all on the front, minus the heroic Jakob Fuglsang who had been brought down on the descent from the Col de Palaquit by a water bottle, which had fallen from Jurgen Van den Broeck's bike. He would make it to the summit some thirty minutes after his leader, suffering from contusions and abrasions and all sorts of other medical terms, which basically meant that he had no skin on his fingers. But – and here was another point of difference – as they entered Uriage-les-Bains for real, there was no time for anyone in the bunch to accuse anyone else of having farted.

Chris and I stopped at the start of the climb to film an intro. We had to wait patiently while an American lady with a particularly penetrating voice marshalled her group of cycling tourists, all decked out in the same Trek livery. Unaware that she was holding up our recording, she stood right next to us, trying to gather everyone together so that they could at least start the climb in one group. We gawped at her, revelling in her pure Americanness. Sometimes you just have to stand back and admire. She wore mirror shades, and a stars-and-stripes bandana 'neath her Giro helmet. She had a voice that could surely be heard on the summit, eighteen kilometres up the road.

'We've lost Diane!' she hollered, repeatedly. 'Has anyone seen Diane?'

'Diane!' we shouted helpfully. Giggling a bit.

At about ten to five, the actual race made the same left-hand turn at the roundabout and started to attack the climb. Astana led the way, with Team Sky locked in concentration behind them. By this point, if you scrutinise the pictures from the day, you can see all the main contenders, and their mountain lieutenants, but there is no sign of Diane.

About six kilometres into the climb, we all had to stop, again. Not for the first time, someone on the climb had recognised Chris and wanted a picture taken. Each time this happened, I jumped in to act as photographer. I was grateful for the rest, but it made getting going again that bit harder. There were twelve more kilometres to go.

It was at this point on the climb in the real race that the camera at the rear of the bunch picked up Richie Porte. He had slipped off the back, and was labouring. It was the moment at which it became clear that he would present no challenge whatsoever to Nibali. So, another rival evaporated. And there were still twelve kilometres to go.

With ten kilometres remaining, Chris and I stopped at the roadside. We had stumbled across a very friendly couple of retirees from the West Country who had supplies of fresh water. Our bottles were dry, and they set about filling them from a five-litre plastic box of mineral water. It glugged all over the place, missing the bottle and splashing refreshingly all over our hands, knees and feet. It was a ridiculously hot day.

This was where, several hours later, the Eastern European duo of Rafał Majka, the Polish climber, and Leopold König, from the Czech Republic attacked the race and went clear. For a while, a group of Romain Bardet, Alejandro Valverde, Thibaut Pinot, Laurens ten Dam and Nibali played cat-and-mouse with each other. But at no point did any of these look for help from a recently retired couple with a plentiful water store.

Five kilometres further up the road, where the gradient suddenly rose again, I attacked Alan.

At about ten past five, Vincenzo Nibali attacked the Tour de France.

Within thirty seconds Alan had pegged me back, and now rode off the front. I could only gasp and watch his receding shape.

Nibali rode across to Majka and König, then he attacked them.

Chris Boardman won, and a little bit later, Vincenzo Nibali won.

And a whole bunch of other people, myself included, didn't. That was the story of the day, except for the shower block, which was as seamlessly perfect this time as a Nibali mountain stage.

By now we were both world-class ablutionists. We had honed the whole routine until it was as perfect as Morecambe and Wise moving around the breakfast room. All Chris needed was a pair of NHS glasses.

Something else happened on the slopes of the Chamrousse. It wasn't immediately apparent how funny it was, but like a pot roast it matured over time. And, also like a pot roast, it kept coming back to amuse me in waves throughout the afternoon.

Every now and then, we would ride past pockets of British support on the mountain: VW campervans with an England flag draped over the front window, or a British-registered caravan outside which a husband and wife from Devon had set out their breakfast stuff. Sometimes, and to their great surprise, they would spot Chris, and identify him as he rode past.

'Chris!' we'd hear them shout as we rode by. And then,

ever receding into the background, 'That was Chris Boardman, I think.'

Not wishing to stop, nor wishing to be rude, Chris would raise a right hand in the air to acknowledge them, or turn and smile back at them.

'Actually, it's quite good for the ego, to get a bit of recognition,' he admitted, with admirable candour. We rode on up the alp.

Then we came to a hairpin bend, on which a family of four had pitched their stall; mum, dad, and two kids. One of them, the twelve-year-old boy, spotted Chris and leapt up from his chair.

'Chris! He shouted. Chris raised his hand in greeting.

But this time, quite audibly, as we rode past, we heard the kid clearly say to his dad, 'That was Chris Broadman.'

Broadman!

The misplaced 'R' killed me. And it carried on amusing me

for days. So much so that I decided it should be his name for at least thirty-six hours, and never failed to address him as Chris Broadman.

It made a change at least. I had not even got to the start line at Leeds before someone had already said to me, 'Are you Chris Boardman?' The problem we both had was the fact that we are about the same height, age, build and hair colour. Our medal collections are a little different, granted, but that is more than compensated for by the fact that every summer for the past five years we have appeared side by side on the Tour de France coverage explaining various aspects of bike racing. For some people, indeed, it seems, for everyone except for me and Chris and our respective families, this makes us entirely interchangeable. It has become a tiresome fact of life that we both must put up with. Especially, as it happens, me.

At least, after about Stage 4, this was balanced out by Chris being mistaken for me. This type of misgreeting is considerably more rare. But in that rarity value, it is infinitely more pleasing. When it happened, I got a text message from him:

> Just been mistaken for Ned Bolting. I just went with it.
> CB.

At least he had the tactical awareness to spell my name wrong. So he retained overall control of the game, by some clear distance.

That text message was just one of a series of messages stored on my phone which are as masterful as haikus or the aphorisms of Kahlil Gibran. One day I will anthologise them, and produce a limited-edition collection, entitled CB. Another text, perhaps his finest of the entire Tour landed in my inbox before the race had even started, indeed, before he'd even reached Leeds. In reply to my harmless question, 'What's your ETA?' he'd written this:

14.48
CB

And that was followed, a minute or two later, by this:

Walk from the station to the hotel is 262ft, which I'm estimating will take one minute. So I'd like to revise my ETA to 14.49. Apologies for the rounding up.
CB

Honestly. The man is beyond parody.

NIBALI

'He'll never give in to bad tendencies.
Not if he ever wants to set foot in Sicily again. Never.'

An almost negligible morning breeze wafted feebly up the mountain to Risoul, where, later that day, Vincenzo Nibali would once again suggest that he might as well give everyone else a head start of an entire mountain, just to make a race of it. This Tour was in his ever-tightening grip. Or, to indulge the imagery of Nibali's nickname, the race was being flung from side to side as it lay helpless and bleeding in the jaws of a shark. Pretty soon, the beast would drag it under, and that would be that.

Just as a high-pressure system had kept that part of France in a locked-down state of suffocation, so too did his yellow jersey keep everyone beneath him pinned down and weakening. The heat and humidity had built rapidly over the last couple of days, even though a long and deepening line of isobars was about to attack from the west. But from where we stood, high up in the Alps and looking down on so much, it was clear that, for now at least, the race was in checkmate.

It was all rather disappointing, if truth be told.

There is no more compelling sight on the Tour de France than seeing the yellow jersey crack. I don't mean that to be nasty, or that it is necessarily admirable to revel in other people's discomfort and failure. I'm just saying, as a matter of routine observation, that when it happens, it makes people stand up, drop their newspapers, place down their cup of coffee, and shout at the TV. Normally, it's something like 'He's cracking! He's gone! He's bloody well cracked!'

It is precisely this spectacle that these three convoluted weeks of racing are built around, the sudden apparition of dramatic change.

Just to clarify: when I say yellow jersey, I don't mean the night watchmen, those guys who are only allowed to keep it for a day or two (Marcel Kittel and Tony Gallopin, on this Tour). I mean the main event, those GC men who, once clad in yellow shorts, with matching socks and a yellow bike with a yellow saddle, will expect to hold it until Paris, come hell or high cadence. In twelve Tours, I have not often seen a genuine race leader fall apart. And yet most days, especially on those stages that finish high up in the clouds surrounded by waterfalls and cable cars, are built around the anticipation of just that: let's watch the *maillot jaune* fall apart.

In 2003, when the race reached the aerodrome at Cap Découverte, Lance Armstrong's perversely altered physiology emphatically let him down and the not entirely natural physiology of his great clodhopping, and, if we're honest, not-quite-good-enough rival Jan Ullrich stole a march on the leader. It was an individual time trial in the middle of a brutal Tour and it was one of the few successes the German ever recorded when it mattered: head to head against Armstrong, with the American in yellow.

The Texan's face had been captivating. It was a blisteringly hot day and unbearably humid. Despite his cyclist's deep tan, his skin had turned pale, and there were great bags under his eyes. His mouth hung open, with no evident flexing of the jaw to suggest exertion. It just hung there, expressive only of suffering. Water ran from the tip of his nose. But that was not the real focus of our attention.

Instead, the eye was drawn over and over to the graphical clock that ticked out on the screen his virtual time loss to Ullrich growing by the kilometre. You could not take your eyes off the story it was ticking out. Armstrong losing time? The race had not seen its like since he started to dominate some five years previous. In the end, he lost a total of one and half minutes to Ullrich, which seemed to crack the race wide open again. Except Armstrong, in his merciless and untrustworthy manner, stamped hard on Ullrich's head at the next available opportunity, dashing any hopes the T-Mobile man might have had. That was when Armstrong attacked after his fall on the slopes of Luz Ardiden.

Three years later, it was Floyd Landis who wore the yellow jersey, the day before his ridiculous, doped charge up to Morzine to burgle the Tour de France. On Stage 16 he had fallen apart in the most emphatic style imaginable on the climb to la Toussuire. It had been totally compelling to watch.

And in 2011, when Andy Schleck tried to rip the jersey from Cadel Evans's shoulders, the Australian retired to some inner reserve of suffering where he meditated in solitary confinement on the nature of human misery, by pushing on his pedals over and over and over again. He lost the jersey, but not permanently. Schleck's hopeless time trail handed it straight back to him a day later in Grenoble.

Flip-flopping jerseys are a rare treat. And the model of 2012 and 2013, when both Wiggins and Froome assumed the race lead early on, and then consolidated it stage by stage, had left us all yearning for a different script. But one Sardinian cyclist wasn't in the mood to satisfy any of our wishes.

Vincenzo Nibali took 'unruffled' to different levels; the calibre of 'unruffled' you might best attain if you laid the imperious Astana rider out on a spirit level-adjusted ironing board, and flattened him with a steam-powered Morphy Richards. He was a silhouette.

Such was the inscrutable steeliness of his demeanour, both on and off the bike, that the TV director for France Télévisions

was feeding off scraps when it came to suggesting drama; there wasn't much to work with. So he went out in search of signs of weakness.

On Stage 14, during the second hour of what was a painfully long prelude to the major climb of the day, Nibali saw fit to execute the following, almost entirely meaningless, manoeuvre: He freewheeled, briefly, moved his left knee to one side, and grimaced. The whole thing lasted two or three seconds.

Instantly, the move was replayed in loving slow-motion. This time, with the video running at about 30 per cent of its natural speed, it seemed to suggest so much more than the casual gesture which, in reality, it had been.

The freewheeling suddenly looked like fatigue, the stretching seemed like muscular pain and the grimace informed the world of a sudden discomfort, bordering on distress. So much for replays adding to the picture. This one simply distorted it, ascribing to Nibali's calm countenance a set of weaknesses that he actually had not demonstrated. By stretching the video timeline, they exaggerated the peaks and troughs of effort.

More information does not necessarily mean that a situation can be better understood. Chris Boardman and I had heatedly debated this exact issue on the night of the World Cup Final, which we watched on an Internet stream while we waited for the Novotel staff in Besançon to bring us some under-cooked burgers. Unusually for football, someone had fouled someone, and the referee hadn't noticed.

'Why not show the referee a replay of that foul?' Chris was perplexed.

'Because it wasn't a foul,' I told him.

'Yes it was,' someone else chipped in.

'See?' I offered this divergence of opinion to Chris as evi-dence against video evidence. 'Two people have both seen the same replay and reached differing conclusions.'

Video evidence in football doesn't solve anything, it just creates a distortion. Every contact looks worse in slow motion. Tackles that were innocuous look like they're full of intent.

'That doesn't make sense.' Chris frowned and took a long sip of his Aflegem (or 'hurty beer' as he later described it) 'How can less information be better than more information?'

Liam and I sighed. We were going round in circles.

'Because football doesn't work like that, OK?' we both said, in differing ways, but with similar layers of patronising over-tones. 'Just stick to cycling, and quantifiable, less ambiguous stuff, Olympic Bloke,' we added. In our heads.

That meaningful/meaningless Nibali replay, in the unlikely event that I am called to appear in a court of law as an expert witness to testify against the use of interpretive video evidence in sport, will be my prize document.

The truth was much less ambiguous. Nibali was not uncom-fortable, at any point. He was simply perfect. Even when a press car got stuck ahead of him on a descent, it did him no harm. And when a member of the public stepped out in front of him, she bounced off him, rather than vice versa. And then she got a quite deliberate wallop from a passing gendarme on a motorbike, just for good measure.

Perhaps as a result of the general sense of a procession, a somnambulance affected everyone on the Tour de France.

A blindly unthinking routine had set in, and with the finishing line in Paris still an almost unfathomable distance away, the Tour had started to acquire an endless feel. Mike, our chief engineer, invented a new tongue twister, which best summed up our growing ennui. He took a look at the long line of Norbert Dentressangle trucks that appear everywhere, every day, all the time and as far as the eye can see. Then he started mumbling to himself, like a minor character from *One Flew Over the Cuckoo's Nest*, 'Red lorry, red lorry. Red lorry, red lorry.'

I too had stopped finding things as funny as I normally did. For example, the appearance of the Belgian sound engineer who looked like Chris de Burgh no longer had the power to delight, nor even provoke me into humming 'The Lady in Red' as close as I dared to him.

The American reporter with the amusing name Steve Schlanger? Well, it was just a name.

Even Chris Boardman's prodigious ability to eat coronary-inducing amounts of cheese had stopped fascinating me, although he was still able to raise a smile, when after helping himself to thirds, he wondered out loud 'if tartiflette had ever been cited on a death certificate'. That evening he followed up his cheese-based lunch by ordering a pizza Roquefort, and declared that his 'centre of mass had just dropped a foot'.

One morning, looking up from his breakfast of croissants and baguette, Matt Rendell had expressed his ennui better than most of us could ever have hoped to. He looked around us all, one by one, taking in our torpor, and then he looked back down at his plate of unwanted food. With his palms upturned and his long arms outstretched, and nearly knocking over a jug of warm milk, he intoned, to whoever was listening,

'Is there not more to life than this?'

Since no one answered him, he was eventually forced to retract his imploring arms, took a bite of croissant, had a swig of coffee, and then scraped his chair back and left the room. 'I'm going to go and watch a bike race, then. Don't know about you lot.'

Out on the road, the lower reaches of the climb to Risoul had been colonised by support from over the border in Italy. Backpackers, daytrippers, overnighters, motorbikers, numberplates from Milan and Turin and further afield, a hubbub of Latin noise, and familial communities forming on the spot. The barbecues soon would be lit, the grappa uncorked, and then it would really get going.

It was true the French occupied the higher slopes, where the local organisation committee had named each switchback after a significant figure from the recent past, however eclectic. There was 'Virage Pescheux', in honour of the recently retired race director, 'Virage Adam et JaJa'; a nod to the French commentary team of Thierry Adam and Laurent Jalabert, and there was 'Virage Quintana', who needed no introduction. Here, the serious planning was in greater evidence. Some of the French campervans must have been parked there for a week, and their families must have holidayed in a lay-by. The grass had grown thick and lush around their wheels.

There were no Americans here. There were few Brits. But for all that, there were a number of Poles, a fair smattering of Germans (welcome back), and ever-increasing gaggles of Slovakians. Indeed, at every finish line there had seemed to be more and more of them, until, by Paris, they'd annexed a considerable length of the avenue with their tall flag poles and boisterous chanting.

But the Italian invasion was a more spontaneous affair, a direct result of Nibali's unexpectedly straightforward romp to a rare Tour de France win for Italy, a nation of cycling fans who are often resentful of the puffed-up status of their French neighbour's Grand Tour and celebrate with insular obsessive-ness, the considerable merits of their own Giro d'Italia. But now that they had a contender for the Tour, all of a sudden their interest had been piqued back into life. And, as a con-sequence, they had arrived.

We were barely a kilometre into our drive up the last climb of the day, heading for Risoul, when I spotted a quite won-derful sight. It lifted my spirits.

There was an elderly Italian man, stripped to the waist,

shaving without looking in the mirror. His gaze was fixed instead into the middle distance, as he sat, bolt upright, stroking his stubble away with a cutthroat razor, his head as still as a jaguar's before it attacks. What prodigious talent! What daring! What concentration! What a show-off! Had he never used a mirror? Was he opposed to mirrors on ethical or environmental grounds? Was he escaped from the circus? Or was he, perhaps, a vampire? Who knew.

What a splendid figure he cut, although we did not get long to admire his magnificence, since we were trying to drive up to Risoul without stalling the car or burning the clutch out.

There was a total calm about his action. Behind him an enormous Italian flag, erected next to his campervan, flopped idly around its wooden pole. On the tarmac in front of him he had painted what looked like a large pair of Y-fronts in the green, red and white of Italy. And on the giant pants, he had, for reasons only he knew, inscribed the word 'Ciao'.

Perhaps that was the last thing he wanted Nibali's opponents to see, as he accelerated away from them, taking with him their hope: a pair of Italian briefs, chalked into the road and bidding them farewell.

By the time the *maillot jaune* repeated his domination of the Alps in the Pyrenees a few days later, winning outright the defining climb up the Hautacam, it was time for the French newspapers to start publishing the definitive Nibali story. There would be no more twists and turns. Now we needed to be briefed fully on who this man was who had won the race with one leg tied behind his back. And, to paint the picture, there really there was only one man for the job.

It fell to the legendary Philippe Brunel to come up with the definitive background story.

Now, Monsieur Brunel is a phenomenon in his own right.

He has been one of *L'Équipe*'s chief cycling writers for as long as anyone can remember. He appears around the race like an apparition: there, but not really there. Certainly, if Brunel ghosts into the back of the press conference (he is always the last to arrive), then the room gains in significance, and the event has an importance conferred automatically upon it, which it might previously have lacked.

Brunel is a pale man, with eyes of the deepest brown imaginable, and a chiselled jaw. He wears a glossy, beautifully shaped bob of black hair, which he is in the habit of flicking nonchalantly over his right shoulder to emphasise a point. He wears nothing but black, save for the occasional, and presumably ironic, splash of frivolous grey. Mostly this takes the form of a black jacket with skinny black jeans and a black V-neck T-shirt underneath. But occasionally, and even in the extreme heat of the South of France, he might be seen propping up a wall and scribbling notes in a floor-length back coat, from which the toes of sharp black boots peep out. It has been known for him to experiment with pashminas and other soft furnishings for his neck and shoulders.

Brunel is a man in love with Italy. He has written a novel set around the suicides of a diva in San Remo. He has written a book about the last days of Marco Pantani. I can almost picture him, in a deckchair on Venice lido, a little hair dye running from the sweat around his brow, taking fevered notes for his latest work as he gazes out across the lagoon.

If anyone was going to bring the Nibali story to life, then surely it was Brunel. The cycling world waited for the moment the Brunel biography landed.

The title certainly augured well: *A Child of Messina. The shopkeeper's son, Vincenzo Nibali, grew up on the streets of Messina in Sicily. Before exile in Tuscany.*

There was much to look forward to here: poverty,

depravation, the mafia, exile? It sounded like a heady cocktail, and it started promisingly, too.

It was in Sicily, at the north-eastern point of the island, amid the oriental glint of an ancient sun, that Vincenzo Nibali was born, in Messina, a harbour city rebuilt in 1908 on the ruins of a terrible earthquake, framed by this age-old sea, both blue and deep, which he would later say 'one can never truly leave behind'.

And yet, Brunel's contention is that, from an early age, it was Nibali's destiny to leave the island and seek his fortune elsewhere. He calls, slightly surprisingly, on evidence here from Tomasi di Lampedusa, who wrote in *The Leopard* that 'for things to remain the same, everything must change.'

In other words, continues Brunel, *you must leave Sicily before it grows roots over you, absorbs you from the ground, with its tentacles and its mafioso shadows.*

Disappointingly, the rest of the article doesn't quite live up to the billing. It transpires that the Nibali parents, far from eking out a living fishing in those immemorial blue and deep waters, or mending nets, or cultivating wine, or pressing olives, ran a video rental shop.

But this rather prosaic truth doesn't stop Brunel's eye for an allusion.

The shelves thronged with ancient yellowing VHS cassettes, of the cult films of Vittorio Gassman, Alberto Sordi and Vittorio De Sica.

And here, helpfully, and just on the off-chance the reader might temporarily have forgotten the precise qualities of those three Sicilian filmmakers, he elucidates:

They bear witness, in their obsolescence, to a distant time of plenty, before the crisis.

His mother is quoted as saying that, with the advent of the Internet, she does a good deal less trade. She nearly had to close the shop. Nearly.

Anyway, to cut a long story short; his mum bought him a bike, he was really good, then he joined a junior team in Tuscany, and got even better. And now here he is, winning the Tour de France. I may have precised the rest of Brunel's definitive article here, but you can probably understand why.

In a desperate last effort to lend Nibali's story a bit of an edge, he resorts to playing up one final Sicilian stereotype, invoking the prospect of a vendetta, should it ever transpire that this son of Messina tests positive for doping. Again, his mother Giovanna Nibali is the source of the quote.

'He'll never give in to bad tendencies. Not if he ever wants to set foot in Sicily again. Never.' A threat, then. How very Sicilian.

By the time we rolled out of the Pyrenees, I had still not been able to get a handle on Nibali. I warmed to him, but I did not know what sort of man he was, not really. I did not have a sense of his foibles, his temper, his humour. There was so little for me to work with, for any of us really to work with (including Philippe Brunel) except the facts of his upbringing, the landmarks of his increasingly impressive career, and his utterances during the race, which shed such little light.

For beneath that peaked cap with its oddly eye-catching Aeronautica Militare logo, there was the alert, steely mind of an exceptional winner; a man who most people had disregarded before the Tour, including, quite possibly, his boss Alexander Vinokourov who had issued him with a very public kick up the backside. And now he was about to join an elite club of riders who could claim to have won all three Grand Tours. Vincenzo Nibali, meet Eddy Merckx.

In summary, then, my impressions from close quarters of the 2014 Tour de France winner: great manners, a restrained smile. Black eyes. Sharp teeth. One eyebrow raised as he talks, to emphasise a point. Sometimes two. And a winning margin in Paris of seven minutes and thirty seven seconds.

And now we're done.

LINGUA ANGLIA

'The new rule is very important for rider because it's not
publication intend finish on the width of the delay
very very long.'

We fell out of the altitude.

At last we left the Alps behind us, dropping down onto a
long plain. We now ran parallel to the coast of the
Mediterranean, in between the two great mountain ranges.

I slept deeply in the car as we drove the road from Tallard
and woke only when we pulled up at a petrol station. I opened
the car door to hot air, infused with that distinctive aromatic
smell of Provence, mixed with unleaded petrol, cheap coffee
and cigarette smoke.

In Nîmes, and all along the road chasing back towards the
Alps, there was an almighty storm, gaining in strength every
minute. The race was engulfed. The sky turned to a biblical

black, and the sheeting rain nearly forced us off air, which in turn made Dave Thwaites, our technical director, run from the satellite 'engine room' at the back of the truck shouting, 'I've pumped the power up as much as I dare.' We all turned to look at him. Was he deliberately trying to sound like Scotty on the USS *Enterprise*? Or did he mean it? A huge crack of thunder suggested he meant it.

On the road, there was havoc. The pictures were extraordinary. There was no longer any point in cameramen trying to wipe their lenses clear, because the water just streamed across the glass, and at times, almost all you could make out were blobs of colour. Martin Elmiger and Jack Bauer were somewhere in that watery blur, almost riding out a heroic victory for the breakaway over the bunch.

But, the storm was the real star. With each darkening of the sky, the headlights of the cars and the motorbikes on the road grew brighter. At one point Richie Porte, whose chastening Tour de France didn't ever seem to diminish his rare ability to smile through adversity, got detached at the back of the peloton, and into a howling headwind, and was fighting to get back on terms, using the cars in the convoy to shelter behind. In the commentary, Phil Liggett produced a gem: 'Any port(e) in a storm!'

In Nîmes, outside the Arena, hordes of Norwegian fans milled about trying to pass the time before they could cheer home the eventual winner of the day. They had obviously decided that this was going to be both the day and the place. I have seen this before with Norwegian supporters. They are very targeted, very precise in their expectations and demands, and they usually get exactly what they want, too. Alexander Kristoff would take the honours, winning a bunch sprint. That much was clear.

This return to the flatlands and the big men of the road, after so much up and down, switchback and mountain vista was a blessed relief. Not only did the topography bring to the fore a whole different raft of names again, it also switched the code entirely. Movistar, AG2R, Française des Jeux and Astana, with their cosmopolitan cadres, receded into the background, leaving the stage clear for the likes of Lotto Belisol, Omega Pharma–Quick Step, Katusha and Giant Shimano to do battle, with minor input from Europcar. These stages were like an eclectic trade fair for hire cars, biofuel, laminate flooring and gear shifters. And for some reason, all the main protagonists spoke wonderful English.

The mountain stages had become a mysteriously, darkly Continental affair, with most of the leading places on GC being populated by speakers of the triptych of great romance languages: French, Spanish and Italian. And in this sense, it was a refreshingly old-fashioned-feeling Tour de France.

But when it came to the flat stages, an alternative set of cultural values suddenly held sway, and with that shift in the temperature of the race, so the lingua franca reverted to English, which has begun to dominate cycling over recent years. Two races, then, within one Tour.

How that has changed. When I started out twelve years ago, you could barely find an English-speaking rider who wasn't Australian, American or David Millar. Certainly, few of the race organisers, or the team managers, would have been able to hold a conversation in English.

Back on the 2004 Tour de France, I was invited (all right, told) to interview a gentleman by the name of Mirco Monti. Mr Monti had an important job. He was the President of the Jury of Commissaires; the very people who adjudicate on the labyrinthine and sometimes impenetrable world of the bike race. Since one bike race is not like another, and indeed one Tour is not much like the next, this is an important job.

Occasionally, because rulings concerning time bonuses and intermediate points are constantly changing at the whim of successive Tour directors, it is not the case that all these new rules are universally understood, at least certainly not by the general public, rarely by the media, and sometimes not even by the teams and the riders themselves.

It was in this context that I sat down to speak to Mr Monti, a perfectly charming, prematurely balding Italian cycling bureaucrat. I asked Mr Monti if he was confident that his English was sufficiently fluent to be able to explain the new rulings concerning the team time trial for an English TV audience. He assured us (albeit in heavily accented French) that it would be. So, we pinned a microphone to the lapel of his padded jerkin, and fired away.

'Mr Mirco. Can you please explain the new rulings in relation to the limitation of time losses on the team time trial?'

I sat back. My job (if you can call it that) was done. Over to you, Mirco. What follows is a precise transcript of his reply.

'The new rule is very important for rider because it's not publication intend finish on the width of the delay very very long. Now it's possible on the new rule it's finish on the top is three minutes. *On peut...*' and then, in Italian, he apologised for speaking French, '...between two team is possible twenty seconds. *En effet*, for example, first team time zero, the second team fifty seconds. Fifty seconds is possible time in the classical general is fifteen seconds.'

It was gloriously incoherent. One could only admire his ability to make a fairly complicated point sound utterly unintelligible. In particular, I admired the phrase 'the classical general', since it brought to mind a man of great bearing and stature, a Napoleonic defender of Reason and Faith, a man not unlike the great Mr Monti himself.

And the best thing about the interview? We actually broadcast it. These were the days when anyone on the race who would speak English to us, aside from Armstrong, McEwen (and for some reason Andreas Klöden, whom we pestered on a daily basis), was a rare and treasured find. And so it was that Mr Monti's garbled explanation made the airwaves, because, if we are honest with ourselves, we just found it very funny. In the finished version of the programme, I then had to explain in slightly plainer English what it was that the Italian commissaire had tried so manfully to articulate.

Those were the days when you could rely on the English translations in the official Guide Historique to leave you doubled up with laughter. This publication is the touristy booklet that the Tour hands out to journalists alongside the route book for the purposes of spreading the message that France is old and beautiful across the world. And it is famed for its incoherent English, which has traditionally relied heavily on Google Translate for its accuracy, even before Google Translate existed.

Yet sadly, these days, the translations make sense. The last thing you want from the Tour is for it to make sense.

The great race is changing its feel and texture all the time. Imperceptibly it is moving from something which was at its heart Mediterranean (with all the lazy stereotypical charisma and chaos that this implies) to something much more straightforward, much easier to read. And by 'easier to read', I mean 'easier to read': the Tour is becoming depressingly Anglophone. This may be our fault, of course, for coming along so late in the day and dominating it just when it was unravelling internally in a never-ending vortex of doping scandal. We are certainly to blame, somewhere along the line, I am sure. Sky, and their sponsorship of the team, have set the tone for the way the race now feels, and other teams are simply aping their approach, internally and externally. And Sky themselves, despite their originator being an Australian, are a very British phenomenon, built on our seemingly insatiable appetite to pay ever more heavily for the right to watch a global potpourri of millionaires arrive at football stadiums in suits and oversized headphones, then pull on Nylon shorts and run around for an hour and a half: the Premier League.

Our 'love of football' has led us not to playing it more, or, God forbid, being any better at it: fewer of us now kick a ball, and our national sides are resolutely melting into international insignificance. But we are admirably equipped at watching telly, and paying for it. That bone-idle, but thoroughly understandable, impulse to spectate rather than participate is where Sky get all their limitless cash from, a tiny percentage of which ends up in the *musettes* of our best cyclists. Their annual spend on the cycling team, despite it being one of the best-funded in the world, amounts to no more than 0.8 per cent of their marketing budget.

And, with their success and funding and aesthetic, they set the tone these days. A decade ago, even in the midst of the Armstrong years, the majority of riders spoke French, or perhaps Spanish and Italian in order to communicate with one another. That's all changed. Sky's largely English-speaking roster (even their Spanish and Italian riders, like Juan Antonio Flecha and Dario Cioni spoke disarmingly perfect English) is no longer the only one in the professional peloton. The Omega Pharma–Quick Step team bus, which echoes to the exhortations of their main man at the Tour, the mostly mono-lingual Mark Cavendish, operates with the same common language. The same applies to Tinkoff-Saxo Lotto, Garmin, Trek, BMC, Orica Green Edge with its preponderance of Aussies, Belkin, Giant Shimano and NetApp Endura (although here English competes with German). The more exotic constellations, Astana and Katusha, rarely indulge in Russian discourse, and fall back on English. Even Movistar and

Cannondale, to some extent the national flag bearers of Spain and Italy respectively, mix and match at will. Certain pockets of total 'foreignness' still exist of course. Lampre is *very* Italian, and most of the French teams are decidedly French, with Europcar perhaps the Frenchest of them all, if you exclude Cofidis, which you might as well, because they are almost totally excludable these days.

But English, where it had been largely irrelevant for the best part of a century, now generally holds sway. You need only dip your online toe into the swirling waters of the twitter-sphere to witness the riders talking to one another in amusingly clunky English, with a vocabulary of about a few dozen words at best, all drawn from a very slim dictionary called 'Cycling English'.

> *The guys did a super strong leadout today. But my legs were not good for the final. #tryagaintomorrow*

> *Beautiful race today. Lost seconds, but it's normal. Team was super strong. #bigchanceforwinmaybetomorrow*

> *Crazy parcours. Dangerous for descent, also legs were not super strong. Now to hotel, long transfer. #TdF #passion #tomorrowforstagevictory*

> *Massage now and after this dinner with the guys. #teamwork #legs #superstrong #pasta #TdF #readytosmashit tomorrowprobably*

I have become something of a connoisseur of these electronic missives to the masses, and I know where to look for the best. Fabian Cancellara's are excellent, and so too are Roman Kreuziger's. Both men are capable of couching their meaning in a wonderful fug of almost correct idioms and slightly off-kilter grammar. They sound endearingly natural, as if they were being spoken out loud in the Euro English of the Tour.

This, from Kreuziger, is typical of the genre. Read it out loud to yourself. Now repeat, panting after every fifth word. You too could give a post-race interview:

> *Ok we didn't won @tinkoff_saxo, arrived 4th ... but I can tell you ... we went very very fast!!! congrats to @opqscyclingteam*

And so too is this from Cancellara. Note here not only the textbook nod to his teammates, but also the exemplary use of the hashtag. Also, I very much like the accidentally generated word 'possibili', since it is neither English nor Italian, nor really an adjective, nor quite a noun:

> *I did my best what was possibili today. I think this was the best i could get. super team effort from all @TrekFactory #cold #Rain #Rain*

Occasionally Cancellara, a truly wonderful man with a naturally generous outlook on life, must sit at his laptop in his hotel room reading the news. Every now and then, the wider world makes its presence felt. I can see his gentle brow furrowing as, for a period of perhaps five minutes, he steps outside of the extraordinary cocoon in which professional cyclists operate, and tries to absorb the dangerous chaos of the world outside hotel lobbies and team buses. Sometimes when he does this, he feels compelled to comment:

> *The world is going crazy. Facebook buy whatsapp for crazy money 15000000000€. politics problem in Kiew were they destroyed theyr own city.*

He's not wrong. Apart from grammatically.

After a month in the company of a race that uses English well, but slightly imperfectly, I have noticed a tendency in all of us to shape our own use of the language to fit the circumstances. It becomes infectious, a way of talking that is perfectly adapted to its environment. Thus, heading for the car park at the end of the day, you might well overhear some of the ITV crew talking to each other as if we were riders.

'It's a long transfer, huh?'

'Yeah, but this is normal, I think.'

'I'm super tired, you know.'

'Aah, but the Tour is long. You get always another chance.'

'#pain'

'#whyarewetalkinglikethis?'

'RT: #whyarewetalkinglikethis?'

So all things will eventually merge. There will come a time when we all understand each other perfectly, because we will have entirely forgotten how to speak a language properly. This is the same creep as we have all witnessed on our holidays evidenced by the sudden proliferation of badly translated menus in French restaurants. On a positive note, this has led to far fewer British tourists ordering andouillette by mistake. No one's going to misunderstand the gist of the English subtitle 'Boiled sausage of the tripe and stomach of a cow with its jus.' But, for many of us who prefer not to understand things fully and consider travel still to be a journey into the partially unknown, this is a great source of regret (Grande Sauce de Regrets).

I am now aware that I sound like my dad. This may be because I am a dad.

So it is that as Western Europe begins to curdle and head for an inescapable cultural plughole, the protagonists of the Tour de France look increasingly like the shop-window mannequins in a branch of Gap: bland, neutered, easy to absorb, culturally non-specific, McSportsmen. The kits, with the honourable exceptions of Lampre, AG2R and Astana, are designed by focus groups intent on making everything discreet and understated. Gone, perhaps for ever, is the 'primary colours are probably the best' principle of design, which served cycling well for decades and contributed in no small measure to the sport being broadly ridiculed by the non-cycling world.

Year on year, the way the race looks and feels becomes less cobbled together, less drawn up on the back of a packet of Gauloises. There are more crowd barriers, fewer demonstrations, more helmets (probably a good thing) and more regulations curbing our freedoms. We are no longer, for example, allowed to roam freely with our cameras behind the podium. We are no longer allowed to run backwards with our cameras. Our numbers on the finish line are limited and heavily policed. It's all probably fair enough, but...

Now the race is called into existence on spreadsheets.

In my mind, I link this inextricably to the shift in its linguistic epicentre. Globalisation = Anglicisation = PR Managers = Restriction. But this is a gradual lapse, its fall into Anglophone ubiquity has been incremental, and I cannot put my finger on any single moment of change. The passing of the years click and clack along their way, like a Rubik's Cube slowly altering its constellation, almost invisibly, so that, where last year the tile was red, now it is white.

The story of Stage 15 was told in English. New Zealand's Jack Bauer wept, after two hundred kilometres of effort, having been swept up by the bunch heartbreakingly close to the winning line in Nîmes. And the impressively Anglophone Alexander Kristoff won, because he was always going to. The Norwegians don't mess around when they have a plan in mind.

Kristoff was brought to me for an interview, just when we

were on a commercial break. Olivier, the French media manager for the Tour, ushered him towards my camera, and I had to hold him there until we were ready to cut live to the interview.

'How long, Ned?' Olivier looked impatiently at me, and then glanced at the long line of other networks, all vying for precisely the same opportunity.

'One minute, Olivier.' And then I turned to Kristoff, 'One minute, Alexander. Thanks for waiting.' Then I remembered to add, 'And well done, by the way. Great win.' Alexander Kristoff is a nice man, otherwise I may not have got away with this.

Two minutes later, I started the interview.

After it was done, Olivier looked daggers at me. 'Why is your British minute always longer than anyone else's minute, Ned?'

'Because we invented time, my friend.' And, on that note, I bid him farewell.

PART 4

PARIS
CHAMPS-ÉLYSÉES ● ÉVRY

● PÉRIGUEUX
BERGERAC

MAUBOURGUET
VAL D'ADOUR

PAU ●
HAUTACAM ● SAINT-GAUDENS

SAINT-LARY-
SOULAN ● BAGNÈRES-DE-LUCHON ● CARCASSONNE

CARCASSONNE

'Sorry, Chris.'
'Probably all for the best.'

We rested up in Carcassonne, where for two consecutive nights I basted my innards in goose fat. This is, after all, the self-proclaimed spiritual home of the world's most unhealthy dinner: cassoulet. And where better to ingest a radioactively superheated earthernware dish full of fat-pimped butter beans and garlicky sausage than within the Olde Citadel of Carcassone, perched atop its fabled hill.

It was the Tour de France that first introduced me to Carcassone's faux medieval splendour. It had not been a place I had visited in my childhood despite a handful of hot holidays spent driving from Calais to the heat of southern France in

an increasingly ageing series of nasty Datsun estates. Once there, 'abroad', the Japanese cars doors would open to occasionally reveal unwilling, car-sick, homesick teenagers, who would then be frogmarched by parents to a Place of Interest in order to be educated and have their minds opened.

This was a process of intellectual emancipation often hampered by the semi-permanent use of a Sony Walkman occluding the natural ambient noise of the quaint French market square/aqueduct/art gallery and overlaying onto the general Gallic hubbub the tortured strains of 'Let's Dance' by David Bowie. In this way my early touristic experiences were compromised by the sense that most things were passing me by. That included, it seemed, Carcassonne.

Some time ago, putting together a clip reel of work I had done on the Tour de France for ITV, I stumbled across a short feature I filmed in 2004 about Carcassonne. The reason for our sudden interest in the UNESCO world heritage site had been the fact that Stage 14 of that year's Tour started there and finished in Nîmes, a long, hot transitional race which was won, as such stages often are, by a breakaway rider. This time it was Aitor González, his final result in a Grand Tour before he was undone by the Operation Puerto doping affair and forced to retire in 2006.

But his victory came sandwiched between two Armstrong wins, one on the Plateau de Beille and the other, hugely unnecessarily, in a sprint finish into Villard de Lans. So, with the probability that the GC race would fall into neutralised torpor for a day while the leaders ate power bars and gave the cameramen cheerful thumbs-up signs, we correctly assumed that the coverage would need pepping up with a little touristy schmaltz. Hence the film about Carcassonne.

So, I found myself with a radio mic pinned to my shirt collar, standing on a drawbridge, talking out loud to a remote camera invisibly situated about a hundred yards away, leaving the flow of tourists passing by to give me a wide berth, in the assumption that I was touched by madness.

'Over the centuries, they've all passed through at one time or another, the Romans, the Visigoths...' (and a slight pause for the rather clumsy punchline) '...and Ryanair.'

The fact that Ryanair had started to fly there from Stansted was entirely in keeping with Carcassonne's twenty-first-century status as something of a glorious fake. Normally there is a world of difference between the pseudo-medieval reproduction armour, chessboards and tea cloths that are sold in the souvenir shops of France's greatest antique wonders and the antique wonders themselves. But, in Carcassonne's case, this is harder to discern, since the whole walled city was partly conceived from the revivalist imagination of the great French architect Eugène-Emmanuel Viollet-le-Duc, whose very name suggested he was never going to be cut out for anything other than dreamily sketching turrets and ramparts and moats with which to adorn France's crumbling stock of ancient fortifications.

It was he, working in the late nineteenth century, who added the third, very spiky and largely gratuitous tower to the roof of Notre Dame Cathedral. It was his work that pimped Mont Saint-Michel and made it look like Sleeping Beauty's architecturally transcribed LSD dream. And it was Viollet-le-Duc's work in the South of France, right in the heart of cassoulet country, that gave Michael O'Leary the idea of sticking pasty British passengers on an aeroplane and flying them (provided they have first printed off their boarding passes at home) to the seat of thirteenth-century Bishop Ranulph.

Not that I mind a fake. One of the great things about Carcassonne is its grossly overstated Bastille Day firework display. In 2006, the evening after Yaroslav Popovych had dispensed with the three other men in that year's irrelevant breakaway move, to win Stage 12 into Carcassonne, the old(ish) city nearly exploded. It was the fourteenth of July, and given that the race had just finished in the self-proclaimed capital of bangers and whizz, they threw everything at it.

In fact, they executed the display with an almost infantile delight, answering the question I have often asked myself: what would it be like to see the fireworks basically all chucked up into the air at the same time? Quite good actually, was Carcasonne's expensive riposte, which they broadcast live to the Republic on TF1. It was over in less than a minute, but while it lasted, all you could do was stagger backwards, shield your eyes and giggle at the wonder of it. Only recently, almost a decade on, have I lost the after-image from my retina.

This year I wanted to visit the Museum of Torture. But instead, Omega Pharma–Quick Step had organised a press conference to announce their new sponsor for next season. There were unexpected parallels.

They chose a location about twenty kilometres out of town, at a campsite populated by a few hundred bewildered Belgian cycling fans, on a hillside overlooking a ruined Cathar fort. There was nothing wrong with this choice of location, except that none of us could find it without backing down a series of narrow farm tracks and executing three-point turns in orchards.

Against this carefully selected backdrop, they erected a small stage, and then obliterated most of the view by inflating two enormous blow-up water bottles with the logo of their new sponsor. The bouncy bidons kept catching in the breeze, straining at their leashes, and threatening to fold over completely and hit the entire OP–QS cycling squad on the head, presumably to the accompaniment of a cartoonish 'boing!' noise.

Meanwhile the chief executive (probably) of the energy drink company who had slapped their logo on big wobbly bottles, was imparting some unlistenable-to jargon about their new deal being 'an important moment in the internationalisation of the brand'. I caught Stage 7's winner Matteo Trentin trying to look interested, while the Australian lead-out man

Mark Renshaw took a surreptitious glance down at his smartphone.

Then, as if sensing they might be losing their audience, onto this stage strolled Mr and Miss Belgium, sporting only their underwear. The rest of their bodies' surface area was painted in the team's black, white and blue colours. They stood, coyly, side by side, holding what appeared to be three giant black space hoppers, with the name of a sugary drink on it. Someone was singing in Flemish. This was the point at which I stopped even pretending to understand what was going on. All that I clearly recall after that was the moment when Mark Cavendish was introduced as the special guest, and the space hopper was thrown into the air in celebration, only to be caught by a violent downward gust, which caused it to hit Cavendish on the head and nearly knock off his Oakleys. And this time, I believe it actually did go 'boing!'

Then we were all invited to eat mussels and frites and drink beer in a tent, which was nice.

Team Sky's press event for the second rest day was at the other end of the spectrum. There was no free food. It did not feature either balloons or mussels or any winners of beauty pageants in their undercrackers. And, perhaps as a result, it hardly attracted any attention, despite the fact that the product it was designed to promote was a genuinely impressive piece of kit provided to the team by their blue chip sponsors. It was a top-of-the-range Jaguar sports car, designed solely for use by the team on time-trial days. The car was, as even I, a self-confessed automobile agnostic had to admit, stunning. It had been converted, I can only imagine, at vast expense, and for almost no reason other than because they could, to carry the spare bikes at an angle on the rear of the car, to save the need for reaching all the way up to the roof. This is perhaps the most expensive ever marginal gain in the history of cycling.

They had intended, of course, for this to be a big showpiece event, unveiling Chris Froome's Tour-winning support vehicle. But instead, with Richie Porte languishing in the lower reaches of the GC, it fell rather flat. We were there, and Sky Sports were there, and one or two other desultory members of the press, but there was no great fanfare. Still, they went through the motions for the cameras, having parked the car up next to the team bus in a drizzly car park outside Carcassonne's Campanile hotel. Porte and Geraint Thomas and Dave Brailsford then duly posed in and around it, pulling up just short of draping themselves languorously over it. And no one had the foresight to provide them with a space hopper to clutch.

One of the Belgian mechanics from Lotto Belisol, who were also staying in the hotel, wandered over to watch the proceedings, wiping his hands on an oily rag. He gazed at the car, and then told me how the people from Jaguar had prevented him from taking a picture of it in the morning.

'I said to them, a little bit, "Fuck off".'

After it was all over, I sat down with Dave Brailsford for a while. He was relishing the lack of attention, and how much more enjoyable the Tour was with the pressure off.

'What do you think of that Jaguar, Dave?'

'I've got one,' he said, casually. 'They're extremely fast.'

Then he told me about his previous sports car, an Aston Martin DB Something, which he managed to lose control of trying to overtake an elderly lady on a country road in Cheshire. He'd booted the accelerator too hard and had ended up coming to a halt, sideways across the road, looking straight at the poor lady in the other car, who'd also slammed on her brakes in alarm. Sir David Brailsford's embarrassment was only complete when she reached over towards him, and from behind the windows of her car, had given him the clear and unambiguous wristy gesture, normally the preserve of white van drivers.

'I put my head in my hands. She'd got me. I was bang to rights.'

We talked about Mark Cavendish. I said that he was back on the race for a day or two, doing some interviews, and generally lending his support.

Then I recalled a distant memory of Team Sky's long-forgotten Plan A. 'Talking of missing riders, where's Chris Froome gone?'

I had tried repeatedly, for about a week, to get hold of him, leaving messages with him, and with his fiancée Michelle Cound, who looks after things like pesky journalists for him. But, unusually, I had heard not a thing in reply. And nor, I gathered, had the team's press officers, who'd also been trying to set up an interview with their man.

'He went off to America.' Brailsford told me. 'They had to get right away from it all, to clear their heads completely, to disengage.' A year of living with the fact that he'd won the race had not been easy for Froome, particularly when it came to the constant need to respond to suggestions that he doped. I got the impression that even when he reached the start in Leeds, he'd been suffering a bit under the immense pressure of his status. Even Brailsford's well-judged attempts to move away from talk of 'defending the jersey' in favour of 'trying to win it again' had not done much to detoxify the situation for him. And then, when it all came crashing down around him, he needed a complete escape. So they disappeared altogether to re-group, and lick their wounds.

Over dinner that evening (pieces of fowl roasted in their own rendered fat and served with butter beans), talk turned to Team Sky and their approach. Matt Rendell suggested that recently they'd tried harder to be more philosophical in their attempts to control the race, and manipulate circumstances to their advantage. But it was only a partial success. They could 'go with the flow', if the rush of water in question ran smoothly like the concrete channel of Los Angeles River. But Nibali was able to negotiate white waters, rocks and over-hanging branches and all. He was tumbling, unscathed, down the Big Sur.

We strolled off into the night, the pulses of heavy rain, the aftershock of that extraordinary storm the day before, having finally relented. Carcassonne was busy.

Much business gets done on rest days, and the race always attracts a bloated number of visitors and guests, some of whom are friends and family, while others are there to talk to and try to sign riders. I sat down for a while with two agents, cousins, from the same extended cycling family. One of them represented Simon Yates, who I had spoken to the day before, just after he had announced the team's decision (and not necessarily one he agreed with) to pull him out of the race.

The Yates twins (Simon has an identical brother, Adam) are an extraordinary proposition. Each one exhibits slightly different characteristics. Adam is perhaps better suited to the long-form climbs of stage racing, whereas Simon sees his future slanted more to the punchier climbing demands of the Ardennes classics. But they are both extremely young, and a cycling career can take many shapes, most of which don't necessarily become fully defined until the rider hits his late twenties.

At the age of just twenty-one, Simon Yates is as sensible an individual as is possible to imagine. Unphased by anything the race could throw at him, he'd got in a break at the earliest possible opportunity, battled through a bout of pneumonia, and then got in another break when he had recovered. Talking to him was humbling. He spoke with such level-headedness, such a total absence of insecurity, that I felt, in comparison, like a shambling fool. The cruelty of youth.

If I were trying to build a team for the future (let's imagine that I was running a team. Just indulge me, please) I'd go out of my way to sign this pair. I think that the rest of the peloton should be genuinely anxious about what they might be capable of a few years from now. They remind me strongly of the Brownlee brothers, who have dominated the triathlon world over recent years: mutually supportive, hermetically sealed, utterly intent, a little dull, talented, winners. It was just that point I'd put to Dave Brailsford earlier that day, having found out that one of the reasons they slipped through Sky's fingers in 2013 was that they'd only offered Simon a contract and not Adam. That struck me as a fairly basic mistake, with twins. I didn't actually pull a face, push my bottom lip out with my tongue and go 'Derrr!' at Dave Brailsford, but I did suggest that it had been an error. In response, he hinted strongly that it wouldn't be long before they would make every effort to bring the brothers back in the fold.

When I recounted that conversation to the two agents sitting in the square, they were on to me in a flash.

'Which one? Simon?' said one.

'Or Adam?' asked the other.

'Both,' I said.

They raised their glasses to each other, and chinked them in celebration of a notional pay-day a year or two down the line.

Refreshed, recomposed, regrouped, the Tour departed the following morning for the Pyrenees in a more tranquil frame of mind. At the start in Carcassonne, there was time for Jens Voigt to stop at the sign-on podium and talk in his richly Germanic French to the crowd thronging the barriers. Would he miss the Tour?

'*Oui. Ça va me manquer.*' I'll miss it. It had been a big part of his life. But he wouldn't miss the suffering.

I watched him struggle down the steps of the podium, trying hard not to slip in his cleated shoes. Then he hobbled across to the horde of people holding out hats and programmes for him to sign. He might miss the Tour, but not half as much as it would miss him, I thought. And then I made a note of that thought so that I could use it in the final programme of the Tour on Sunday, which I duly did.

Behind where I stood, at the side of the podium, two of Voigt's compatriots, André Greipel and Marcel Sieberg, sat with their feet up on a sponsor's table, which looked like cheap garden furniture, stuffing themselves with Haribo. This, for the big Germans, was preparation.

And Thibaut Pinot (who Chris Boardman kept referring to as Pinot Thibaut, or even Tibu Pinu) was at work, talking to the press. Before the race, he was telling anyone who cared to listen that these were important days in the mountains for him, as he tried to dispense with the trio of threats from Romain Bardet (the increasingly worried-looking young climber), Alejandro Valverde (the not-in-the-slightest-bit-worried Spanish veteran) and Jean-Christophe Péraud, who, at the age of thirty-seven, simply couldn't believe what was happening to him.

They got on their bikes, and we headed for Luchon in the car.

The hours passed in a sunny daze. The town was bright, breezy and delightful. Pinot even managed to make Nibali look momentarily uncomfortable on a climb, at which point France briefly held its breath and dreamt the impossible. But then Mick Rogers managed to bring the country back down to earth by out-thinking, out-manoeuvring and out-riding the Europcar duo of Voeckler and Cyril Gautier, to win comfortably from a breakaway.

My principle task for the day had been to chaperone Mark Cavendish from the finish line to the studio. He would be on the race that day, travelling in the first Omega Pharma–Quick Step team car. The operation sounded simple enough. I would meet him, at an agreed point, just before the finish line, and bring him into the cordoned-off 'Zone Technique'. The problem was logistics. The official entrance to the Zone was about half a kilometre away from the both the studio and the spot where we'd agreed to meet Cavendish. Thinking ahead, we'd managed to preserve a gap in the fence, before it had been totally closed. This would be our chink in the armour through which we could smuggle in the Manxman. That way he need only walk fifty metres, rather than five hundred. It was fiendishly clever, devilishly brave, and not without risk.

At the allotted time, I snuck out of the secret gap, and stood on the road, waiting for Cavendish. Just when I expected it, his car screamed round the corner and then, seeing me in his mirror, running after them, slammed on its brakes. A door opened and out got Cavendish.

'How far do we have to go?' He looked impatient already.

'It's over there.' I pointed over there. 'We can get through the fence just there.' Then I pointed just there.

Now he looked distinctly unamused. 'Bloody hell. Shall I get back in the car, then?'

'Um . . . If you want to. But it's only over there.' We started walking towards it, as his car pulled away. He was clearly in one of those moods, during which, I have learned, you don't speak unless spoken to. There's just no point.

We reached the gap in the fence. Except it was no longer a gap. To my horror I discovered that in the five minutes I had been gone, one of the guards had spotted the breach and tied the two panels of security fencing together with cable ties. I stared at them in disbelief. I did not dare to glance at Cavendish. But I knew that there was no chance at all I would be able to persuade him to walk all the way round the compound to the official entrance. He'd only extremely grudgingly walked this far.

I looked back at the cable ties. Then I placed my right hand inside the sharp plastic loop. I had just enough room to fit in three of my fingers, and bracing my left hand against the fence, I screwed my eyes up and pulled with all my might. All the while I was aware of Mark Cavendish's close scrutiny.

To my complete astonishment, the cable tie pinged open, and I was able to lever the two fences apart, so that the famous sprinter could pass, unhindered.

'There you go, Mark.' I gestured as if I were a *Downton Abbey* footman.

He stepped through without a word, as if it were the most natural thing in the world that I had just single-handedly (literally) burst open an industrial-strength cable tie. But after he had gone ahead, I winced to myself in pain and glanced down with pride at the hand that had performed such a miracle.

By Stage 16, you do not realise how strong you have become. Especially with him watching you.

Yet my strength was short-lived. Chris and I hatched a plan to get away from Luchon that revealed itself as hubris. It was a fine, sunlit evening as we left the spa town, bound for that night's accommodation in Saint-Lary, some thirty kilometres away. We scrutinised on a map the distance we would have to travel to get there, and how long it might take us. This was important, as it was already getting quite late, and riding our bikes without lights on narrow Pyrenees roads didn't seem like a good idea.

Unfortunately, as we soon discovered, the map to which we had referred didn't show gradients. We set off along the main road in Luchon, and turned left. No sooner had we done that, than the road began to rise. In fact, it carried on rising for about forty minutes, by which time we reached the foot of the actual climb. It even had a sign on it, which displayed the fearsome name of the Col de Peyresourde. Our gentle little ride home, it seemed, had turned into an ascent of one the most famous passes in the great mountain range. Only on the other side of the Peyresourde, and over another shorter, but perhaps steeper, climb, would we finally descend into Saint-Lary.

The climb was endless. After some time, we rounded a shoulder of land, and the full extent of its horrors was revealed to us. Admittedly, now, we could at least see the summit, but that didn't greatly improve the mood. It lay five or six kilometres away still, at the end of a road that wriggled crazily up the side of the mountain.

On and on we ploughed. It was beginning to get dark. Clouds had drawn in, and it was threatening to rain. The rest of our crew, as well as hundreds of other Tour de France colleagues, started to overtake us in the comfort of their cars. We let one or two of our team pass us by with a beep of the horn and a merry wave, but by the time we knew that there was just one more of our cars to come, a terrible realisation began to dawn. This was our last chance. If we didn't stop it, then we were committed to riding the entirety of the route. Besides, there was no mobile phone reception up there in the mountains.

And then, with sober certainty, I knew I couldn't do it. I was going to bail out.

Chris, I am sure, would happily have ridden on at his own considerable pace, but opted, out of solidarity, to join me in my feeble-mindedness. And before we knew it, we'd flagged down Liam at the wheel of the car, and were busy taking the wheels off the bikes so that we might fit them in the boot space of the Espace. It was humbling.

In the space of just a few hours, in the Hautes-Pyrénées, I had known great triumph, and abject failure. Such is the frailty of human endeavour. One man's cable tie is another man's mountain.

'Sorry, Chris.'

'Probably all for the best.'

No one spoke much after that.

SAINT

'He was born between Anquetil, his senior by one year, and Poulidor, his junior by several. With him in the middle, who knows how the famous duel between Anquetil and Poulidor might have turned out?'

In 1974, the same year that the Tour first visited British shores, with a much derided circuit of the Plymouth bypass, Raymond Poulidor won his final-ever stage on the race in which he had forged his great reputation. It was a 209-kilometre mountain stage through the Pyrenees, finishing with the uncategorised ascent of Saint-Lary Pla d'Adet.

On the approach to the climb, and sensing some weakness in the yellow jersey of Eddy Merckx as they entered the village of Saint-Lary in the valley, Poulidor had already forced a small gap. Then, as they hit the slopes in earnest, he started to prise it open further, driven on by a partisan French crowd who were willing him to win for one final time at the impressive age of thirty-eight.

'They gave me great support. I almost forgot about the pain in my legs,' Poulidor recalled after the event.

When he crossed the line, he was able to tell French TV that he had waited years to rediscover the feeling of winning again on the Tour de France. But when I asked him about the stage win, forty years later, he suddenly, surprisingly, recalled it for a very different reason.

'Yes, yes. It was a memorable day. But, do you know what? That was the first day that Daniel Mangeas became the Speaker of the Tour! It was his first day on the job. And do you know why? Because the man who was supposed to do it broke down on the way there, and his car was stranded. So Félix Lévitan asked Mangeas to fill in for him. He never looked back.'

That morning in 1974 Daniel Mangeas walked up the mountain, accompanied by the most famous daughter of Saint-Lary, the great French downhill skier Isabelle Mir. Only when he got to the top did he find out that he would be anointed, from that moment on, the Speaker of the Tour, a position of great honour, and one that he has turned into an art form.

Mangeas himself sees it as fate. 'One man's misfortune is another man's stroke of luck.'

Besides, it was destined to happen. For, according to him, 'you don't become a speaker. You are born a speaker.'

Just as everyone on the Tour knows Poulidor, so everyone knows Mangeas. He is tall, loping, faultlessly polite, and always smiling. His long flaxen locks belie his real age; he looks ten years younger than he is. In the mornings, at the start, he will welcome the riders onto the stage, reeling off their Palmares from the top of his head. Although he always carries a clipboard with his notes, he seldom needs to refer to them. He recognises all the riders without fail, and they all know him. Every now and then he'll stop them for a quick word, which they know will be just that, a quick word. They trust him not to keep them detained for too long or to ask daft questions.

Then, later in the day, at the finish line, Mangeas will sit in a booth, in front of a microphone, entertaining the crowd, as first the publicity caravan comes through, and then the race itself. Hours of talking. He can talk for hours, all alone.

He weaves a narrative that seamlessly moves from weather forecasts, to race reports, historical narratives, cultural observations, sponsors' announcements and riders' biographies. It is entertaining, observant and informative. It is the background noise of the Tour, and when it ceases to be heard, then it will be noticeable by its absence. For, after the conclusion of this Tour, Mangeas has decided to quit. Forty years of talking, it seems, is enough for any man. Even for the Speaker himself.

So, on Wednesday 17 July 2014, the race roared once again into Saint-Lary. It snaked along the valley and then hit the foot of the climb to the ski station and started to writhe uphill. Looking down on this procession, tooting and parping its way to the top, one man stood, a microphone in his hand, connecting with his past. He never struck me as a sentimental man, but I wonder if Daniel Mangeas took time out to consider the twist of fortune that changed the course of his life, as he gazed down from his perch at the top of the mountain.

'Rafał Majka, le grimpeur de l'équipe Tinkoff SaxoBank, s'approche de la ligne d'Arrivée!' He roared his commentary as the Polish sensation Rafał Majka, winking to the cameras, approached the line. Majka won all alone on the Pla d'Adet, having distanced the yellow jersey, just as Poulidor had done in 1974.

Both men, Mangeas and Poulidor, were there to see him do it, forty years after their shared moment; the great speaker's first stage, and the great rider's final win.

They were both there a short while later to see Vincenzo Nibali pull on yet another yellow jersey. Poulidor was on the podium alongside the Italian, and Mangeas sat on the tarmac in front of the stage, so as not to block the view of any of the spectators.

'Vin-Cen-Zo Ni-Ba-Li. Le maillot jaune et le leader souverain du Tour de France!' The pitch of the speaker's voice reached its definitive level. As if to say, 'Ladies and gentlemen, thank you, and good night.'

A little while after that I watched Raymond Poulidor making his way to the car they kept waiting for him. He and his wife were teetering across a wasteland of thick TV cables, trying to pick their way through, accompanied by a small army of assistants.

Suddenly I remembered that I needed to talk to Poulidor. I still didn't know who the other rider was, the one who was said to be as good as him and Anquetil. When I'd spoken to him about Roger Rivière, he'd mentioned that other name, and then my battery had died. Who was it?

'Monsieur Poulidor!' I went chasing after him, as he disappeared from view behind a truck. 'Monsieur Poulidor!'

But when I got there, he had vanished.

I woke the next morning to a shuttered room in a familiar hotel in Tarbes. The light had been so effectively removed from the room, the darkness so complete, that it took me a long time to reassemble the constituent parts of my psyche. Eventually, they came together; my consciousness dropped down from the ceiling, my conscience crept back in under the door and my memory picked itself up from the pile of socks in the corner. I dressed and went down for breakfast.

The road from Tarbes, past Lourdes ('a Mecca for Catholics' according to Phil Liggett one year in the commentary) and into the Hautes-Pyrénées, is one I have grown to know well. Familiar landmarks flash by, like a devilishly dangerous-looking nightclub on the fringes of Lourdes. There's nothing terribly godly about this establishment with blacked-out windows, and a forecourt dotted with broken-down cars. It goes by the name of Le Mylord. I am not sure how much trade it gets from the flow of pilgrims through the holy town.

The wheat fields of the lowlands were already cut and baled up in neat drum-shaped stacks. Seemingly on top of each one, a single magpie stood sentinel. And behind them, getting ever closer, the blue-tinged edifice of the Pyrenees. From down here they always look unreachable.

Further along, as the mountain road started to rise up the famous climb of the Hautacam, and the crowd thickened with each passing hairpin, we drove by a British fan who had chosen to pull on an inflatable 'fat lady' suit and over that a yellow tutu. A rather touching sequence of events unfolded as we came near his (her) swaying figure. Two young Frenchmen ran up to her with a bunch of wildflowers they had picked from the side of the road. She gratefully received them, and then offered each of them one of her inflatable breasts which they might kiss. This they duly did. Then they left with a Skoda hat that they pinched from her head, which didn't matter greatly, as she appeared to be wearing two more under that.

Eventually we arrived, and parked the car at a ridiculous angle on the steep grassy side of a ski slope. Up here on the mountain, the last summit finish of the Tour, all we could do was wait. Mike, who had by now stopped counting his red lorries, and I watched a helicopter far beneath us. It scurried noisily through the valley, its shadow appearing to flit across the ground faster than it was cutting through the air. We debated the physics of that particular optical illusion, until we had both reached the limits of our understanding, which was pretty soon after we had begun the discussion.

Then we turned our considerable attention to the physics of gravity.

'What is it, exactly?'

'Well, it's obvious.'

'Is it?'

'Yes, mass attracts mass.'

'Why?'

I stared down at the steady flow of cyclists riding up the mountain far below, straining to prise their mass away from that of planet Earth, and I completely failed to understand what lay behind it.

I could feel the giant effort of the race, lifting and lifting itself against the pull; this was what awaited the clutch of riders battling behind Nibali to claim a place on the podium in Paris. This is where Valverde, Bardet, Pinot and Péraud were heading.

Above us, all along the very top of the Hautacam, lined up on the ridge that defines it, and differentiates rock from sky as you look upwards, there was a kilometre-long string of campervans. From the finish line, placed at a distance below, they looked like teeth, pointed upwards and set in the jaw bone of the mountain. A part of a desiccated sheep skull.

The temperature was twitching like the flame of a candle caught in the breeze. When the sun came out it turned instantly hot, but no sooner had it come out than it disappeared once again, washed away by a sudden rolling mountain mist.

Next to us a team of TV engineers from Luxemburg had set up a makeshift barbecue, on which half a dozen unnaturally pink sausages sat impassively. The men stood around despondently, every now and again poking hopefully at one of the bangers.

Right now that seemed to be a fitting image for the race itself. It was not sufficiently hot. The contenders lay on the grill, side by side, occasionally spitting a little hot fat at one another, but hardly sizzling. It was a race that smelt of damp charcoal in the mountain mist.

Apart from an impulsive, aggressive, but ultimately completely pointless, attack by Alejandro Valverde on the descent before the final climb, Stage 18 mostly conformed to expectations. The Spaniard eventually cracked, and, along with Romain Bardet, lost time to Jean-Christophe Péraud and

Thibaut Pinot. The young Frenchman came second on the stage, beating by two seconds the effervescent Rafal Majka, who sewed up the mountains competition.

And the winner? Vincenzo Nibali, completing his quartet of victories, in Yorkshire, in the Vosges, in the Alps and now in the Pyrenees.

Once the main business of the day was done, we started the long descent off the mountain. Just as I was making my way back to the car I saw once again the Poulidors, this time alone, looking out into the milky sunshine in the valley far below. I took my chance, and reintroduced myself.

Then I explained my predicament to him, and asked him for a second time who these riders were. Rivière, he said, and then something that sounded like Gérard Senne.

'*Est-ce que vous pouvez repeter son nom, si'l vous plaît?*'

'*Gérard Senne.*' I couldn't make out the surname.

'*Semme?*'

'*Non, Senne.*'

'*Senne.*'

'*Oui, comme le Senne.*' What did he mean?

'*Merci, Monsieur Poulidor.*'

Senne? Semme? Sainne? I tried to search for every possible variation of what I thought I had heard, but drew a blank each time. I replayed Poulidor's strange Auvergnat pronunciation over and over, but could not make head nor tail of it.

Perhaps it was Seine, like the river? Nothing.

And then, suddenly, I found him.

On 11 March 1960, Paris–Nice was due to be run in two stages. The first half of the day's racing was scheduled to be a 130-kilometre race from Manosque to Fréjus, but it was raining so hard that the organisers cancelled the half-stage, and instead the riders were ferried across to Fréjus in cars so that they could at least ride the second and final stage of the race to Nice the following day.

Roger Rivière, along with his Rapha-Géminiani teammates Pierre Everaert, Luis Otano and François Mahé was travelling in the team car, looking out at the rain, and listening to the radio. Suddenly the music was interrupted by a speaker who announced the death of Gérard Saint, their teammate. He had been killed in a car accident near Le Mans.

Raymond Louviot, the team's manager, brought the car to a halt. No one moved, and no one spoke. When they finally got to Fréjus, the news had spread across the peloton. 'I got out of the car,' recalled Rivière, 'and I started to tremble.'

Saint was just twenty-four when he died, and had barely started out on a career which people believed would take him to the very top. He was a huge man, nearly six foot four, by far the tallest in a peloton that boasted a fair number of giants. He was also spectacularly good. As Louison Bobet said of him when he rode Paris–Nice–Rome in the spring of 1959, 'In my opinion, Gérard Saint is the fastest. He is a great rider.' That race, extended into Italy for one year only, was supposed to have been all about Anquetil and Rivière. But instead it was Saint who stole the show, with *Miroir-Sport* describing it as '*étincelant*', or 'sparkling'.

His one and only participation in the Tour de France came in 1959, where he finished in ninth place, seventeen minutes down on Federico Bahamontes, and some twelve minutes behind the pair of Anquetil and Rivière. That bald fact doesn't tell the whole story. Twice, he punctured on Stage 13 at just the time that Ercole Baldini launched a ferocious attack that ripped the race to shreds. That misfortune cost him thirty-two minutes. But by the time the race reached Paris, he'd reclaimed fifteen of them.

At the age of just twenty-three, that season of 1959 was enough to suggest that he had a great future ahead of him.

If you unpick the records of the day, they make him sound like a kind of turbo-charged Geraint Thomas. He was elegant, placing his hands on his handlebars, according to Louison's brother, Jean Bobet, 'like a pianist at a keyboard. His body remained motionless, even during the most violent of efforts.'

He won races from breakaway groups or a solo attack. He had, in the quaint parlance of the day, 'a jump'. Everyone feared his accelerations. 'When Saint goes, it's like trying to stop an express train,' according to one of his adversaries in the 1957 Tour of Luxembourg. It wasn't just his prodigious talent on a bike, it was also his character off the bike that endeared him so greatly to the press, and through them to the public. He understood, intuitively, that the media could help him build a career. In fact, here too the Geraint Thomas model fits like a glove, for the Welshman has always had an easy, unencumbered relationship with the media. Saint's younger brother, Jacques, remembers how Gérard couldn't help but smile during interviews, and always appeared genuinely surprised by his own successes.

But there was more to his story than that. He had grown up in poverty in Argentan, in Normandy. His mother was a maid, and his father an agricultural labourer. In fact, Gérard Saint was barely educated. He took an agricultural attitude into his racing, too. The 1957 edition of Liège–Bastogne–Liège was raced in freezing weather that had whittled the peloton down to just twenty-seven survivors, of whom Gérard Saint was one. The riders were no longer identifiable, as their woollen racing garb had frozen solid and turned white with ice. But it was possible to make out Saint pulling away at the rear of the group, stepping off his bike, and sheltering behind a tree while he urinated on his fingers in an attempt to defrost them. It was rudimentary, you might even say it was vulgar, but it was effective, and was born directly from his experience of working on the land. Even before then, writes Jacky Desquesnes in his biography *Gérard Saint ou l'espoir anéanti* 'he knew that he belonged to a world where sometimes your own urine was the only way of combating frostbite, and where the presence of pain meant that everyday decorum was sometimes optional. He didn't become a cyclist to put an end to his suffering, but rather to bring light to the discreet self-sacrifice which he had learnt growing up among people who had little.'

Fame and success brought huge rewards to cyclists of his generation. In June of that year, the magazine *Sport et Vie* featured a colour photo spread of Louison Bobet, posing with his wife, wrapped up in mink fur, in front of their own private aeroplane. Saint would never live long enough to benefit from that kind of remuneration. But he would often talk to journalists about the wonderful opportunity the sport had afforded him, and of the great virtue of social mobility in post-war France.

It was a story that told itself well, and the country wanted to hear it. The new Republic had been founded, in a way that mirrored the welfare state over the water, on fiercely wished-for principles of equality of opportunity. He dressed well, spoke well, charmed people. He seemed for all the world like a paid-up member of the upper bourgeoisie and yet, if you read his story, his origins could hardly have been humbler. He was cherished.

France still had military service in force during those years, and Saint had been called up once already, but then released. A kidney condition, with which he had lived since childhood, exempted him from the exertions of a life in the army. However this non-participation caused some embarrassment, not only to Saint, but also to the French army. The public spectacle of him riding the Tour de France seemed to sit uneasily with his medical reports suggesting that he would not fare well during the rigours of military service. So, after the 1959 Tour had implied that he was exceedingly fit, they re-tested him, and the following year, he was assigned to the 153rd Company. The army agreed, however, to allow him to continue his sporting career pretty much unaffected. And that would include riding the Tour de France.

It was as he was returning to barracks after a day's leave, in March, just as his new St Raphaël teammates were finishing off Paris–Nice, that it all came to an end. He had enjoyed a short break, during which he'd visited his wife Nicolle and his three young children, and was in a rush to get back to the company, given that he was running an hour late already. He lost control of his Citroën (one of those classic beauties of the late 1950s), swerved to avoid an oncoming motorbike, and smashed his car into a poplar tree.

The impact was catastrophic: side-on into the driver's door. Saint lived long enough to plead with his rescuers to release him from his 'metal straitjacket', but he'd broken both his arms, both his legs and his pelvis, as well as rupturing his femoral artery. He was dead on arrival at Le Mans hospital.

We left the mountains, and headed north. The next day would be a flatland gallop towards Bergerac, and from there just the time trial remained before the podium positions would be confirmed. France hoped dearly that the brave old warhorse Péraud might hold on to his exceptional third place, and become the first Frenchman to make it onto the podium since 1997. But more than that, the white jersey and second place, which was the property of young Pinot, that mattered more than anything else. Should Pinot maintain his place, then at last, and after so many years, in which generations of French riders have fallen away, they would have a hope for the years to come.

As Raymond Poulidor made his way off the mountain and into the final days of another Tour, he might have thought about those around him, who were no longer there. Anquetil, who would never allow himself to be beaten by Poulidor when it mattered, died long ago. He only made it to fifty-three, taken away in 1987 by stomach cancer, without knowing the long drought that France would have to endure on the race he had dominated. Rivière was younger still when he died, aged just forty. But the youngest of that great generation to go might just have turned out to be the best of them all.

As Bobet puts it, 'He was born between Anquetil, his senior by one year, and Poulidor, his junior by several. With him in the middle, who knows how the famous duel between Anquetil and Poulidor might have turned out?'

Two days later, in the bright sunlight of Périgueux, Thibaut Pinot and Jean-Christophe Péraud achieved their objectives. French tricolores were draped from the balconies of townhouses looking onto the podium. Péraud had smashed his own expectations, as well as the nation's, hauling himself up into a remarkable second place overall. Now, he would be allowed to eke out what remained of his career with great pleasure and pride: the highest-placed Frenchman on the Tour de France since Bernard Hinault.

But Pinot's future shone even more brightly, that same unknown potential with which both Rivière and Saint had ridden their too-brief careers. You could almost sense, in the caution with which he expressed his satisfaction at the end, that a shadow of expectation had fallen over him already.

The secret is out. It's no longer the subject of conjecture or whispers or shrewd predictions over fish and chips on cross-Channel ferries. Pinot is the anointed one, for France. Now.

KITTEL

'The Armstrong years are cycling's great memorial.
We shouldn't forget. We mustn't forget.
It must stand there as the symbol of an
era that must never return.'

It had been days since I'd spoken to Marcel Kittel. I'd glimpsed him, from time to time, mostly looking increasingly shattered. And, at the top of the Hautacam, as he hauled his massive frame up the mountain, flanked by the other sprinters in the *grupetto*, he'd completely changed to look at. He looked haggard, drained, gaunt. All that beaming energy of his opening salvo of wins had been bled out of him by the rigours of getting over the mountains.

But now I stood opposite him again. I asked him how he was. He told me that he was very tired.

'Is today a day for you?'

He glanced heavenwards, at a sky that threatened yet more rain. 'I think maybe not so much.'

'Is Paris your next objective, then?'

'Paris is, of course, my goal.'

Stage 19 threw everything at the race again. From swollen black skies above the sand dunes and pine forests of Les Landes, tongues of lightning appeared. Then the rain followed. Once it started, it did not stop.

Ramunas Navardauskas rode away from everyone on a difficult final climb, surging past his teammate Tom Slagter, and with half the bunch crashing just inside the final three kilometres, they never saw him again. Meanwhile, Kittel was flexing his enormous legs and rolling into the finish, worrying not about this stage.

He was worrying only about Paris. His mum and dad would be on their way by now, having locked up their home in Arnstadt, handed instructions to the neighbours, packed the car and left for France. They wanted to go and see their son win on the Champs-Élysées. They did it the year before, and they saw no reason why they shouldn't do it again this year.

Marcel Kittel was born in East Germany, but only just. He was raised in the heartland of a region that has produced most of the talent that has hauled the sport of cycling in Germany back from the brink of obsolescence.

To use the English term, Thuringia is rather fun, in a medieval revivalist sort of way. It calls to mind rain-soaked mountain passes and dark forests, punctuated by the flickering yellow lights from tiny settlements of timber-built cottages, on whose mantelpieces elaborately carved oak-faced clocks tick and slumber, tick and slumber, to the gentle snoring of the village blacksmith asleep by the fire, a dog at his feet. And, despite the obvious and enduring blight of its remaining GDR-styled high-rise housing estates, it does indeed retain something of that far-flung cosiness, if you squint.

Of all Germany's vast interlocking interior, Thuringia, or Thüringen to give it its correct German name, remains the most hidden from sight. Gaining admission to it normally requires the passage of an ICE express train from Western Germany, arrowing into its arcane, occluded heart.

When I lived in Hamburg in the early nineties, shortly after reunification, I knew of Thüringen for one reason alone: it had given its name to the safest and most palatable of all the nation's bewildering array of pork sausages. The Thüringer was the default banger, as safe and unchanging as an autobahn, greyish, brownish-white in hue and flecked with the correct amount of unthreatening spice, suitable for any occasion, and far less risky than its vivid red, altogether angrier cousin the Krakauer, whose salted flesh would go to work immediately on the lining of your stomach. I felt warmly towards Thüringen, taking it to stand for comfort. I thought it might be a land of delicate wonder and quiet delight.

Of course, contemporary events of that time were doing their very best to undermine my schmaltzy imaginings. I was, in the early 1990s, a devotee of the impeccably left-leaning anarcho-syndicalists' football club F.C. St. Pauli. Occupying a space near the infamous red-light district of Hamburg, this football club was supported by a ragamuffin horde of Autonomen, Germany's unique race of dreadlocked squatters and weed-addled, black-trousered, dog-wielding dreamers. These were the people who rather wonderfully turned out to support this fabulously idiosyncratic football team (they played, and still play, in a brown kit) at home matches. And some of them would make the away trips to the newly assimilated ex-East German clubs, a few of which lay in Thüringen.

These early cultural exchanges between recently reunited eastern and western brothers and sisters generally did not end well. Trains pulled into the tumbleweed, put-upon towns of the East and disgorged hordes of reasonably unsavoury anti-fascists to meet and greet the resident Ultras, some of whom might actually have spent the previous night torching refugees' accommodation, as they had done so shockingly in places like Rostock and Hoyerswerda. These were rough-and-ready times, and territories such as Thüringen found themselves on the political front line, as their local economies, propped up by feeble central planning, fell apart.

And in the midst of all this, Thüringen's latest and most brilliant son, Marcel Kittel, was taking his first steps in the world. It was a world that was shifting beneath his tiny, not yet cycling, infant feet.

Shortly after, I turned my back on Germany, when I realised that it had stopped feeling like a foreign adventure. In fact, I only returned to its chintzy yet minimalist surroundings when, at least a decade later, ITV sent me to cover the 2006 World Cup. I scarcely recognised the place.

It was as if a spell had been cast on the entire population. Gone was that laconic air of the latent resentment that had curdled the goodwill of reunification. By now, the fear of total economic collapse had subsided (although the credit crunch had yet to hit), and a new generation had grown into adulthood; the first post-war cohort without any immediate need to preface all their attitudes with rehabilitative thinking in light of a recent Nazi past, and the nagging worry that their parents might indeed have been the bad guys. The country was visibly, tangibly freeing itself from the neuroses that had defined it for half a century, a kind of national angst that had made it both enviably strong and laughably uncertain. I found this change exhilarating, exemplified by the moment when a Turkish taxi driver, with a TV screwed to his dashboard, nearly crashed into a Nuremberg lamppost with delight when Germany scored a last-minute winner against Poland. In the Germany I had known, such an affiliation would have been unimaginable.

And at around about this time, Marcel Kittel was coming of age.

If ever there was a man suited for his time, then it is him. This is how I think of him, and these weighty values are what I invest in him, the poor sod. He is, for me, a standard bearer for a better world, a totem of enlightenment, a modern-day Tristan, as well as being a professional bicyclist with magnificent hair. It is blond, intricate, layered, bouffant, quiffed, sensational. Even his Twitter profile reflects the purity of his purpose on this planet: 'I love speed, sprinting and hair.'

Once, when, lifting off his helmet after a stage win, and running his fingers through his hair, he looked at me for confirmation that his blond locks, flattened from hours of compression, were doing him justice. This had to be ascertained to his satisfaction before we could do the interview.

'You look just fine, Marcel.'

'OK, let's talk.'

'I have only one reminder of the old East Germany.' He smiles to himself. 'I've got my immunisation records from when I was a baby. They've been stamped with the hammer and compass.'

To Marcel Kittel, this scarcely believable symbol of the old country into which he was born is simply a curiosity, filed away somewhere in a drawer back at home along with some old telephone bills and an instruction manual for a DVD player. He was just eighteen months old when the hammer fell apart and the compass got stuck. That was the end of the GDR.

Thus he was spared the kind of uneasy compromises that were foisted on his devoted parents, both of whom represented their country.

'As an athlete you were supposed to respect the state, and I am not sure the state had much respect for the athlete. You were supposed to represent the values that the state wanted to be invested with.

'My dad was a cyclist and my mother was a high jumper. Her personal best was something like one metre seventy-five. They were both at the Sports Academy in Erfurt. The parents weren't rebels. As a family, we escaped the worst of the GDR, we didn't suffer.'

Matthias, his father, was also a sprinter. He's a tall, muscular man, who looks to this day like he'd be able to give most of the peloton a run for their money in a battle for the line. He represented the GDR on the odd occasion, but never at the World Championships. His greatest success came in the 1982 Tour of Poland, at which he won the points jersey. This is the kind of peripheral achievement that is lost almost permanently from public record. No website accurately records it. To verify it, you'd have to travel to the offices of the organisers of the Tour of Poland itself and open up the dusty ledger marked '1982'. Even Marcel Kittel, who has grown up with the deepest respect for his father's career, and never fails to cite him as his inspiration, cannot precisely remember which year it was that his dad returned from Poland clutching a sponsored jersey.

'Dad was never a professional, he rode at a different level altogether. But his training was just the same.' This was not necessarily a good thing. 'Of course there was state-sanctioned doping in East Germany. I've spoken to him about that.'

I imagine this delicate conversation. Perhaps it took place on a training ride, up on to the range of wooded hills that fringe the southern aspect of Erfurt, and freewheeling down the other side. A teenage Marcel Kittel, his physiology beginning to match his ambition as he burst into adulthood, and starting also to question all that he saw around him, what he watched every summer on the TV. He was just eighteen when Germany's last great cycling hero Jan Ullrich disappeared ignominiously from the 2006 Tour de France, before the race got underway, and without turning a pedal. Kittel might have been forgiven for wondering what his father had witnessed during his racing career; what his father might have done.

'He told me that he'd never knowingly doped.' That is the simple form of the answer, its singularity of meaning fuzzed up with the qualifier 'knowingly'. Such was life in East Germany. Such was life, everywhere in cycling, perhaps. There's a 'but' coming...

'But he couldn't be sure that he hadn't been given stuff unwittingly, in tablet form.' It must have been the hardest of admissions. It must have been the hardest of questions. But there is no judgement in Kittel's words, as he recalls his father's testimony.

'For riders back then, there was a certain ignorance. It was never injected, but they took tablets. He grew up in this system. He never knowingly took anything, because he trusted his milieu.'

They have their eyes wide open, this latest crop of German riders, and in that regard Kittel is not alone. The post-post-war generation has Glasnost in its DNA. As teenagers, Kittel and Tony Martin, the pre-eminent time-triallist of his generation, were teammates. They, along with Sebastian Lang and John Degenkolb, both rode for the legendary development team Thüringer Energie. If British Cycling has its Manchester Academy, then this, informally, is a close as Germany gets to replicating that kind of serial success. But being a cyclist in Germany is not a mainstream pursuit, particularly in what are still referred to as the Ost-Länder.

Tony Martin is, to some extent, shaped by the same cultural inheritance as Kittel. Martin was only four years old when, just as Erich Honecker's palsied grip on a moribund nation was starting to slacken, his parents took the decision to leave Thüringen and head for sanctuary. They left the country on a tourist visa and, when they returned, the East German state had collapsed, in no little part because of their next move.

The Martins joined the hordes of families who camped out in the grounds of the West German embassy in Budapest, demanding political asylum. It was this group's public dissent, which more than anything else led to the chain of events that brought down the Berlin Wall.

Against this historical background, it is perhaps unsurprising that both Martin and Kittel, as professionals in a sport still wriggling free from corruption, continue to tear down the edifices. There is no equivocation.

'The Armstrong years are cycling's great memorial. We shouldn't forget. We mustn't forget. It must stand there as the symbol of an era that must never return.

'I still think it's very important to continue to expose the facts, and to work out the connections, and to learn lessons for the future.'

Germany couldn't really give a damn about Marcel Kittel, still, even now. This has to be understood. It's a big part of his story.

It is in this environment that Marcel Kittel has pursued his passion, surrounded by scepticism and distaste. In his country, a 'professional cyclist' rates as highly as 'banker' does back home. A generation of EPO dopers has come and mostly gone, and has left behind them the wreck of a sport that had grown very suddenly from a very low base when Jan Ullrich won the 1997 Tour de France. That rapid surge in popularity for cycling was not dissimilar to the Wiggo effect on these shores. But one by one, from Erik Zabel, through Ullrich to Patrik Sinkewitz and Stefan Schumacher, a series of riders had either been ensnared by the dope testers, or had their confessions beaten out of them in the court of public opinion. Cycling in Germany is still struggling to cope with such a deluge of bad news, as well it might.

*

In February this year, I went to visit Kittel. It was a journey that involved a thrilling number of trains, and convoluted changes at remote railway stations. Once I stopped at Fulda, where I headed for the nearest newsagent in the hope of picking up some cycling literature. After all, their great sprinting hero had just returned from the Tour of Dubai, where he'd beaten Mark Cavendish not once, but on three consecutive occasions. I searched the shelves. There was not one cycling magazine. And before you get the impression that this was a tiny corner shop, or newsagent, let me tell you that I stood there and counted the titles. There were exactly fifty-one. Yachting, kite-boarding, kayaking, skating, snow-boarding and scuba-diving, about a dozen football magazines. All these were on the shelves, hawking their glossy wares, but cycling wasn't among them.

'No one knows who I am.' Kittel smiles at my disbelief when I sit down opposite him in his agent's offices high above the banked track of Erfurt Velodrome.

'What do you mean?' I ask him. I am genuinely amazed. Apart from anything else, he could hardly be more recognis-able: six foot something, tanned, blond, big hair. 'If you walk down the street, surely people ask for your autograph?'

'No one talks to me.'

'That can't be true.'

He laughs at me, amused by my astonishment. 'It's a bit different over here.'

And indeed it is, still, a bit different. The perma-sulk that started to afflict German TV after the shambolic start to the 2006 Tour, and which reached its sulkiest apotheosis with the horror show of 2008's filthy Tour, continues unchecked. The public service broadcasters, which used to devote whole afternoons and much of their evenings to the Tour de France when they were in the grip of cycling fever a decade ago, picked up their microphones and left, without any intention, seemingly, of returning.

Except, there may be a glint of light. I noticed, working on the 2014 Tour, the return to work of the famous Volp brothers, Gernot and Hartmut. I had not seen them for years, but there they were again, one a cameraman and the other a sound recordist. They appeared to have slid themselves back into contention, even though they had no obvious outlet for what they shot, as German TV was still boycotting the race.

'Volp! What are you doing here?'

'Sssshhh. We may be coming back,' whispered Gernot to me one afternoon, looking around furtively. 'A decision will fall in September. But don't tell anyone I told you.'

'My lips are sealed.'

And if they do return, it'll be down, in no small measure, to Marcel Kittel.

'We've hit rock bottom and we're on the way back. We're on an upward curve. But it's difficult. Until TV shows the race, then we can't really grow. We need to be on the free-to-air channels, to appeal to those people who perhaps aren't even remotely interested, but enjoy watching the countryside. At the moment we're only being watched by sport freaks on subscription channels.'

The German newspapers did indeed report on Kittel's swashbuckling 2013 Tour triumph, but they did so much in the same way that *The Times* still publishes the Court Circular in dutiful but hardly celebratory words. After that race, for example, he'd not once been invited onto a chat show, nor been asked to appear as a guest on a mainstream TV station. His accomplishment, like his physical presence in the land of his birth, is almost invisible.

Later that afternoon, Kittel drove me to Erfurt railway

station in his ridiculously new, ridiculously low-slung and menacing black Mercedes.

Our leather-cosseted backsides were suspended millimetres from the cobbled ground, as he glided unnoticed through his beautiful hometown. The roads narrowed as we left the offices behind us and closed in on town. Once we passed inside the perimeter of the old city walls, the houses either side of the road grew taller, four storeys now, with scaled-down Disney turrets and ornate Weimar Republic decoration. The tramlines shimmered with drizzle in the sodium wash as people made their way home, unfolding umbrellas. It all dripped with Mittel Europa gentility, and I get a kick out of that kind of thing. My eyes were on stalks.

'It's never crossed my mind to leave here.' Kittel was waiting to turn left at a set of red lights. His indicator clicked rhythmically as he thought about his decision to buy a flat in the middle of town. The wipers moved once, silently across the glass in front of us. I turned to look at him. 'I've never seen anywhere in the world where I've thought, I have to move there. This is where I'm from.'

Through the Bose loudspeakers, a typically unconvincing German R&B track was coming to an end, and Sputnik Radio sputtered into a sudden gear change; a different jingle. It was the sports news. Kittel lent forward and turned the volume up.

'*Nach drei Tagen sind die Olympischen Spiele immer noch clean. Bisher sind keine positiven Tests vorhanden.*' Three days in and the Olympic Games are still 'clean'. Still no positive tests have been recorded.

He turned to look at me as if he'd just proved a point. The local radio reports from the Sochi Winter Olympics, in which the Germans were expected to return with a significant medal haul, were leading with a doping story. Or rather, a lack of a doping story. The fact that there had been no positive tests so far was the headline, behind which, if you listened hard enough, you might be able to detect a hint of disappointment. Or was I imagining it?

It became very clear that Kittel had turned up the radio for a reason. He'd wanted me to hear the background noise to his life. To relieve the sudden tension in the car, I changed the subject.

'And the Classics?' I wondered what his wider ambitions were as his cycling career entered its best years.

Kittel shook his head and waved a dismissive hand in my direction. 'Why should I bother with them? They're fine for Boonen and riders like him, who haven't got the power to compete at the top end. But why would I be interested? Only one thing matters for me, and that's the pure, flat sprint.'

And as if to prove a point, he eyed up a light a hundred metres away that was just turning amber. He dropped a gear and stamped on the throttle. The Mercedes roared terrifyingly back at him in response, and we shot forward. I was temporarily pinned to my seat, knocked back by the acceleration.

We made the light, a fraction of a second before it turned red, and he had made his point.

He dropped me at the station. 'See you in Leeds!' I had said.

'Why? Where's Leeds?'

'The Tour starts there.'

'Really?' He looked politely interested, amused. 'Leeds. Sounds good.'

'Bye, Marcel.'

I watched him drive off. His hair was in A1 condition. It was the colour of late-harvested oats, and stacked so high from his rangy forehead that it bent slightly with gravity at its tallest extreme, lending it a jaunty don't-care-how-you-judge-me nonchalance.

And, five months later, here we all were, in Paris.

ARRIVÉE

'A person of little importance, a man of nothing,
or at least so very little.'

If my introduction to the Tour de France in 2003 had been
giddy, daft, confused, then my appreciation of it, as I headed
for the finish of the 2014 edition, had ripened on a window
sill, probably like a big fat Camembert. Left out in the sun
it had gone soggy at the midriff and acquired a fullness of
flavour that was almost too rich to consume.

It was a La Vache qui rit.

There had come a point in time, hard now to define with
anything like accuracy (I could well be five years out, either
way) when all that distinctive otherness that so defined my early
brushes with the bike race had become cosily familiar. For me,
working on the Tour was like wearing an ambitious new pair
of shoes, a little over-styled for comfort, whose leather suddenly
gives way as you slide your foot into place. The period of court-
ship had, at some indefinable point, imperceptibly ended.

Quite when this happened, though, is hard to ascertain.
It maybe took hold when Lance Armstrong bowed out in
2005, taking his gear with him, and leaving chaos behind.
Those testing (normally positively) Tours which followed
taught me much about my role on the race: poking away,
prying, insisting, making myself unwelcome.

Or perhaps it was at the moment, in 2008, when Mark
Cavendish declared that it was possible for a Briton to thrive
on the Tour de France; his first stage win into Chateauroux
was akin to planting a flag on the moon. Certainly, the

following four or five years, in which the race was under his spell, allowed me, by sheer power of association, to puff my chest out. And when Bradley Wiggins decided it was time to have a go at actually winning the thing, then all our previous and well-founded assumptions about what was and what wasn't possible turned to dust. So maybe 2012 was some sort of Rubicon, which, once crossed, meant that we might never again return to a state of innocence.

Like turning forty. Not that turning forty is a bad thing. Forty-five is still OK, I am amazed to find. There is plenty of evidence out there to suggest that everything you imagined you had achieved and believed you had understood prior to these ages is just so much froth.

No, forty was certainly not an issue.

I just never once imagined that I'd celebrate that particular birthday, on 11 July 2009, by trying vainly to interview Luis León Sánchez, after his stage win at Saint-Girons, in a dysfunctional hybrid of Spanish, French and English. I gave up. (On the interview, that is. Not on life.)

Perhaps that was the moment, on the very anniversary of my birth, when, turning to the camera, and ignoring my interviewee completely, I confessed to the viewers that I hadn't the faintest idea what he was talking about. I believe that may well have been the instant when at some unfathomable level I understood how much I loved this race, with all its frailties, quirks, lack of coherence and grand scale.

On my first few Tours I would have been left in deep shock by such an inept interview, too traumatised to make light of it, too disappointed with myself, and too sure that I had failed. But by the time I turned back to Señor Sánchez, and, bidding him farewell, shook him firmly by the hand, I had no such concerns. For by now I understood that the Tour de France is home to everything; farce, drama, intrigue, slapstick, tragedy and comedy. And I embraced it all.

Yet the problem with these things, when great attachment arises, is the sense that nothing stays the same for ever. The strings that bind are there to be tugged at. For example, Euskadi Euskaltel, the Basque team of Luis León Sánchez, would eventually fail to attract a sponsor, and fold. They had been a perennial fascination for me during those early years, culturally distinct, linguistically apart, and really very feeble on a bike.

So things pass into history, and it's hard to think that what replaces them is ever quite as good. The happy playground eventually clouds over. Drizzle will fall. I miss things.

We made our way to Paris.

All of us who work on the Tour have a special shirt. It remains folded and unused all the way around the lap of France, unmoved and unmoving at the bottom of the suitcase while less important items of clothing come and go at higher, less significant, levels. And all the while, invisibly, it bides its time, only to emerge, blinking into the bright Parisian sunshine to mark the completion of another July in France.

This year mine was black. It was a simple polo shirt, but made of a soft, breathable material, and of a cut that I felt good about. Every now and again, during the month on the road, I had lifted it out of the suitcase to access something deeper still, and then very gently placed it back, still folded. All the while, as I did this, I probably thought to myself, there now. You can go back in there. You will be worn, of that you must rest assured. But only when we reach the capital city, when the Eiffel Tower winks out its Morse-code greeting, under those tall Parisian summer skies, at the very end of the race. Until then, my shirt, you must wait.

Talking to polo shirts, even if not out loud, was one of the many indications to suggest that I may have been doing this job too long already.

I think the last time I cried with laughter was because of a special shirt. And when I say that I cried, that's exactly what I mean: face creased and red, eyes wrinkled shut, hot tears streaming down my cheeks. It was the kind of feverish, unstoppable, cascading laughter that leaves you clutching your midriff, moaning with cramp when it finally subsides. In this regard it reminded me, awfully, of those cataclysms of distress at school when an unheralded fart escaped the buttocks of an unwitting classmate just at the wrong moment in a geography lesson, provoking the kind of laugh that scares you by dint of its own innate violence. Such things can land you in trouble.

Even now, many years later, when I am simply detecting the background microwaves, the distant echo of that Big Bang of a laughter attack, I cannot recall the incident without the corners of my mouth turning up at the edges, and a rogue chuckle bubbling to the surface like an Icelandic geyser.

It had come about because of a simple clothing choice. Matt Rendell, my dear friend and companion, with whom I have passed a dozen summers tramping the super-heated tarmac of the Tour in search of unwilling bike riders, decided to wear something which he thought looked good. Fair enough, you might think.

But he was gloriously, marvellously mistaken.

Another Tour was done, my second, I believe, in 2004. As a perfect high-summer dusk descended on the city, we finally packed away our things and we made the short, blissful, annual walk from the finish line to the Place de la Madeleine. Here we would stop off briefly at our hotel (the same one we have always used, out of neurotic, obsessive-attachment neediness) wash hands and splash water on faces in an attempt to lose some of the dusty grime which kicks up from the sandy margins of the Champs-Élysées, and then quickly reconvene in the brasserie at the corner of the square where we'd arranged to meet.

Time was not on our side. Paris has a baffling habit of closing up extremely early on Sunday nights, even the last Sunday of July, when every year the Tour descends. Frequently this results in desultory packs of Tour personnel loping thirstily through echoing closed-down side streets, jaws hanging and a degraded look in their eyes; in search of a beer and a magret de canard. Each second matters, as Paris becomes alive with black-aproned waiters stacking chairs and removing cutlery as if they were expecting a storm.

One by one we sat down, our circle swelled by the addition of partners and friends and family from home, who had made the trip over to join us in Paris. Those of us who had passed the last three weeks on the race, and intimately in each other's company had no need to talk. We suspended all conversation, until the beers had not only been ordered but placed in front of us. Only then did it occur to us it might be polite and thoughtful to talk to the various guests. Our finer manners had long since been left by the side of the road, and after the full duration of a Tour, where communication amongst the crew was concerned, everything had been reduced to a barely functional level of monosyllabia.

But where was Matt?

The tall, muscular frame of the erstwhile language lecturer, jazz-funk bass player and adventure cyclist was notably absent. There were no large gesticulating hands, nor ill-fitting baseball cap atop his handsomely wide and grinning face. Put simply: the big man had not yet arrived. We cast our eyes around the square wondering where the formerly Colombian-based lin-guist might have got himself to, not without irritation, since we had a table booked for nine-thirty and needed to be over the other side of town.

A sip of beer. A glance at a watch. 'Shall we go on without him?'

And then, suddenly, he was upon us. Emerging from around

the corner, showered, spruced, with perhaps the subtlest note of aftershave, came Matt Rendell. But this was not Matt as we knew him. This was a heightened Matt, an enhanced version. For Matt had decided to wear something very special. And it was this utterly splendid T-shirt, sitting tightly over his considerable but wiry frame, which instantly brought us helplessly to our knees. That a simple garment (and believe me, it was simple) could bring about such instant, unquenchable hilarity, I had not known. The wonder of cloth, when badly conceived! The power of fabric, when poorly suited to the moment, to entertain! To this day, I thank Matt from the depths of my heart for choosing to pull on this appalling shirt, because it STILL casts its spell. No matter now what may befall me, what hammer-blows of fate await me as I trundle towards the latter part of my life, I shall face them down with good humour and I shall know that all is not perdition and horror, because I was there when Matt inexplicably decided to wear the Worst T-Shirt in the World.

It wasn't just the colour; the thing was banana yellow. It wasn't simply the cut; horribly, it was sleeveless. It was, in summary, a banana-yellow sleeveless T-shirt. It was the kind of shirt that possibly Leroy from The Kids from 'Fame' (google that one, children) could pull on to offset his purple day-glo leg warmers and still emerge with dignity. Matt failed dramatically. He just looked very, very silly.

But what elevated this moment from routinely amusing to unspeakably funny was his attitude vis-à-vis The T-Shirt. Confronted by the tidal wave of laughter and abuse now being heaped on him and his beloved *maillot jaune*, he couldn't hide his hurt. There was a painful sense of wounded pride in his reaction to the ridicule that came his way, which, I am sorry to say, just made it funnier still. He simply had not seen this derision coming. In fact quite the opposite. It became evident, as he headed wearily back to the hotel to change out of it, that he must have thought he'd pulled off something of a sartorial *coup de grâce*. This T-shirt had been kept back as a special flourish for the end of the Tour, carefully chosen both to show off his considerable biceps, but also as a nod to the hundred-year history of the Grande Boucle (i.e. it was yellow). It was his special shirt.

And, on this point, I can identify with him.

There were two races on the final day of the 2014 Tour, Stage 21, with its inevitable bunch sprint, and the inaugural edition of the women's circuit race, La Course. They had placed an extra podium on the Place de la Concorde, in the middle of the roundabout, near the fountain. That was where the buses and campervans belonging to the women's teams parked up too, laying open for public scrutiny the gaping disparity between the levels of funding in men's and women's cycling. Only one of the women's teams, United Healthcare, had turned up with a full-sized bus. And that was only because their men's team didn't need it that weekend.

But the race was tight, and aggressive, and produced a notable winner in the great Marianne Vos, who had to pull herself inside out to get the better of her compatriot Kirsten Wild. Lizzie Armitstead fell heavily inside the final kilometre, and limped back to her team bus, pushing her bike, and bleeding from the knee and the elbow. The waiting posse of British journalists, of which I was one, stood to one side and let her pass. No one dared to ask her a question.

There was then a long lull in the action, while the avenue filled with people. It had been sparsely populated for La Course, which was disappointing. Perhaps it was too early in the day, or maybe lunch just got in the way for too many people. This new race may take some time to establish itself.

Our crew were joined, as they always are, by a smattering of family and friends, visiting Paris and taking in the bike race, often for the first time in their lives. Watching live cycling can be a puzzling experience, if you are not familiar with it. There is a lot of standing around to be done, while nothing's happening. On this occasion, the effect was exacerbated by a long, sleepy lull in the action. We had come on air for the women's race, and then we had gone off air again. It would be hours before the men's race finally hit the Champs-Élysées. Our visitors sat around, trying not to look bored. We, on the other hand, tried to look busier than we actually were, to justify ourselves, and to stand up our often-cited contention that the Tour was exhausting. We were, undeniably, all very tired. But now that we stopped and thought about it, why were we? What did we actually do all day long? You could read these questions passing through the minds of the various visitors. It was a little uncomfortable, like a having a mirror held up in front of you, when you least want one.

I stood up, unable any longer to bear the scrutiny. 'I'm just going to, um . . .' I looked around '. . . Recce. Something.' And I walked away, in the direction of something.

Instead of doing anything useful, I went to look, for the final time, at the long list of obsolete French words, which somebody in the Zone Technique had been thoughtfully collecting during the Tour. Each day they'd add to the list another archaic verb, adjective or noun, which had fallen into disuse. Then the following day, they'd publish its definition. It was strangely fascinating, especially since the growing list was photocopied daily, and then Sellotaped up all over the place, but with an emphasis on the urinals.

Not for the first time, as I stood there, educating myself, my eye was caught by Stage 3's word. *Un crapoussin* meant 'a person of little importance, a man of nothing, or at least so very little'. That was roughly how I felt, standing there have a pee against a plastic urinal in Paris.

Just then there was a thunderous roar overhead, as the eight jets of the Patrouille de France shot through the sky, leaving patriotic smoke trails to fall gently and disperse before they reached the cobbles of the avenue. I looked up to see them receding already into tiny dots, and heading over the Arc de Triomphe.

The race had arrived, and with it the most predictable move of the whole Tour: an attack from Jens Voigt.

Only the previous day, after his time-trial effort in Perigueux, I had sat down to discuss the race with him, definitively, for one last time. He'd made time for me, even though I was the last in a long line of people hoping to speak to him ahead of his final-ever stage on the Tour.

With his expressive over-articulation, and his usual playful hyperbole, he indulged in all the trademark Voigt stuff. He talks about suffering on a bike like no one else. But, on this occasion, he also spoke of the beauty of the race, the country that hosts it, and the people whose presence turns it into the spectacle it is. Few riders have ever 'got it' like Voigt. His ability to see the bigger picture, while being in the middle of the landscape, has always been extraordinary.

I stood by the barriers, and watched him riding flat-out off the front of the bunch, strung out single file on their first circuit of the Champs-Élysées. Just once during that interview had he appeared annoyed, when I had asked him to reflect on the chaos of the years he had ridden, through perhaps the very worst of cycling's long, inglorious history with drug cheats.

'Now, why can't we talk about the beautiful things? Why always this?' He glared at me.

'Because it's extremely important, Jens?' I countered.

He sighed deeply, then launched into his withering verdict

on his peers who had almost destroyed the sport, 'OK. Since we *have to* talk about it, let's talk…'

At the end of the interview he asked Liam to keep recording. Then he posed, 007 style, with an imaginary pistol, and said, 'My name's Voigt. Jens Voigt. And I like it shaken, not stirred.' Then he roared with laughter, clapped us all on the shoulder, picked up his kit bag, and left.

His attack on the Champs-Élysées didn't last long. Pretty quickly he was back in the pack, just one of 164 men who'd made it to Paris.

The next time I saw him it was dusk. He was pedalling slowly up the avenue, detached from the rest of his teammates, and wiping a tear from his eye. He must suddenly have become aware that this was real, now. That he'd never be back.

Marcel Kittel really shouldn't have won that sprint. Kristoff was the man on form; Kittel was tiring. Kristoff timed it perfectly; Kittel left it horribly late. Kittel shouldn't have won.

But he did. He had waited ever since Stage 4 for that moment, riding 2,953 kilometres, just so that he could edge out Alexander Kristoff in the final few metres. Some run up, that.

He found a moment, away from all the madness at the finish line, to walk a few yards up the avenue, quite alone. He looked along the length of it, from the podium, up that gradual rise to where the Arc straddled the inside of the Place d'Étoile, presented to the world's gaze is if on an upturned palm, Paris, offering this spectacle. Then he turned, had stopped momentarily for a picture, and walked back, slowly to where the chaotic throng of media, photographers and assorted crowds of others still waited on his presence. Some roadies were trying to unfurl a yellow carpet, along which the riders would soon be asked to walk. They were struggling to get it into the correct position, which seemed to fascinate Bernard Hinault. He stood over them, giving advice. He probably knew how to unfurl carpets correctly, or would at least have been extremely confident that he knew.

As Kittel walked back, I saw him hold the first two fingers of his right hand fleetingly in front of his eyes. He mouthed to himself the simple number 'Zwei.' With that tiny gesture, I took in again the strangely human, small-scale sight of such private pleasure on such a grand and public canvas. He'd won the race in Paris for the second time.

It is almost certain that far away, on the Isle of Man, Mark Cavendish was not watching. Nor too, I would suggest, were either Alberto Contador or Chris Froome.

In their absence, Vincenzo Nibali, clutching a script for a speech of such banality that I feared he must have downloaded it from a 'Speeches for All Occasions' website, was left to enjoy his victory. The Italian anthem played, and for the first time the wider world saw Nibali without either a cycling helmet or that ever-present light blue hat. At a stroke, it made him more approachable. He just looked like a bloke who'd worked really hard at getting something right, and was standing back to look at what he'd done. A carpenter, perhaps. Or a decorator.

Nibali was flanked by the emotional Péraud, and the more reserved, slightly hunched shape of Pinot. Only one of those two Frenchmen would have been wondering to himself what the air feels like at the higher altitude of the top step. And he was keeping his thoughts to himself.

A short while later there were the usual processions, as darkness began to gather.

One by one, the teams rolled up along the avenue, to warm applause from those fans who had waited by the side of the road. The NetApp Endura riders, almost to a man, had their phones out and were filming themselves as they rode. Zak

Dempster came past. In his first Tour he had finished 148th, four and three-quarter hours behind the winner. He radiated pleasure, relief and deep, deep satisfaction.

Peter Sagan rode along, still pulling wheelies, still locking up his back wheel and skidding to impress everyone like a hyperactive ten-year-old past his bedtime. The Tinkoff Saxobank team meandered along, Rafał Majka riding more slowly than any of them, and unable to contain his grin. The Française des Jeux riders had their young children balanced on their handlebars, the Bretagne team each carried those heraldic-looking black-and-white flags aloft. Marcel Kittel was at the centre of a knot of Giant Shimano riders, draped in his country's colours. Luca Paolini grabbed hold of a passing motor-bike, mimicking Rafał Majka's controversial attack up to Risoul, much to the delight of Joaquim Rodriguez. Even Team Sky looked relaxed. Dave Brailsford stopped at the barriers where we stood, and exchanged a few warm words with Chris Boardman, and Geraint Thomas wanted to know where we'd got our beers from.

And then they all departed. Riders wandered off into the night, in search of their hotel rooms. Or they rode back to their team buses, where the mechanics had already got the parties started.

The race had clattered into life, noisily, angrily. It had torn into the first week, and then, tiring even itself, it had settled into something more sedate, more contemplative. But, aside from the riders, and with equal intensity, it had delivered an opportunity once again to reflect on the passage of the years, and the land that rose up and fell away under the riders' wheels. It had asked us once again to reflect on the tribes to which we think we belong, the values to which we think we aspire, and how it is we want to be remembered.

The Tour asks riders to go beyond what they most fear, and encourages us all to search out questions that lurk behind the surface of what we think we understand. It is, as I knew it would be at the outset, uncontainable.

And so it proved again.

The loose affiliation of the peloton dispersed. Its form was only ever temporary. The binding forces that had brought them together on Headrow in Leeds, when they first bunched up at the start line, suddenly slackened and let the race unravel. It was over.

EPILOGUE

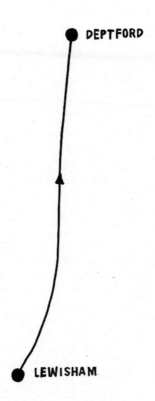

THE BUTCHER

'Did that Italian bloke win it then?'

The day after the Tour de France ended I rode to my local butcher's shop to buy a chicken.

It is a ride of some one and a half miles, which crosses a busy road, then meanders along a riverside path before reaching Deptford, where it ends. There are no climbs of any note. I rolled up one trouser leg, flung a rucksack on my back, and set off, turning the pedals slowly and relishing the unencumbered pace of the day. There were no pressing demands, save for the need to buy some poultry and roast it. There were no interviews to conduct, no scripts to write, no race to follow. There was no Tour de France.

In fact, passing under the railway arch, and onto the cycle path by the river, I realised that not much of the Tour had come back home with me. Normally it takes me days to get it out of my system, to stop reliving stages, remembering images, feasting on memories. But this time? Not so much. That's not to say that it had not been a bewildering, intense experience. But it had been remarkably easy to leave behind. Once it had finished, it had folded itself neatly away, tied up with a yellow ribbon and labelled 'Nibali. 2014'. More quickly than normal, I had moved on.

The path divided into two. I chose the right-hand fork, which hugged the riverbank, and led past the solitary bench which is invariably occupied by drinkers of premium-strength cider. This time there were two of them, so deeply engrossed in a muttered conversation that they barely noticed me passing, and would not have registered my cheery 'Good afternoon.'

I was feeling extremely well disposed to the world: morally refreshed, chipper, almost bumptious. How good it was to be riding a bicycle with no particular purpose save for the acquisition of a chicken! I could only surmise that this general sense of harmony with the world was the direct result of a race that had, for three weeks, been devoid of brattishness, deceit or rancour. In place of those three, the opposing values of endeavour, courtesy, humility had risen to the fore. It was all most unorthodox. I blame Yorkshire.

For the 'goodwill to all mankind' had flowed from the start. Mark Cavendish, for example, had crashed and then apologised for bringing down his opponent in the sprint. This was not standard. No one had attacked a teammate. No one had been caught doping. No one had a bad word to say about anyone, save for the one occasion when Andrew Talansky lost his temper with Simon Gerrans, but even that was kind of understandable. The poor lad had just crashed for the hundredth time. Even the rain had been honest.

It had been a refreshing race. Those who could rise up and make a name for themselves did just that: Kittel, Martin, Kristoff, Pinot, Yates and Majka. A new generation was taking centre stage. And no one could find fault with Vincenzo Nibali.

But for all that, it was a Tour that simply whetted the appetite for the next edition, and drew a thick line under so much, denoting an end. No Millar, no more Voigt. Would Voeckler ever win again? Had Cancellara finally faded? Could Cavendish ever really recover? Would Froome triumph again? Next year's race could not come round quickly enough.

Arriving outside the shop, I leant my bike against the display window, and I walked in.

Here I found and greeted the estimable William Wellbeloved. Will is a laconic man, whose family has purveyed lumps of dead animals to the people of Deptford for generations. He quite likes golf, or at least playing it. He sometimes watches the football, but only out of a weary sense of duty, and normally only if there's a World Cup on. He has far too much on his plate just running the business, and can't really be bothered with much else.

Mostly, sport leaves him unmoved, except by a general sense of disappointment, which he expresses by wiping his bloodied hands up and down his apron, up and down.

'Hello, Ned,' he said, wiping his hands up and down his apron.

'Hello, Will.'

'How did it all go then?' (He knows, after all, what I do for a living.)

'Good, thanks, Will.' I took in the rich smell of kidneys, cooking down in the back room for the next day's pies. 'In fact, it was amazing. Have you got a nice big chicken?'

'Shame about Cavendish, and that Froome fella.' He rummaged around in the window display. 'This one big enough for you?'

'That's fine, thanks.' I got my wallet out. 'Yes, it was a shame.'

'Still, you've got to have luck on your side, I suppose. Six pound fifty please, Ned.'

I handed the money over.

'It didn't really do it for me, this year, if I'm honest with you, Ned.'

'I'm sorry to hear that, Will.'

This was already the longest conversation I had ever had with him about cycling. But, just as I imagined it had come to close, he asked me one more question.

'Did that Italian bloke win it then?'

'He did.' I wondered at the sudden depth of his knowledge. 'Nibali,' I added.

'Yeah. That was him. Nibali.'

I told him it was good to be back. Then I cycled home to get the meat in the oven. As I pedalled, I smiled to myself at the strangeness of it all. I never thought I'd be talking to the butcher about an Italian rider from Messina. But, history will record, I just had.

So, to return to the question: had I enjoyed the Tour?

Let me think about it.

ACKNOWLEDGEMENTS

My first duty of thanks goes to those who work on the Tour de France production for ITV, especially at the London end, where there is a great deal of hard work for meagre reward. Rita Ballanca, Carolyn Viccari, Peter Wiggins, Peter Hussey, Dave Reynolds, Chrissie Jobson, Rob Blake, Jonathan Long, Ron Bradley, Nick Pratt, Phil Long, Mark Harris, Will Butcher, Simon Crombleholme, Leon Glover, Adam Rose, Marcus Cooper, Charlotte Villiers-Smith, Ola Olu, Alex Uszkurat, Angus Sutherland, Chris Nicholson, Chris Roberts, Chris Littleford, Rosie Shaw, James and Brian Venner, Tony Davies, Nick Etherton, Harry Hesp.

In France I depend daily on the efforts of Richard Gaines, Philippe Grelat, Odette and Romain Selva, Dave Thwaites, Mike Tope, Steve Blincoe, Phil Liggett, Paul Sherwen, Rob Llewelyn, Liam MacLeod, Jim Sefton, Steve Docherty, Gary Imlach and Richard Haywood. Thanks, too, to Jill Douglas for joining us for the first three stages of this edition. And, as ever, to Matt Rendell, Chris Boardman, and literally unforgettable Sally Boardman whose photography I have been known to plagiarise.

Plenty of people have given up time for this project and have been of great assistance in many different ways. Jim Clayton tried manfully to unearth a rare publication for me, one which I was only made aware of after reading a fine article by William Fotheringham. In particular, though, I would like to thank Lara Thornton and Gary Verity from Welcome to Yorkshire, whose tireless work was amply rewarded when the Tour de France finally came to town. Paul and Ghada put me up, and put up with me visiting them in the lead-up to the race more times than

I can remember. Peta Cavendish surrendered the best part of an afternoon to talk to me, as did Joe Fisher and Pete Kennaugh.

But in the end, it's the riders who make the Tour, and to whom I owe the greatest debt: Mark Cavendish, Chris Froome, Richie Porte, Geraint Thomas, Peter Sagan, Tony Martin, Jens Voigt, Tony Gallopin, Thibaut Pinot, Romain Bardet, Vincenzo Nibali, Thomas Voeckler. In particular, I would like to thank Marcel Kittel for the welcome he extended to me when I visited him in Erfurt. And, not for the first time, I am grateful to David Millar for his friendship and candour. I wish him well in the next phase of his career, whatever that may be.

Raymond Poulidor was extremely patient with my enquiries, as he always is. Without his input I would not have come across the stories of Roger Rivière or Gérard Saint, and their respective biographers Jean-Paul Ollivier and Jacky Desquesnes. Thanks also to Philippe Brunel, Sir Dave Brailsford, Bernard Hinault, and the man whose race it is, Christian Prudhomme. I am also indebted to the powers that be at ITV who continue to showcase the race, and send me off 'on my summer holidays' as Chris Boardman puts it.

The excellent team at Yellow Jersey Press have helped (insisted that I) deliver a book very rapidly. I am certain I would not have been able to do so without their support and encouragement. But particular mention must go to Justine Taylor, Alice Brett, Kris Potter, Fiona Murphy and Matt Phillips, who continues to demonstrate a rare ability to know my mind better than I know it myself. Thanks also to Mark Stanton, for his ability to craft a proposal based on a total absence of story.

Kath, Edie and Suzi continue to feign occasional interest in my work. Actually it's only Kath. The other two have stopped caring/never cared at all.

And the staff at the Caird Library in Greenwich continue to turn a blind eye to my unwanted presence at their desks. Good on them.

LIST OF ILLUSTRATIONS

14.1 The river in Besançon.

15.1 Production manager Rob Llewelyn asleep in the bowels of our truck.

15.2 Bernard Hinault being interviewed.

15.3 The front page of *L'Équipe* featuring Tony Gallopin's stage win.

16.1 A poster advertising a biography of Roger Rivière.

17.1 Chris Boardman and me, filming an insert for the ITV coverage.

17.2 Chris Boardman fettling a bike.

17.3 Chris Boardman and me on the top of the climb to Chamrousse.

18.1 Vincenzo Nibali talking to the press.

18.2 Liam and John Tinetti asleep on the set.

19.1 The sky on the road to Nîmes.

20.1 Carcassonne at dusk.

20.2 Miss and Mr Belgium posing for the cameras.

22.1 Marcel Kittel preparing to race.

23.1 The Eiffel Tower at midnight.